Liza! Liza!

Liza! Liza!

An Unauthorized Biography of Liza Minnelli

Alan W. Petrucelli

KARZ-COHL

New York · Princeton

Library of Congress Cataloging in Publication Data

Petrucelli, Alan W., 1958–
     Liza! Liza!: an unauthorized biography of Liza
Minnelli.

     Filmography: p. 157
     Discography: p. 163
     Bibliography: p. 167
     Includes index.
     1. Minnelli, Liza. 2. Actors—United States—Biography.
3. Singers—United States—Biography. I. Title.
PN2287.M644P4   1983   791.43'028'0924 [B]   83-16278
ISBN 0-943828-57-0
ISBN 0-943828-58-9 (pbk.)

Designed by Abby Goldstein
Set in type by Columbia Publishing Co., Inc.
Printed by Interstate Book Manufacturers, Inc.

Published in the United States by
KARZ-COHL PUBLISHING, INC.
24 Brookstone Drive, Princeton, N.J. 08540
and 320 West 105 Street, New York, N.Y. 10025

Printed in the United States of America

For my Mother and Father,
because I never really said thank you.

Contents

Acknowledgments

When I began writing this book, many of my friends loved Liza Minnelli. Months later, when it was completed, very few of them wanted to hear her name again. All I had done was talk, eat and sleep Liza Minnelli! I am very grateful for the patience, kindness, generosity and understanding of my friends and dozens of others, who were helpful to me. I am indebted to them all.

To those who took time from their busy lives to share memories with me: Peter Allen, Charles Aznavour, Ray Bolger, Mary Bryant, Wayne Cilento, Max Eisen, Mike Ellis, Elliott Gould, Robert P. Haseltine, Jim Henson, Pat Hipp, Al Hirschfeld, Lainie Kazan, Walter Kerr, Stanley Lebowsky, Rex Reed, Chita Rivera, Mickey Rooney, Mrs. Murray Silverstone, Liz Smith and Elizabeth Taylor.

To those who willingly opened their minds and files and allowed me unlimited access: Val Almendarez (Academy of Motion Picture Arts and Sciences); Jo-Ann Amantea; Laurel Amedei; Elliott Ames; Nancy Barr; Roberta Boehm (Photoreporters); Donald Bowden (Wide World Photos); Dolph Browning/Chen Sam (Chen Sam Associates); Seth Cagin; Carlos Clarens (Phototeque); Mindy Clay/David Greenstein (Bettmann Archives); David Sorin Collyer; Mary Corliss (Museum of Modern Art); Helene Curley (*TV Guide*); Craig Dawson; Patricia Diehl (CBS); Bruce Dressler; Michael Franks (Solters/Roskin/Friedman); Dudley Freeman/Kerry McCarthy (New York News Service); Isabel Giardina/Lin Tazmann (Rogers and Cowan); Pat Hayward/Julian Weber (*National Lampoon*); Shirley Herz/Sam Rudy (Shirley Herz Associates); Etty Inmna (Retna); Paula Klaw (Movie Star News); Nettie Kritch (Eastchester Public Library); Madeline Luchini (Ferncliff Cemetery); Josephine Macchiarola; Pat Marcus; Walter McBride (Retna); The Staff of the Mt. Vernon (NY) Public Library; Bill Murray (Celebrity Service); The Staff of the

Museum of Broadcasting; Anthony Paige/Joseph Riccuiti (NBC); Joanne Powell; Denise Rampulla; Marilyn Reeser (Sarah Lawrence College); Carol Richards; Welton Smith; Denise Specktor; John Springer; Heidi Stock (Billy Rose Theatre Collection/The New York Public Library at Lincoln Center); Marta Tarbell; Ray Terone and The Staff of the Will I. Grinton Library in Yonkers, NY.

And special thanks to: Arlene Alda, for her advice; Lyn Amedei, for her motherly concern; Ethel Bargellini, for always believing in me; Barbara Britt, for her unrelenting support; Izora Cohl, for her acumen in smoothing the rough spots; Jackie Collins, for taking time from her writing dynasty and encouraging me to take chances; Jeanne Drewsen, for her inspiration and guidance; Bette Fragola, for sticking by me when others did not; Gary Kriss, for his thoughtfulness; Jane Olivor, for urging me to grab the golden ring; Elizabeth Pearson-Griffiths, for the kind words that comforted me during troubled times; Ric and Sue Riccardi, for bringing new meaning to the word *friend*; Dr. Alan Schwartz, for helping clear the path; and Stephanie Schwartz, for helping me stay on it. I must also thank my brother, Dennis M. Petrucelli, for our renewed relationship; Vita, Nicky and Myra, and the rest of the 5 Star Donut Shop for the Swiss cheese omelettes.

And to Kevin M. Boyle, who went through hell during the writing of this book. If it weren't for his unending support and tireless patience, it may never have been written.

We wish to acknowledge the following photographers and companies for permission to reproduce their photographs.

Oscar Abolafia: page 103. Irv Antler: page 95 left. Nancy Barr: pages 11, 52, 69 bottom left and top right, 91, 101, 108 left, 112, 150. From the Collection of Nancy Barr: pages 18, 23, 25 bottom right, 36, 37, 42, 46, 55, 85 bottom right, 92. Nancy Barr/Retna Ltd.: page 145 right. The Bettmann Archive: pages 66 left, 78. The Billy Rose Theatre Collection/The New York Public Library at Lincoln Center: pages 61 left and center. Ron Galella: pages 2, 63, 76 left, 97 top, 98, 99 top, 106 right, 107 left, 133, 143 right, 144, 145 left, 146 left and right, 151, 154. Globe Photos Inc.: pages 58 left, 90, 105. Darlene Hammond/Retna Ltd.: page 148. The Museum of Modern Art/Film Stills Archive: pages 6, 9, 12, 13, 20, 21, 23, 25 top left and bottom left, 30 right. The National Broadcasting Company Inc.: pages 64 top left and bottom left, 66, 80, 96. Louis Nemeth: page 76 right. From the Collection of Alan W. Petrucelli: pages 17, 35, 40, 42, 43, 56 top, 57, 60, 64 right, 67 top and bottom, 71, 72 top and bottom, 73, 74, 75, 84, 85 top and bottom left, 93, 107, 108 right, 111, 115 right, 119, 120 top and bottom, 135, 137, 138, 139, 140. Photoreporters, Inc.: page 99. Phototeque: page 18, 115 left, 116 bottom, 117. Springer/Bettmann Film Archive: pages 19, 26. United Press International: pages 30 left, 46, 47, 48, 56 bottom, 58 right, 68, 116 top, 128. Thomas J. Wargacki: pages 76 center, 88. Wide World Photos: pages 11, 14, 22, 24, 25 top right, 32, 47, 59, 61 right, 82, 89, 95 right, 97, 100, 102, 113, 125 top and bottom, 126, 129, 131, 134, 142, 143 left, 147, 152. Richard Young/Retna Ltd.: pages 153, 156.

We also acknowledge the following film companies for their stills: Allied Artists, American International, Metro-Goldwyn-Mayer, Orion, Regional Films, Twentieth Century-Fox and United Artists.

A Fan's Notes

I first met Liza Minnelli in 1969. I was a twelve-year-old junior high school student. She was Judy Garland's daughter.

Liza was peeking at me from page three of the New York *Daily News*. She was actually staring at the camera, but an infatuated adolescent does not discern the difference between peeking and staring. I found myself staring back.

The photograph I'm talking about is a strange one. It accompanies full-page coverage about Judy's death. Judy, son Joey and second daughter Lorna form a grinning triangle, but it is Liza — alone, on the left — who stands out. Blame it on her toothy smile or the exaggerated collar of her white turtleneck sweater, or my own empathy. Somehow, that day, Liza was the center of attraction. She still is.

Liza and I "met" again nearly eighteen months later. It was Christmas time, 1970, and we were having dinner together at the Empire Room of Manhattan's Waldorf-Astoria Hotel. Rather, my parents and I were having dinner. Liza was performing.

My mind never digested what we ate for dinner (I believe it was chicken divan), but I have never forgotten the dessert: two hours of sweat and silk, drama and dance, sequins and song. Liza live! Saturday, December 19, 1970, marked the first time I had seen Liza in person. It would not be the last.

After the show, I approached Liza for an autograph. A towel was wrapped around her neck to absorb the excess perspiration from her face. She was exhausted. She took one look at my outstretched hand, pen and paper and cried, *verbatim*, "No, no, please! I can't."

It was the best turn-down I ever received.

✂   ✂   ✂

One does not become a fan overnight. It may seem like that—one film or one concert, and you're hooked for life. But celebrity adulation takes weeks to recognize, months to develop and years to nurture. Just like falling in love.

I fell in love with Liza Minnelli fourteen years ago. Since then, I have watched her grow from a gawky young woman into a Halston-clad superstar. I have witnessed the highs and the lows. Applauded when I wanted to; booed when I had to. I have never cheated Liza. I may be just a fan, but I'm a damn good one. I know it; Liza knows it.

Over the years, I have also discovered that Liza and I have some things in common. We both have the same four last letters in our surnames. We both are of Italian-American extraction. We both love Coke—although I don't use a straw, and Liza prefers hers mixed with Grand Marnier. Liza and I also share the same favorite author: Dorothy Parker. And it was only very recently that I discovered we both appreciate the same Parker poem, *Résumè*:

> Razors pain you;
> Rivers are damp;
> Acids stain you;
> And drugs cause cramp.
> Guns aren't lawful;
> Nooses give;
> Gas smells awful;
> You might as well live.

✄ ✄ ✄

Liza Minnelli did not want this book written. When she heard I was doing it—shortly after I had hand-delivered a letter to her Manhattan apartment—she let it be known that she was not cooperating with me. Several of Liza's friends would not speak to me; letters went unanswered; phone calls were never returned. Word was out that *Liza! Liza!* would be an unauthorized biography, and those who fear the Minnelli wrath stayed away.

A few weeks before I began writing this book, I contacted Allen Eichhorn, Liza's New York press agent. Since Deanna Wenble is no longer her manager (she was "let go" soon after Liza married Mark Gero), Allen is now handling most of Liza's private and professional affairs.

I phoned Allen one cold winter day and explained my story; he explained Liza's. "She wants to preserve the memories of her mother for her own book," he told me. I then mentioned the card Liza sent me from France in January, 1970, the one in which she wished me *"Bonne année."* I told him about my collection of Minnelli memorabilia and reiterated my fan's devotion. Couldn't Liza share *something* with me? Allen listened patiently. He promised to call me back. He never did.

As early as 1977, I had been cautioned not to write a book about Liza Minnelli. Nancy Barr, a celebrity photographer who has known Liza since 1962, warned me in a letter. "If you contacted a publisher in regard to a book on Liza and she heard about it," the letter reads, "your name [would be] forever tarnished with her. Liza is *not* the same person you met at the Waldorf; she is a woman now; not the same naive, vulnerable little girl she always gave the appearance of being. Things have changed with Liza, and you could easily put yourself in a position in which you could be deeply hurt if you made the wrong moves."

I never answered the letter.

✄ ✄ ✄

Liza Minnelli has been my addiction for fourteen years. It has not been a waste of time. In fact, Liza has become one of my greatest teachers. From her, I have learned how to discern between a good entertainer and a great one. I have learned how to deal with people on an active, energetic level. But the most important lesson I've learned from Liza is how to recognize—and welcome—change. And it is that change which brought about this book.

Since 1969, I have gone from a professional fan to a professional writer. With *Liza! Liza!* I have meshed the two together, hoping to cast new light on that galvanized, impregnable star lost in the ambiguity of fame.

For too long, I have held back. This book is my push forward.

Alan W. Petrucelli
July, 1983
Bronxville, New York

Liza! Liza!

Naming a Star

Judy Garland could not sleep. Perhaps it was the unfamiliar bed. She was on a business trip with her husband Vincente Minnelli, and they were staying in Suite 904 of Boston's Ritz-Carlton Hotel. It was a weekend in 1945.

Judy tossed and turned: she was pregnant and felt edgy. She finally gave in to her insomnia and nudged Vincente.

"I have a name for the baby if it's a girl," Judy said. "How about *Liza?*" Judy pronounced the name with a hard *i*, *Lie-za*.

Even in his sleepy state, Vincente liked the idea. Ira Gershwin was a dear friend and naming a child after his song would be a touching tribute—Judy and Vincente had decided on Vincente Junior if the child were a boy.

Vincente agreed, *Liza* would be fine. Judy smiled and fell asleep.

A few moments later, Vincente was the restless one. He began nudging his wife. "But you know," he sighed, "I always wanted to name a child after my mother. Couldn't we call her *Liza May?*"

Judy beamed. *Liza May Minnelli*—perfect!

With that, both drifted to sleep.

Preface

Whenever she is nervous, Liza Minnelli bites her nails to the quick. Sometimes the cuticles even bleed. It is a habit Liza acquired in her youth. The traumas she suffered as an adolescent —hiring and firing servants, and living with her mother's suicide attempts and erratic behavior—became too much of a burden, so nail biting became a habit that expelled Liza's nervous energy. It was certainly less masochistic than the drug addictions of her mother.

On Tuesday, March 27, 1973—the night of the Forty-Fifth Annual Academy Awards—Liza was nervous. She was nominated as Best Actress for her role as Sally Bowles in *Cabaret*, and the competition was tough: Maggie Smith for *Travels With My Aunt*, Cicely Tyson for *Sounder*, Diana Ross for *Lady Sings the Blues* and Liv Ullmann for *The Emigrants*.

Outwardly, in her clinging, low-scooped, two-piece yellow dress, her sterling silver Elsa Peretti teardrop pendant and triple-strand gold bracelet, Liza looked calm. But inwardly, Liza was beyond nervous—Liza was hysterical. And now, more than ever before, Liza wanted to bite her nails. But she knew she couldn't. Tonight, Liza's nails were fake.

Oscar Night, 1970

Cabaret marked Liza's second Oscar nomination. In 1970, she was nominated for her poignant performance as Pookie Adams in *The Sterile Cuckoo*. But that night, unlike the night that would follow three years later, Liza was in no position to be nervous. Liza was drugged.

The week before, Liza was in a motorcycle accident on Hollywood's Sunset Boulevard. After dining with actor friend Tony Bill, Liza decided to go for a ride. She hopped onto the cycle and, before she knew what was happening, it spun onto an oil slick. Liza was hurled through the air. She remained unconscious for over an hour.

Today, Liza laughs at the incident. She all but dismisses it, something she often does with painful events in her life. "All I remember was this big light shining in my face," she says, "and a policeman telling me I was going to be all right. It wasn't even a good accident," she adds, "because it wasn't even a big cycle, but a motor scooter."

The accident was more serious than Liza likes to admit. She was rushed to the hospital in near critical condition, suffering from a broken front tooth, fractured shoulder, and kidney damage. It took twenty-five stitches (and later, some plastic surgery) to mend her lacerated face. Yet there was humor in such a frightening situation. When Peter Allen, Liza's husband at the time, found out about the accident, he phoned the hospital and asked to speak to "the East Coast branch of the Hell's Angels."

Liza was as resilient as her mother had been, and she was determined not to be hindered by the crash. She left the hospital within five days. "I just couldn't be bothered staying in bed anymore," she remembers. Liza had less than one week to recover before the Oscar ceremonies. She was often in pain and the drugs she took to help alleviate the discomfort left her lethargic. Yet Liza would not miss the Oscars—after all, it was her first nomination—so Liza hired Charles Schram, the man responsible for her grotesque makeup in the film *Tell Me That You Love Me, Junie Moon* to make her swollen and sore face presentable. Schram had also done Judy Garland's makeup in *The Wizard of Oz* nearly forty years earlier. Using his movie magic, Schram was able to hide the raw scars under layers of makeup.

"I was kind of all patched up," Liza recalls, "though to people I looked all right. I had my right arm in a sling. The doctor had given me a shot—he said it was a minor painkiller—and I was in a daze. So I just hung onto Daddy—you should have seen us, a real hot twosome!"

Obviously Liza's drug-induced stupor was not as minor as Liza was led to believe. When the Best Actress was named—Maggie Smith and *not* Liza Minnelli—Liza hooted and applauded, almost as if she were *rooting* for her competition. This is something most nominees (in the same category, no less!) just wouldn't do.

Later, when she realized what she had done, Liza explained: "I didn't even know it was the Best Actress category. I applauded and Daddy said that was it. I had been in such pain—whatever the doctor gave me made me a little woozy—so I just sat there not knowing what was going on."

Oscar Night, 1973

But on that warm night in March, 1973, Liza, as tense as she was, knew exactly what was going on. She and Desi Arnaz, Junior (her fiancé at the time) picked up her father and his date, Lee Anderson, in a studio limousine at 5 P.M. It took nearly an hour to get from Vincente's Beverly Hills home to the Dorothy Chandler Pavilion in downtown Los Angeles. For the length of the drive, the foursome laughed and giggled at vapid, often-repeated jokes. Laughter was the defense mechanism Liza chose that night so she wouldn't have to deal with what was about to happen.

If anyone was more nervous than Liza, it was her father. Vincente (himself an Oscar winner in 1958 as Best Director for *Gigi*) was better at hiding his frayed nerves than his daughter was; the six years he spent married to Judy Garland provided him with ample techniques to mask his anxieties. And tonight, his paternal pride shook his techniques. On the way to the Pavilion, Liza would frequently laugh; but somehow, Vincente's laughs were always just a bit longer and louder.

By the time the limousine screeched in front of the theater, the rows of curious bystanders were dozens deep. This was nothing new. Every year, die-hard fans camp out overnight on the wooden bleachers set outside the building where the Oscars are being held. This Tuesday night was no exception: people began arriving at 6:30 the night before. As each personality left a limousine or elegant car, Hollywood columnist Army Archerd shouted out the name in true movie premiere style, and the crowd of over two hundred, like a chorus, acknowledged both presence and popularity. The louder the applause, the more deafening the shouts, the more famous the person. That night, Groucho Marx was squealed at, Natalie Wood and Robert Wagner were shrieked at, and Liza Minnelli was screamed at.

Television reporters pestered Liza for on-the-spot interviews. Questions, questions. Everyone had them. And everyone demanded different answers, answers that would make good copy. What will you say if you win, Liza? Are you going to marry Desi, Liza? What would your mother have said tonight, Liza? The bombardment went on and on by newsmen seeking good quotes.

One got one. As Liza was entering the theater, she turned to a reporter and matter-of-factly said, "Well, if I don't win, I can always think of it as a nice party."

After posing for the endless blast of photographers' flashes, Liza and Desi were ushered to their choice, roped-in seats. Desi sat to the left of his fiancée, Vincente to her right, and Lee Anderson sat on Vincente's right. Shortly before seven o'clock, the houselights dimmed. The golden ceremony was beginning.

Liza was too nervous to realize that *Cabaret* was sweeping the Oscars; by the time Joel Grey and Bob Fosse won for their work, seven other *Cabaret* contributors had also won golden statuettes. Fosse, a dear friend and ex-lover of Liza's, would also win an Emmy Award two months later for his direction of Liza's NBC-TV special, *Liza With a Z*.

When Marlon Brando was named Best Actor for his role in *The Godfather*, an aspiring Indian actress, Sacheen Little-feather, stepped to the podium. At Brando's request, she delivered a forty-five second tirade on the harsh treatment of Indians by the Hollywood community. Her speech was originally three pages long. Littlefeather's comments—greeted by a sprinkling of applause and some boos—put a damper on the festivities. The fact that the show was running nearly an hour late didn't help, either. Later, when questioned about Brando's remarks, Liza simply said, "Sending someone else is a bit of a cop-out."

The bad mood didn't prevail for long. Immediately after the Best Actor was announced, Raquel Welch (who appeared onstage to announce Best Actress with Gene Hackman) brought some levity to the evening. "I hope the [Best Actress] winner doesn't have a cause, too," the buxom star quipped, much to the audience's delight.

A Star Is Born

The time had come. Vincente Minnelli remembers it well. "All during the proceedings," he has said, "I felt as if I were watching them through seven layers of gauze and listening to them through an echo chamber. I felt like I was going through World War III. My only touch with reality seemed to be those nervous moments when Liza squeezed my hand. Lee and Desi seemed to be enjoying the show immensely, but I'd occasionally catch their sideway glances to see how Liza and I were holding up under the strain."

Liza held up surprisingly well. "I was holding onto Desi's hand," she remembers, "and I was also holding onto Daddy's hand. When Gene Hackman said, 'The winner is Liza Minnelli,' Daddy let out a yell in my ear, enough to deafen me for life. Now, I'm not used to this from him. It was just the *shriek* of the century—hysterically funny—and I will never have perfect pitch again because of that yell. Oh, Desi let out a yell too, but it didn't compare to Daddy's."

After hearing her name, Liza rushed to the podium. She was excited, relieved and, yes, surprised that she had won. "I thought they were going to give it to Diana Ross because she did a really good job," Liza admits. "But when I saw her change her dress in the middle of the show, I felt she knew something I didn't know."

That night everyone—the invited audience and the television audience of more than eighty million—knew. Liza Minnelli was Best Actress. More than that, Liza Minnelli was now a *superstar*.

As she clutched the golden statuette to her chest, Liza said, with just the right amount of pathos in her voice, "Thank you for giving *me* this award. You've made *me* very happy." What makes Liza's acceptance speech so memorable is the way she emphasized the word *me*. It was a subtle emphasis, but few people had to strain to catch it. Even fewer people were shocked by her self-indulgence. They knew Liza Minnelli had made it. That night, a star was born.

That was one decade ago. Today Liza Minnelli's life and career are both still, as they say, a cabaret!

PART ONE

Rainbow's Child

If Vincente Minnelli had not been anemic, he may never have met Judy Garland. And surely there would be no Liza Minnelli—at least not the one we know today.

The year was 1943 and Arthur Freed, the genius producer of M-G-M movie musicals, wanted George Cukor to direct his new property, *Meet Me in St. Louis*. The film was to be based on the childhood memories of a writer named Sally Benson, stories that had been originally written for *The New Yorker*. M-G-M paid $40,000 for the film rights and wanted a success, much like Cukor's *A Philadelphia Story*, three years earlier. But Cukor was unavailable to direct *St. Louis*—he had enlisted in the army and was going off to war.

So Freed appealed to Vincente Minnelli, then the studio's up-and-coming musical director (Minnelli's first film, the all-black *Cabin in the Sky* made in 1942, had been a surprising success). Minnelli read the *St. Louis* script and agreed to do it. Why not? He had the time—he too had volunteered for the army, but, unlike Cukor, was turned down. He was anemic.

Judy Garland did not want to make *Meet Me in St. Louis*. She read the script and hated it. Then twenty-one years old and recently divorced from her first husband, bandleader David Rose, Judy thought the role of seventeen-year-old Esther Smith was too "Dorothy Gale from Kansas." Judy Garland, in real life, was growing up, and the characters she portrayed on the screen had to grow up too. Besides, the script seemed pointless; it was boring.

She complained to Louis B. Mayer. The curmudgeon of M-G-M (his roar was feared by some of the studio's biggest stars) paid little attention to most of Judy's whinings. This time, however, he listened. He read the script and telephoned Arthur Freed.

"Judy is right," Mayer told Freed. "Nothing much happens in the film." Freed and Minnelli would not give in; both wanted the film to be made. Minnelli had already envisioned the way he would use color and lighting to achieve the beauty the film would later have.

Whenever he was puzzled by a script, Mayer sent for his prized reader, an unyielding woman named Lillie Messenger. Mayer would ask her opinion; whatever she suggested, he would follow through on. Lillie read the *St. Louis* script, loved it and urged Mayer to do it. That was enough for the studio head to hear. *Meet Me in St. Louis* would be made. Arthur Freed would produce, Vincente Minnelli would direct, and Judy Garland would star.

When Judy was told the film was to begin shooting, she arranged a meeting with Vincente. She burst into his office, the *St. Louis* script in her small hands. "This isn't very good, is it?" she asked in a voice so hushed it belied her anger.

"I told Judy it was marvelous," Vincente recalls. "I said, 'I see a lot of great things in it. In fact, it's magical.' But Judy could not see the magic in my approach nor, I suppose, in me. She looked at me as if Arthur Freed and I were planning an armed robbery against the American public."

Meet Me in St. Louis has become a film masterpiece, a 14-karat Technicolor slice of Americana. But forty years ago, some people felt it would never be completed.

Trouble began the first day of shooting. The initial scene to be shot was between Judy and Lucille Bremer, but Judy would not say her lines as written. "Judy was making fun of the script," Vincente recalls. "Her intelligence showed through and she didn't come off as an impressionable young girl. However, Lucille was wonderful—you believed every word she said—and was doing a far better job than Judy."

Minnelli shot that scene twenty-five times, but never once to his liking. He would demand take after take, but his demands were done subtly, very unlike the harsh directors Judy was used to working with. Judy could not handle Minnelli's quiet stubbornness. Years later Judy would write, "Vincente made me do that scene until I was ready to scream."

One day during a lunch break, Judy broke down, sobbing uncontrollably. She phoned Arthur Freed. "I don't know what Vincente wants," she wailed. "He's making me feel I can't act."

At the time she was filming *Meet Me in St. Louis*, Judy Garland was a big star. *The Wizard of Oz*, made four years earlier, had turned Judy into a household name. Between 1939 and the release of *St. Louis*, Judy appeared in eleven other films. A studio car brought her to the M-G-M lot each day (usually last—and late), and she led the life of a celebrity: from dressing room to set to her Hollywood home. It was a pattern Judy found comforting—and one Vincente, the film's demanding director, found disturbing.

Vincente would always insist on call backs, even when Judy thought her work was perfect. He was never satisfied. There were always scenes to rehearse, new lines to go over. On days when filming ended early, he would call Judy back for more work, just as her car was leaving the studio gate. She resented Minnelli's perfectionism—and made it clear to him.

Judy would arrive late on the set, if at all. Once, she was scheduled to show at eight in the morning, but arrived more than five hours late, costing the studio nearly $30,000 in overtime. Whenever she felt the pressures mount, Judy would walk off the set. She often found solace in Mary Astor, the actress who was playing her mother in *St. Louis*. Astor would pacify her fuming friend with her homespun philosophy, saying, "Judy, Vincente knows what he is doing. Give him a chance."

Judy, raised by her own standards of discipline, did not realize that Vincente was trying to teach her to become a true professional, a disciplined actress from whom he could extract truth and beauty. Only when she saw a screening of *Meet Me in St. Louis*, only when she witnessed its ageless splendor, only when she saw the confident and in-depth performance Minnelli nurtured out of her, did Judy realize the man's genius. By that time, she was also in love with him.

"Towards the end of filming *St. Louis*," Vincente recalls, "fashion designer Don Loper decided Judy and I should get to know each other better on more neutral territory. He arranged a double date for Judy and me with his lady friend, Ruth Brady. We all hit it off immediately!"

Minnelli reveled in Judy's wacky sense of humor; it made him forget the problems this lady was causing him during the day. In turn, Judy found herself warming up to the man she never really allowed herself to know.

Less than a week after their first date, the quartet dated again. But when they attempted another date a few nights later, Loper couldn't make it. "I'm sorry, Vince," he told Minnelli, "but will you phone Judy and call it off?"

Vincente phoned Judy. "Don is sick so I guess we'll have to postpone the evening," he told her. Judy listened carefully, then let out a guttural laugh. "We don't have to go out with

Don and Ruth *every* time, do we fella?" she asked. "Let's do it alone."

It was easy for Vincente Minnelli to fall in love with Judy Garland. They shared similar backgrounds: she was pushed onstage by the time she was two years old, and he was performing children's roles at three-and-a-half as part of his family's Minnelli Brothers Tent Theater. Judy admired Minnelli's good taste; his impeccable sense of style. Vincente and Judy would meet often, alone at his home, and he would teach her about art and literature.

He gave Judy books on music and introduced her to the worlds of Cole Porter, Josephine Baker and Dorothy Parker. He taught Judy about life.

At the time Judy met Vincente, Judy was also dating film director-writer-producer Joseph L. Mankiewicz. She once even thought Mankiewicz made her pregnant. The tests were negative. In April, 1944, while *Meet Me in St. Louis* was being edited, Arthur Freed treated the film's cast and crew to an all-expense trip to New York City. Vincente and Judy went together and, for several weeks, shared living quarters. But Judy's demands were too much for Vincente to handle. The lovers broke up and Judy drifted back to Mankiewicz.

Shortly after he broke up with Judy, a lonely Vincente plunged into work on *Ziegfeld Follies*; he would direct ten of the film's fourteen vignettes. Minnelli wanted Greer Garson to mock her Mrs. Miniver/Madam Curie image in the vignette titled "The Great Lady Has an Interview," but the music proved too challenging for Garson to handle. Kay Thompson and Roger Edens, the couple who wrote the special material, suggested their friend Judy Garland. Minnelli loved the idea.

Minnelli recalls, "Any pain I might have been dreading in seeing Judy again simply didn't come to pass. We were no longer lovers, but we could be friends."

"The Great Lady" filmed smoothly (even though some critics thought Judy was spoofing Bette Davis spoofing Greer Garson). Soon after it was completed, Judy invited her director to lunch at the Players Club. Vincente and Judy spoke easily, a surprise to him since he was sure the more intimate setting would make him uncomfortable.

Judy talked endlessly about her next film, *The Clock*, a war romance which offered Judy her first real dramatic role. *The Clock* was temporarily shelved—director Fred Zinnemann was fired in an unprecedented move. Some said the reason was because of script problems, but Hollywood sources

insisted Judy wanted Minnelli to direct instead. It seemed that Judy was, again, taken by Minnelli and wanted to be near him; and it was no secret that he wanted to be near her. He read the script for *The Clock*, wrote Zinnemann a letter and asked M-G-M for permission to direct the film. Because *Meet Me in St. Louis* was such a success, the studio bigwigs consented and three days after Judy's luncheon with Vincente, *The Clock*, for the second time, began filming in September, 1944.

The Clock was completed in less than a year; upon its release in May, 1945, it, too, was a big success. Again, Vincente and Judy were deeply in love, this time it seemed for good. Judy moved into his home. And Vincente gave her an engagement ring he designed himself: an exquisite pink pearl set in an ebony shadowbox. Vincente would also design their wedding rings: gold bands studded with pink pearls and set in ebony shadowboxes. Years later, Liza would fall in love with her mother's engagement ring and beg her father for a copy.

At first, Judy was so eager to marry Vincente that she suggested they elope to Mexico. But Vincente was well aware that Judy's divorce from David Rose had not been finalized yet, and vetoed the idea. Minnelli went to work on *Yolanda and the Thief*; Garland on *The Harvey Girls*.

Judy wanted a traditional wedding with organ music, rice, flowers and tears. She wanted it in the most romantic city she knew: New York. But Louis B. Mayer would not be able to attend if it were on the East Coast (supposedly problems at the studio were mounting), so Judy was forced to marry her second husband at her mother's house in Los Angeles. The wedding took place on June 15, 1945, one week after her divorce, and five days after her twenty-third birthday.

The ceremony was small: Ira Gershwin was best man, Betty Asher, Judy's publicist and best friend, was maid-of-honor. Louis B. Mayer gave the bride away. Arthur Freed was there, as were M-G-M publicity chief Howard Strickling and Judy's sisters, Virginia and Suzy.

Almost immediately after the ceremony, the couple drove to the train station to embark on a honeymoon in Manhattan. Judy and her new husband rented a duplex apartment on posh Sutton Place, which boasted a magnificent view of the East River, and they began to live together again.

Although she wasn't totally free of M-G-M's demands (Judy was forced to go on publicity rounds to promote the upcoming release of *The Harvey Girls*), it was a good time for Judy. For

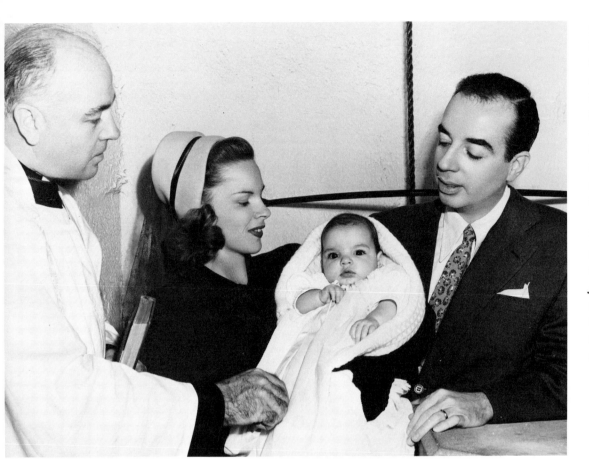

the third year in a row, the Gallup Poll named her one of the five most popular actresses in the country. She had given up pills, or so she hoped. A few days into their honeymoon, Judy had thrown a vial of pills into the East River, vowing, "I'll never take them again." In the later years of her life, Judy claimed her dependence on drugs began during her early days at M-G-M. She said the studio forced her to take diet pills and she even complained that Louis B. Mayer was having amphetamines ground into her food. "M-G-M gave me pep pills to keep me on my feet long after I was exhausted," Judy said. "Then they'd take me to the studio hospital and knock me out with sleeping pills." But that weekend in New York, Judy had no need for drugs. For Judy, love was the greatest narcotic.

Ten days before the newlyweds left New York to return West, Minnelli took his wife to a Park Avenue doctor. Their suspicions were correct: Judy was pregnant.

A Beautiful Baby

Judy Garland gave birth to her first child nearly three months before her twenty-fourth birthday. It had been an easy birth, except for some very painful calf cramps and delivery through Caesarean section, because Judy's pelvis was too narrow to allow a normal delivery. There were no physical postpartum complications.

Liza May Minnelli—May adapted from Vincente's mother Minna, who had died shortly before her son's wedding—debuted at 7:58 A.M. on March 12, 1946, at Los Angeles Cedars of Lebanon Hospital. She weighed in at 6 pounds, 10½ ounces, a pink-faced, wrinkle-free baby with a robust cry that rang throughout the nursery. Even at her birth, Liza Minnelli demonstrated the determination she inherited from Judy.

"Liza was the most beautiful baby in the nursery, a perfect child. When I first saw her, she was letting out a healthy cry—projecting! I couldn't wait to get home to her each night!" Vincente recalls.

Like all proud parents, Judy and Vincente thought their baby was beautiful. So did godparents William Spear and his wife, the part time actress, Kay Thompson; as well as Louis B. Mayer, Arthur Freed and the rest of the M-G-M honchos. Kay

11

Thompson would later base Eloise, the fictional character from Thompson's best-selling children's books, on Liza's childhood antics.

Liza was born with a surprisingly large amount of auburn hair on her head. It may have looked adorable on her as a newborn baby, but in later years the hair also developed on her face (in the area where men grow sideburns) and on her arms. It is a problem many women have and a problem Liza inherited from Judy. But today, it's rare to catch a hirsute Liza. She has the excess hair removed on a regular basis.

Growing up, Liza never thought she was beautiful. "I was the Queen of Ugly," she says, "real weird looking, with brown oxford loafers and lots of fat. I remember dancing on our front lawn and as this car passed by, a woman leaned out the window and vomited. Now how's *that* for rejection? I figured

that was proof how ugly I was. But when I told Daddy the story," she adds, "he laughed and told me it was all right. Daddy told me I didn't make the lady throw up. Isn't it nice to have someone take the pain away? My Daddy always did that."

Liza is still self-conscious about her looks, even today, and she's often admitted that she would love to get her nose cosmetically altered. Liza spends hours painstakingly applying her makeup and asterisk spider lashes to achieve what she calls "my professional face." But it doesn't always work.

When Liza opened in *The Act* on Broadway in 1977, John Simon, reviewing the lackluster show for *New York* magazine, wrote: "I've always thought of Miss Minnelli's face deserving of first prize in the beagle category. [She has] a face going off in three directions simultaneously: the nose always

inside and at least I don't have to worry about staying beautiful for my fans."

Ask Liza what she thinks the best part of her anatomy is, and she smiles. Sometimes she picks her "huge brown eyes"; other times it's her "phallic tits."

Not being beautiful is just one of Liza's physical problems. The other one is her weight. "When I was little," she explains, "I was always pudgy. By the time I was thirteen years old, I weighed 165 pounds! A real *el chubbo*!" In recent years, Liza has often been mistaken for pregnant when it was merely extra poundage. Until a few years ago, she would order her clothes in three sizes, assuring her five-foot-five-inch frame a perfect fit despite her fluctuating weight. And of course, since 1970, Liza has had Roy Halston Frowick make her clothes. "Baby"—as Liza calls the fashion maven—knows how to handle Liza's weight problem and can hide, when necessary, her excess flesh (Liza claims she has a metabolism problem).

Liza also has a tremendous sweating problem and often has a towel waiting for her in the wings. Halston comes to the rescue again; by using lots of sequins and rhinestones, he can keep the unsightly sweat stains undercover.

"I see Liza as a lady Fred Astaire," explains Halston. "She looks great in shirts, pants and a snap-brim hat. I gave her confidence years ago. I made her realize how attractive and womanly she really is." Liza adds: "Baby is my friend, and because of him, I became one of the Best-Dressed Women in the world. He believed in bosoms when bosoms weren't in."

Hollywood Childhood

If Judy Garland and Vincente Minnelli were the reigning queen and king of Hollywood during the late forties and early fifties, then Liza Minnelli was its princess.

Liza grew up surrounded by the best in food, fashion, art, music, furnishings and people. "Daddy would read me all kinds of bedtime stories," she remembers, "from Colette to

en route to becoming a trunk, blubber lips unable to resist the pull of gravity and a chin trying its damnedest to withdraw into its neck, apparently to avoid responsibility. It is, like any face, one that could be redeemed by genuine talent, but Miss Minnelli has only brashness, pathos and energy."

Simon's description left Liza devastated. At the same time the review broke, Liza was undergoing marital problems with Jack Haley, Junior, her second husband, and the rather poor notices *The Act* received only compounded her depression.

"The longer someone knows me, the better I look," insists Liza. "Anyone who's known both Mama and Daddy has always said I look more like Daddy. Yet when I was living with Mama, I looked like *her*. But in all honesty, if you compare me with your average beauty, I just ain't it. If I was spectacular looking, maybe I wouldn't be able to act so well. Still, beauty is what's

H. G. Wells. He'd tell me about the Bois de Boulogne in real little details. Daddy gave me Paris this way, and it didn't disappoint me. Daddy was ethereal while Mama was more adamant."

Liza's birthday parties were always given at Ira and Lee Gershwin's house. The Minnelli home was simply not large enough to handle the crowd of 100 children, who usually attended the festivities. Neighbors Lana Turner, Lauren Bacall, Edgar Bergen and Oscar Levant would bring their offspring, and as the children played, the adults took turns watching to make sure everything went along without a hitch.

Liza's parties were no intimate soirées: each one was carefully choreographed by her father, who remembers: "In those days, the object wasn't to see how money could be spent, it was to find things that would delight the kids." One rule was that none of Liza's gifts could cost more than four dollars. But it took money—and lots of it—to supply the parties with their diversions.

"There might be a choo-choo train," adds Vincente, "in which the kiddies would get in the five or six cars and ride from one end of the block—which the Beverly Hills police had to block off—to another and back. Then there might be a Punch and Judy show, Disney shorts in the projection room, clowns, a female magician, pony rides and a taffy pull in the corner. The children's nannies would all sit guard by the pool while the kids, who never seemed to talk to each other, would go through all the attractions and come back for their ice cream and cake."

Liza's parties continued throughout her childhood. Even when Judy divorced Vincente, Liza's dad would still throw them, with Lauren Bacall often acting as surrogate mother. Liza has fond memories of them. "When I think back, I say, 'My God! I was so lucky to be able to have all that—even the drunken clown who worked every year!' My parties were not average; they weren't part of the ordinary life. But they were terrific times and I feel so grateful that I wouldn't change my life for anything."

Candice Bergen was a frequent guest at Liza's birthday parties. As a pampered Hollywood child herself, Candice was also

Vincente Minnelli did not direct the film Funny Face, *but he might as well have. "I love Daddy more than anyone in the world," gushes Liza, who, even today, refuses to let go of her father.*

given lavish parties by her ventriloquist father, Edgar. Her memories are not as attractive as Liza's.

"Our environment was on the highest level of the absurd," she says. "The birthday parties were organized follies—with trained dog acts, cartoons, triple screenings of new movies—we had every imaginable extravagance. It was all highly surrealistic, like living in a big playroom."

As Liza grew into womanhood, the parties grew less lavish. Now, her birthday is usually celebrated with a few close friends, Liza's husband and, of course, a visit or phone call from Vincente.

Two Minnelli milestones occurred at these parties—the first and only time Liza hit her father, and the first time Liza fell in love. Vincente remembers them both. "One year, I was talking to Betty Bacall and some other mothers. Some little girl came over and sat on my lap. I kissed her, but I didn't know Liza was watching. She came right over and punched me right in the nose! Did I see stars!"

The next incident—Liza's first romantic rendezvous—took place at her fifth birthday party. Lee Gershwin pointed out a quiet redheaded tot who was paying too much attention—at least in Vincente's eyes—to little Liza. When Vincente found out the boy was Timothy Getty, the son of oil heir J. Paul Getty, Vincente remembers thinking, "just for a minute, that we would all retire to the South of France."

Liza's version of Getty's crush differs. "I remember falling in love with this four-year-old boy and wanting to desperately neck with him. But all he wanted me for," Liza says, "was so he could jump on my trampoline!"

Crash Course in Growing Up

Liza does not like to talk about herself. She will do it when promoting a film, concert or album (being the shrewd businesswoman she is, Liza realizes it's all part of the business called show), but ask her about her life, specifically her childhood, and she will sometimes be evasive.

"I'm a private person and I don't give a damn what people write about me," she says. "Don't get me wrong—I *love* gossip and reading about other people's pasts. I just don't like talking about my own. People are always asking me, 'How was it?' What they can't get through their heads is that the past is finished for me—I've lived it. So I cannot think of why it should be so interesting."

Liza will admit that she had a childhood that was not normal. "I had a crash course in growing up," she says. "I learned too much, too soon, too fast. But I'm not a freak. I remember going through a period of my life when, if anyone laughed at me, I'd burst into tears. There were all these pressures going on around me—the broken marriages, the court appearances, the suicide attempts—but somehow I seemed to thrive on them. People think it's easy because Judy Garland was my mother. Boy, I've got news for them! Sure, it was tough being her daughter. But Mama was a friend of mine, a trying friend, but a friend. She never denied me anything and once she cried because she said she had no money to leave me. But Mama left me her guts and integrity."

Liza continues, "When I grew up and found out that nobody has an absolutely happy childhood, I was really assured. The kind of childhood I had could make you or break you. Luckily, I made it. Sure, my childhood was weird—it may have even been crummy sometimes—but it was never dull." How could it be? Although she was an accomplished swimmer by age two and often used the pool in her own backyard, the studio sets were better to make waves in. Liza's playground was the M-G-M backlot, and movie stars were her best friends.

Almost every day after she finished school, "which was so dreary," Liza would scurry to M-G-M in Culver City. The guard would let her in with a smile—everyone smiled at Judy's little girl—and Liza would seek out her mother and father and watch them work. But the waiting periods between the scenes of Judy's films were too boring for Liza, so she would spend some of her free time riding the camera boom and lining film shots with her father. Liza often found her father's work more exciting than her mother's: "I can hear my Mama sing around the house anytime," she once told a reporter on the set.

"M-G-M seemed like a factory to me," Liza recalls with glee in her voice. "I loved it. I got to know every inch of the studio, all the short cuts to the different stages and all the underground passages. And all the people knew me there. I would run around and chat with everyone." Studio executives, film stars and M-G-M personnel welcomed Liza, the pony-tailed lass with the wide-eyed sense of wonder and lively sense of curiosity.

"What really interested me the most," Liza adds, "was watching people dance. The musical numbers were so wonderful and I wondered if I could do them. I'd go over to Re-hearsal Hall B or C and watch Cyd Charisse, Gene Kelly and Fred Astaire. I'd study them, learn their numbers, then go home and practice for hours in front of the mirror."

Liza put to use her newly-acquired dance expertise. She performed mini-extravaganzas for her parents. Dressed in one of the many costumes Vincente had copied for her from actual movie star gowns (studio designers Adrian and Irene Schraff designed these), Liza and her pals would recreate musical numbers from some of M-G-M's best films (as Liza grew older, the costumes would be passed down to her half-sister Christina Nina, whose mother, Georgette Magnani, was Vincente's second wife).

Oscar Levant's daughter Amanda would often participate, as would Mia Farrow (Maureen O'Sullivan's daughter), Tish Sterling (Ann Sothern's daughter), Portland Mason (James Mason's daughter) and Juliet Colman (Ronald Colman's daughter). "My pals and I would work on the numbers during recess at school," Liza recalls. "One of the first ones we did was from *The Band Wagon*. We did it for Daddy and later for Mama on her birthday."

Gayle Martin, Dean Martin's daughter, always participated in these shows and remembers them well. "We'd put on lots of shows," she says, "because some of us had lots of parents. We would rehearse like pros until we got it right."

They usually did. Judy was enthralled by her daughter's enthusiasm (if not yet her singing ability) and would often shout bits of criticism—"Kick higher! Sing out!"—to the children during the shows. Sometimes, Liza would be given a post-performance singing lesson from her mother. "After the variety shows," Liza remembers, "Mama would teach me the music to songs, but not the lyrics. So I just sang my name, Liza May Minnelli, in place of the words."

Unfortunately, Vincente had a demanding work load and rarely witnessed the best of Liza's mini-musical epics. The one time he did catch a show—held outside after a light rain—he was so awed by his daughter's creativity that he not only missed a dinner party he was invited to, but he soiled his tuxedo from sitting on the wet ground.

Liza was spoiled by her father. "Spoiled rotten," she gig-

Judy, in elaborate dress for The Pirate, *holds her beautiful baby. Liza was often bored when she visited Judy on film sets. "Too much waiting around," Liza recalls. "And who wanted to hear Mama sing? I got that at home for free!"*

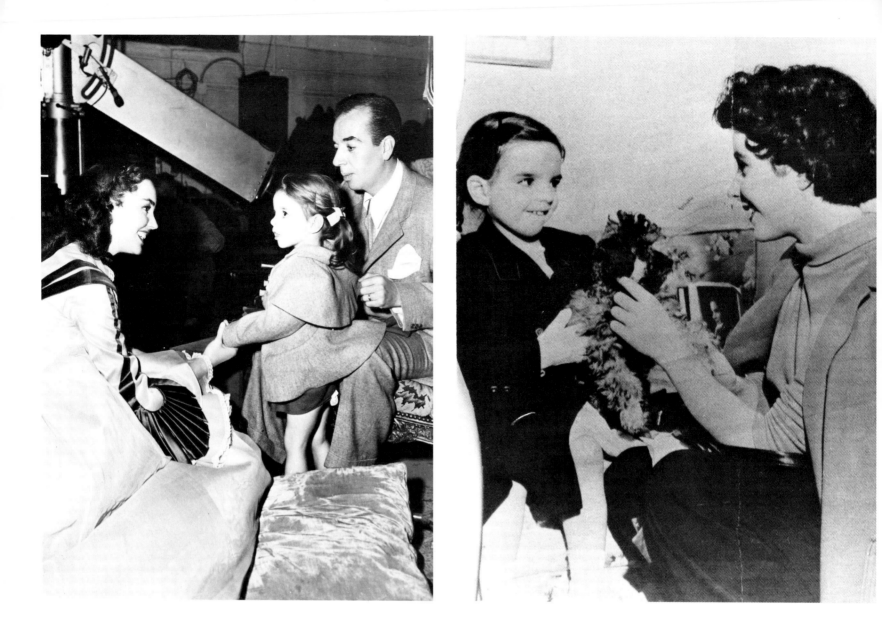

gles, "but with love." Vincente adds, "If I spoiled Liza outrageously, it was done to achieve a balance with the starkness of her life with Judy [after the divorce]. Much as Liza loved her mother, Judy represented duty and worry. I required nothing. As a result, I shared Liza's most carefree times. Judy was sadly short-changed." Vincente, it should also be noted, spoiled Judy as well. Writing in the by-lined article, *The Real Me*, in the April, 1957, issue of *McCall's* magazine, Judy said, "I cannot call my marriage to Vincente Minnelli a mistake. He spoiled me and babied me."

In return, Liza spoiled her father with devotion. "Daddy always treated me like a lady," she says. "I remember him taking me to the Ice Capades one day when I was four years old. When we arrived, I had a frilly white dress on. I looked

around at the other kids and realized I wasn't dressed right. I said, 'Daddy, I don't want to go. I don't feel right.' Well, it was a long drive back home, but Daddy took me and let me change my clothes. Then he took me back. Even back then," Liza adds, "when I was so very young, Daddy dealt with me on a feminine level. He always trusted me; to do that to his little girl is probably the most valuable thing that could have happened to me."

Judy's Breakdown

It all began to happen when Liza was just nine months old. Under Vincente's acute direction, Judy began filming *The Pirate* on December 21, 1946. She was making nearly $1,000 a day —her M-G-M contract stipulated that she be paid $5,619.23 a

Actress Jennifer Jones (far left) greets Liza on the set of Vincente's film Madame Bovary. *Nearly two years later, Liza and Elizabeth Taylor saw eye to eye as they played with Vincente's toy poodle on the set of* Father of the Bride. *When Liza dropped by to visit Judy between film shots, she brought along a new member of the Minnelli household, her favorite doll. Liza is still Vincente's favorite doll, although she's now a bit too large for him to cradle in his arms.*

week for five years—but offstage, Judy was paying dearly. She was suffering from colitis and was painfully thin, a fact even Irene Schraff's lavish costumes could not hide. Her addiction to pills had started again, much to the chagrin of her husband, who kept trying to rid Judy of her addiction.

When Judy would show up on the set, after days of being gone (absenteeisms Vincente dismissed to the studio heads as sicknesses) and more often than not in a stupor induced by Benzedrine or Dexedrine. She would either be gay and fun to be around, a down-to-earth hard worker, or she'd harshly criticize Vincente in front of the film's crew.

"Judy, in her paranoia, became jealous of the time Gene Kelly and I were spending together," Vincente recalls. "We would be so concerned with getting the choreography right that we excluded Judy from our discussions. I'd felt it wasn't necessary for her to have to deal with such problems. But she felt neglected."

Tensions mounted at the studio, and Judy brought them home with her to the Minnelli house, a mock-Mediterranean, pink stucco edifice high in the Hollywood hills. She and Vincente fought often; the loud arguments screeching to a halt only when Judy would storm out of the Evansview Drive home to sleep on Ira and Lee Gershwin's spare living room sofa. Days later, Judy would meekly seek out Vincente's guidance and support. But the reconciliations were temporary; soon

Liza never found ballet practice "tutu" difficult. At age three, she demonstrated grace and flair, and Liza could plié *with amazing agility. "I still take dance classes," Liza says. "I love to act and sing, but I consider myself a dancer first." Liza's first professional dance lessons came from Nico Charisse, who took Liza through her paces on Saturday mornings. "I'm sorry Mama didn't see me make it big," Liza adds. "But at least she saw me dance. Mama loved watching me dance."*

there was another fight, another night on the Gershwin sofa.

Judy was having such difficulty finishing *The Pirate* that Louis B. Mayer forced her to see Dr. Frederick Hacker, a noted Viennese psychiatrist, each day she worked. Mayer, obviously more concerned with bringing the film in on time than his star's mental health, paid Hacker's fees himself.

Judy played tricks on Dr. Hacker. "He really was a darling old man," she said, "but I could never 'associate freely' with him. In fact, sometimes I used to rehearse lines. I'd whip out of bed, dash over to the doctor's office, lie down on a torn leather couch and tell my troubles to an old man who couldn't hear, and who answered with an accent I couldn't understand. Then I'd dash back to Metro and make movie love to Mickey Rooney. No wonder I was strange."

Vincente would drive Judy to her fifty-minute sessions with

the doctor and wait in the car. Other times, Hacker would sit with Judy and Vincente and watch the daily rushes of *The Pirate*. But the therapy failed to work, and Judy's depression grew. About these times, Vincente recalls, "Judy's mood was unaltered, and our spats and bickerings became more magnified. I tried to control my own volatility, but occasionally failed. The lashing out left raw scars."

Liza was not then aware of her parents' fights. Judy and Vincente fought in their bedroom; Liza was safely ensconced downstairs in her nursery suite. When Judy was pregnant, Vincente spent almost $70,000 redecorating his home for his wife and soon-to-be-born Liza.

Sometimes Judy would wake up Liza at all hours of the night, when she was lonely and needed someone to speak to. One night a severely depressed Judy woke Liza, then less than

a year old, at 4 A.M. so actress Joan Blondell, who was visiting, could see her. Joan tried to talk Judy out of waking the soundly sleeping tot, but she failed. After lifting the baby from her crib and presenting her to Blondell, Judy warbled (at that hour and in her manic state, it was anything but singing) Liza back to sleep with "Over the Rainbow."

At a very young age, Liza suffered from excruciating earaches. It was an ailment that also plagued Judy as a child. Whenever her baby was sick, Judy would cancel all appointments and nurse Liza back to health. She would drop warm camphorated oil in Liza's ear and sit by her side until she felt better. Yet not everything was handled by Judy.

As she was growing up, most of little Liza's demands and needs were met by Mrs. MacFarlane, a British woman Vincente had hired to be Liza's nanny. Liza would be taken to the park

There was time for horsing around in Liza's childhood. At pal Monica Henreid's birthday party, two-year-old Liza (left) rode a merry-go-round horse thirty times! Monica's dad, actor Paul Henreid (below) was a good friend of the Minnellis. Liza loved making waves in the family pool (right).

by Mrs. MacFarlane. And while Liza played with playmates Mia Farrow and Gayle Martin, Mrs. MacFarlane would join the other nannies and watch sternly from the sidelines.

At night, Mrs. MacFarlane would prepare Liza for bed. The only thing the nanny did *not* do was tuck Liza in; that was a job reserved for one person—Judy, who took a great deal of time in bidding her daughter a loving good night.

Liza hated her nanny. "She treated me like a kid," Liza exclaims, "and beat the hell out of me." Liza's accusations may be hyperbole, but one thing is certain: Judy did punish Liza, but only on extremely rare occasions. Whenever she misbehaved, Judy would spank Liza quite severely. Then, perhaps to absolve the guilt she felt for hitting her child, Judy would kiss Liza's tears away. Later, Lorna would receive the same treatment, but Joey would rarely, if ever, be spanked.

Like all youngsters, Liza suffered from childhood fears. One thing she hated the most—indeed, the thing she was terrified of—was the dark. It was also a fear that Judy shared. Several nights a week, Liza would climb out of her crib and crawl up the flight of stairs leading to her parents' room. Once she reached the second-floor landing, Liza would crawl to Judy and Vincente's bed. "They'd put me in the middle and we'd all go to sleep," Liza remembers. "But sometimes, during

the night in their sleep, Mama and Daddy would hold hands across my stomach or head. I didn't dare move for fear I'd get tossed out. I didn't want that to happen because it was so warm and safe in there."

Ragged Edges

Except for a ballet number that belonged to co-star Gene Kelly, *The Pirate* completed filming on July 10, 1947. Judy and Vincente hosted a huge party on M-G-M Soundstage Ten; invited guests included Louis B. Mayer, Arthur Freed, Cole Porter (who wrote the music and lyrics to *The Pirate*) and Irving Berlin, who would begin work with Judy on *Easter Parade* that December.

It was a festive occasion. Judy and Gene entertained for hours, and Judy seemed in the best of spirits. Yet, if anyone carefully observed her, if anyone searched her deep-brown eyes, they could not have helped noticing how sick Judy Garland really was.

A few days after *The Pirate* gala, Ethel Gumm, Judy's mother, paid a visit to the Minnelli household. She was playing with her granddaughter Liza in the child's nursery, desperately trying to distract her from the commotion that was going on in her daughter's bedroom. Judy and Vincente were

having another scream fest; this one ended abruptly as Judy ran into the bathroom, crying that she was going to kill herself.

After hearing the sound of breaking glass, Ethel demanded, in an unusually ugly voice, that Judy open the door. When she did (even in her sobbing stupor, Judy knew her mother's rage was more real than her own), Ethel and Vincente rushed in and found Judy crying, her wrists cut by a broken glass. The wound was superficial—Ethel stopped the bleeding with a simple Band-Aid—but Judy's actions were severe enough for Dr. Hacker to suggest hospitalization. Worn and on the verge of nervous collapse, Judy Garland, M-G-M star and twenty-five-year-old mother and wife, was sent to Las Campanas.

"The only thing that I have carried over from the old Holly-wood days is my reputation for giving glamorous parties," says Liza. Growing up, Liza's birthday parties were spectacular mini-extravaganzas. On Liza's fourth birthday, Judy and Vincente gave their petite princess a puppy (above). At pal Candy Bergen's Christmas party, Liza screamed for ice cream—and got lots of it (top, right). Liza's first "beau," Timmy Getty, shared his seat with Liza and had a ball (bottom, right). And when Liza attended Candy's fifth birthday party, her pals Michael McLean and Vicki Danzig and Candy's father Edgar Bergen taught a visiting dog some new tricks (top, left)—one of which was not to follow Liza and pal Juliet Colman (Ronald's daughter, bottom, left).

Located in between Long Beach and Los Angeles in Compton, California, Las Campanas was a sanitarium that catered to the rich and privileged. Patients had their own bungalows and the sound of laughter from patients, from doctors and nurses, from friends and visiting family often could be heard echoing through the spacious grounds.

Las Campanas was an expensive hospital—in 1947 $300 a day was expensive, except, perhaps, for the head of a Hollywood studio—and it offered Judy superb treatment.

Judy referred to Las Campanas (and the institutions that would follow) as the "nuthouse." In the January and February, 1964, issues of *McCall's* magazine, Judy remembered her first days at the hospital. "It didn't take me long to realize that my bungalow was next to Ward Ten, the violent ward," she said. "I met some of the most charming people there—sensitive, intelligent, humorous people. As far as I could gather, none of them were demented in the common sense. Most of them were too highly strung for reality. I realized I had a great deal in common with them."

The day after Judy was driven to Las Campanas by Dr. Hacker (he felt it would be easier on Vincente if he took her himself), Vincente told Liza, then barely fourteen months, that her mother had gone away. "I told our daughter that her mother would be back very soon," Vincente recalls. "I'm thankful that Liza had a very capable nurse during these years. Between the two of us, we hid the unhappy truth from her until she was old enough to cope with it."

Judy demanded that Liza be given visitation rights. "I developed a terrible case of melancholy over not seeing my baby," she said. "I kept asking, and they wouldn't let Liza visit me. Finally, I put my foot down. I *must* see Liza. After many conferences, they decided to bring her."

Liza's visits were emotional ones, mixed with tears and laughter, wet kisses and affectionate hugs. The gushing—baby talk, slobbering, *et al*—was kept at a minimum. Even in her emotionally crippled state, Judy did not believe in too much gushing.

"Liza would toddle into my bungalow and into my arms," Judy recalled. "I just held her, and she just kept kissing me and looking at me with those huge, helpless brown eyes. I didn't know what to say to her."

As happy as Judy was when Liza visited, she was equally devastated when her daughter left. Years later, Judy would recall one all-too-brief visit. "After they took Liza away," she said, "I lay down on the bed and started to cry. There have been many blue moments in my life, but I never remember having such a feeling. It was physical pain, pure torment at not being able to be with my baby. I almost literally died of anguish."

Judy's stay at Las Campanas helped her mental state, but not her marriage. The fights still came; in addition, Judy was now suffering from severe bouts of insomnia and woke Vincente almost every night seeking comfort. It was easy for Judy: she wasn't working and could sleep late in the mornings. But Vincente was working steadily at M-G-M and needed his sleep. Still, he always gave in to Judy's midnight pleas for help.

A major blow to the Minnelli marriage occurred when Judy's doctors suggested that Vincente not direct Judy's next film, *Easter Parade*. Judy, they said, was associating her husband too closely with M-G-M; in fact, Vincente had become her personification of the studio. Charles Walters, who demonstrated his directorial capabilities with *Good News*, was given the assignment.

Judy's leading man in *Easter Parade* was Fred Astaire, a man Judy respected, admired and feared because of his total professionalism. They had met only once before, when both stars were serving on the Hollywood Cavalcade of Stars for War Bonds in 1942–3. Although Astaire was nearly twice Garland's age, he agreed to replace Gene Kelly (who had broken an ankle playing baseball), because he admired Judy.

When *Easter Parade* was released in July, 1948, it was such a success that M-G-M decided to reteam Judy and Fred for *The Barkleys of Broadway*. It would be, however, a film Judy would never make.

Filming *Easter Parade* was troublesome for Judy. She would arrive on the set late, struggling from the effects of the amphetamines she had taken that morning to help her lose weight. "I wouldn't ask Judy where she got the pills," recalls

Liza's heart may belong to Daddy—she still calls herself "Daddy's little girl"—but one thing is certain: Liza's profile belongs to Judy. When they didn't spend time riding camera booms and lining shots, Liza and Vincente discussed one of his favorite pastimes: women. "You always spoil them," Liza once told him. "You let Mama and all the others walk all over you. You let them take advantage of you." Vincente's reply: "Isn't that what women are for?"

Vincente, "because she'd become highly offended when I brought the matter up."

Easter Parade is the first Garland film in which there are noticeable changes in the star's weight. For most of the film she is thin, but watch the "When the Midnight Choo-Choo Leaves for Alabam'" number and you will notice a pudgy Judy.

On July 19, 1948, Judy received a registered letter from M-G-M, informing her that they were suspending her for her erratic behavior. It came at a bad time: Judy was still recovering from the sudden death the month before of one of her doctors, Ernst Simmel, and on the advice of her other doctors, she moved out of Vincente's Evansview Drive home.

The house Judy was living in was at Ten Thousand Sunset Boulevard in Los Angeles. She moved there to get away from her husband, who she claimed caused, along with M-G-M, most of her problems. It was a huge house—not far from her old one—and she rented it at $1,000 a month for one year. Liza would visit often with Vincente. But Judy was not well. She was beginning her three-month studio suspension and her weight had plummeted to 85 pounds. She was forced to drop out of *The Barkleys of Broadway* (Ginger Rogers replaced her). Once again, Judy Garland was down.

Liza was three years old when she began to be affected by her mother's mental breakdowns and the parental separations. True, her father was always around; even when he was too busy, he found time for his precious princess. Liza was thrilled when she spent days with her father, who often took her to the circus and on carnival rides. Liza would spend Saturdays with Judy's mother, Ethel, whom Liza fondly called "Nanna." Nanna Gumm would take her granddaughter to Nico Charisse's dance studios, where the tiny tot would sway to the music and, later, utilize what she had learned in her at-home mini musicals. About those early "training" days, Liza says, "There wasn't a moment I wasn't dancing. I thought my brains were in my feet!"

Although Judy hated her mother—"She's the real-life Wicked Witch," she told more than one reporter in her lifetime—she knew Ethel Gumm would keep Liza good company. She was obsessed with the notion of Hollywood fame and fortune and instilled this in Judy. She badgered Judy to become a star and practically ran much of her daughter's early life. Until the day she died, Judy felt she had betrayed her mother. Although she may have later resented it, she also knew Liza loved her

Nanna. Liza never met Judy's father, Frank Gumm. He died in 1935, almost eleven years before his granddaughter's birth.

These were hard times at the Minnelli home and Liza felt the burden. She passed the time watching television (she was only allowed to watch a few hours a day), nibbled at the dinner Mrs. MacFarlane set out for her or, when the rage became too great, smashed her toys.

"My first real horrendous recollection happened when Daddy and I were taking Mama to the train station," Liza recalls. "She was going away and crying so much because she didn't want to leave that Daddy ended up going with her. I wanted to go too, but all I did was stand there watching the train pull out of the station." Eventually, a tearful Liza was taken home by her nanny.

Baby Takes a Bow

It was inevitable that Liza would continue the legend set by her mother and father and follow her parents into show business. Yet who expected her movie debut would come when she was just two-and-a-half years old?

In the Good Old Summertime was Judy's first feature film for M-G-M since her suspension. She had sung just two songs in *Words and Music* a few months earlier. She was now to play Veronica Fisher, a music shop clerk who carries on a first-class love relationship—via US mail—with co-worker Van Johnson.

At the end of the film, Judy and Van marry, and Liza plays their little girl. As the closing music soars, Van picks up the tiny child and Liza, wearing a dress created by Irene, weakly smiles—Van had suggested Liza for the role.

It is less than a cameo—Liza appears for just a few seconds—but a memorable one. Says Liza, "I dressed myself and wore a pretty white outfit. But when Van picked me up, I remember feeling his cool hand on my rear end. I forgot to wear underwear!"

Her moment in *In the Good Old Summertime* was, even in its brevity, more important than Liza's role as the Virgin Mary in a school play two years later. Judy and Vincente came to the play, only to watch Liza "drop the baby Jesus" center-stage. Then, five years later, Liza made her second film appearance in her father's film, *The Long, Long Trailer*. Her wedding scene cameo was later cut, but Liza got to meet the film's stars, Lucille Ball and Desi Arnaz, whose son would later play an important role in Liza's life.

While Judy was making *In the Good Old Summertime*,

Vincente had been approached to direct a film version of Gustave Flaubert's classic novel, *Madame Bovary*. He jumped at the chance—first, because he had remained idle since his release from *Easter Parade*, and second, because he loved the *Bovary* story.

Judy's reaction to Vincente's choice assignment was less than supportive. "Here you are working with these great talents [Jennifer Jones, James Mason, Van Heflin]," Judy told her husband, "and what am I doing? Still playing the shopgirl around the corner!" Vincente remembers Judy's comments sounding "unexpectedly bitter," but he blamed them on the pills she was taking, and immersed himself in *Madame Bovary*. Vincente did not want to face the fact that his marriage had crumbled. There were reconciliations, but no matter how many or how joyous, it was only a matter of time before the marriage disintegrated altogether.

By the time *Summertime* was released to good reviews—critics found Judy's voice sweet and vibrant—Judy wanted to take a long-needed vacation with Liza. But Louis B. Mayer called her into his office and asked her for a delay, promising her the script he was handing her was to be her best film ever. M-G-M was planning on a $3 million production of *Annie Get Your Gun*, and Judy would star.

Mayer gave Judy $5,000 as a bonus on the contingency that she postpone her vacation to record one of the film's songs. Mayer told her that he wanted to begin the film while she was away. He promised Judy the "song" would take only a couple of days. Judy was fearful something was wrong, but she wanted to play Annie Oakley badly, so she agreed.

On March 25, 1949, Judy recorded one of the film's songs, "Doin' What Comes Naturally." Later that same day she also recorded "You Can't Get a Man With a Gun." The one day led into six weeks of work (Judy recorded the entire score), and Judy, who had been lied to by Mayer, was again on the verge of a breakdown.

She rarely slept, the Nembutals she took kept her jittery and nervous, and her hair was starting to fall out. "Dear God," Judy would joke, "I can hear it dropping to the floor!" She weighed a scant 90 pounds and that spring was given her first series of shock treatments, in the hope of combating her deep depression.

The wardrobe test shots taken of Judy during this time show a wan star, her eyes tired and unfocused, obviously resulting from the drugs she was taking and the lack of sleep. Mayer realized Judy could not continue filming and on May 10, because production costs were soaring, Judy was fired from *Annie Get Your Gun* (Betty Hutton, on loan from Paramount, later replaced Judy and M-G-M lost more than $1 million).

Vincente recalls those days of horror. "Judy was in terrible condition," he says, "yet she continued to take more pills. I caught her using them and took them away from her. Her reaction was enormously angry and, for the next few days, her treatment of me was cold and contemptuous."

As gruff as he was, Louis B. Mayer had a soft spot for Judy, his favorite actress. Upon her suspension, he met with Carleton Alsop, Sylvia Sidney's husband, who would later become Judy's manager, and they decided to send Judy to Boston's Peter Bent Brigham Hospital. M-G-M would pay the bill. "That's the least we can do," said Mayer.

On May 29, 1949, Alsop took Judy by train to Peter Bent. Once she was admitted the star told her doctors, internist George W. Thorn and neurologist Augustus Rose, that she had "only a physical problem." But Judy was there to withdraw from amphetamines and barbiturates.

Quitting drugs was a painful experience for Judy. Alsop would visit her daily (he was staying nearby, at the Ritz-Carlton) and find Judy sprawled under her bed, agonizing screams piercing the air. However, no matter how much hurt Judy was in, Alsop refused to give in to Judy's pleas for release.

In her 1964 *McCall's* article, Judy recalled those days at Peter Bent. "I was put on a diet of three great meals a day and lights out at nine o'clock at night, whether I slept or not."

During her stay, Judy was deluged with gifts and fan mail; almost every day Frank Sinatra sent presents, from perfume to flowers to records. Once the crooner even flew to Boston for a visit and, with the hospital's permission, he took Judy out on the town. Several days later, even Louis B. Mayer himself paid a call.

Judy had to undergo an electroencephalogram—a test to see if the brain is tumor free—and the only place to perform it was at Boston's Children's Hospital. Once there, Judy visited the retarded and rheumatic children who lived on the first four floors. At first she was reluctant—"It won't do me or the kids any good," she said—but once the children recognized her (as all children do, from *The Wizard of Oz*) and greeted her lovingly, Judy could not get enough. It was obvious that Judy missed Liza. Some of these children were her age, and they only reminded her how lonely Liza must be.

Judy later recalled in *McCall's*, "If I was cured at Peter Bent Brigham, it was only because of those children. All I can remember are their eyes. They were so friendly and waved at me from their little cribs." Judy summed up her experience in one sentence, "I loved feeling I was helping someone else for a change."

Judy was given a very special present on June 10—her twenty-seventh birthday—a visit from Liza. She flew to Boston (with her governess) from Los Angeles and was picked up by Judy and Alsop. The quartet spent the day at the Ritz-Carlton Hotel; ironically, in Suite 904, the same room where little Liza had been named years earlier by a sleepless Judy. On other visits, Vincente would join Liza and the three Minnellis would spend quiet afternoons in Fenway Park, watching the Red Sox practice baseball.

Four weeks after she entered Peter Bent Brigham Hospital, Judy was pronounced cured. She was no longer dependent on pills, and began to live a routine fit for Jane Doe: normal

sleeping habits, normal eating habits, normal drinking habits. It was time to celebrate, so Judy, Liza, Sylvia Sidney, Carleton Alsop and their son spent the July Fourth weekend in Gloucester, Massachusetts. Liza and Judy rode the carousel, and fought off gathering fans who wanted a closer peek.

When she returned home, Judy tried to rebuild her marriage to Vincente. They seemed content and often dined out at La Rue Café. But it was more a public illusion than a private truth; both knew their marriage was over, yet they felt they had to stay together for Liza's stability.

One of Liza's most cherished memories of this time was the first time "my father *really* spoke to me." One day, after a taxing day at M-G-M, Vincente, reclining on the living room sofa, turned to his tiny daughter and told her his impressions about de Gaulle's political tribulations in France. This was too much for Liza to handle, so she ran to the pool to find her mother. "Mama!" Liza cried. "Daddy is talking to me!" Vincente's seemingly innocuous remark became a milestone in

"I guess what's saddest [about life]," Liza says, "are broken dreams. But at least they leave room for new ones to come and take their place." Judy took us over the rainbow—and Liza is keeping us there. Judy could become quite affectionate with Liza (here she steals a smooch for the camera) but when Liza stole her mother's spotlight, whether at the Palace or Palladium, that affection turned to anger and hurt.

Liza's life because, for the first time that she was consciously aware of it, the most important man in her life—her father—had treated her like an equal, without any of the baby talk usually reserved for tots. Today, it is an incident Vincente still laughs at.

Recovery or Rage?

Gene Kelly did not want to make *Summer Stock*. He relented only as a favor to his friend, Judy Garland, who gave him his first break by helping cast him opposite her in *For Me and My Gal* eight years earlier.

Summer Stock was to be Judy's first film after her Boston hospitalization; although she was fifteen pounds overweight, she feverishly dieted throughout the filming (for most of the film, Judy is pudgy; the "Get Happy" finale, which boasts a svelte Judy, was filmed and tacked onto the film after all her weight was dropped).

Trouble developed very soon. Judy would call in late. She felt the film was beneath her talents; she was suffering from chronic migraines and would sometimes arrive on the set at the end of the day. Other days, when she did appear, she locked herself in her dresssing room, screaming for Vincente, who was also on the M-G-M lot, to take her home. Although their marriage was "over," Judy still needed Vincente, who acted as her surrogate father in times of trauma.

Judy continued to behave like this despite the fact that her actions were being meticulously watched by doctors from Peter Bent Brigham Hospital. Eventually *Summer Stock* was completed and, upon its release, was well received.

While Judy was working on *Summer Stock*, Vincente was completing *Father of the Bride*. The 1950 film starred Elizabeth Taylor, and Liza would often visit her on the set. Elizabeth was fourteen years older than Liza and treated Liza like a sister. They got along famously.

Today, Liza is still close to Elizabeth Taylor. "I love Elizabeth dearly," says Liza. "She's great fun and childlike, yet very much a woman. And what a beauty! Even when she's

heavy, she has that radiance that every woman—even me—longs to have."

Elizabeth is equally complimentary. "Liza as a little girl was both shy and precocious," she says. "She was also tender and intelligent. As a mature woman, she retains all of these virtues. She embodies all of the talents of her gifted parents and adds her own measure of pizzazz. I love her! She's like my daughter!" Elizabeth probably did a great deal to make Liza feel more secure, at a time when Judy was desperate and unhappy.

"Get Happy," *Summer Stock*'s finale, is an ironic title because that year, 1950, Judy was rarely happy at home. She tried to make the marriage work, but nothing—not dining out, not attending parties, not even Liza—*nothing* could save it.

Judy's rage went even further. One day, it was finally directed at her mother. After a fierce argument (perhaps one of the worst Judy ever participated in) with Ethel, Judy kicked her mother out of her house and forbade Mrs. MacFarlane, the nanny, to ever take Liza to "Nanna's house again." That afternoon, when Ethel Gumm stormed out of her daughter's rented house, marked one of the last times Liza would ever see her grandmother.

Liza remembers the first time Judy's rage was directed at her. She was lying on the upstairs family sofa, waiting to show her parents a cowboy movement she had recently learned. There was little Liza, outfitted like a little cowgirl—set and ready.

Judy had had a bad day at the studio and was pacing back and forth in front of the sofa. She was unaware of her daughter's planned surprise. Liza was timing herself. At the right moment—when her mother walked in front of her—she would arch her spine and spring forward, finally landing on her feet. The time had come. Up sprang Liza—a split-second off. The heel of her boot hit Judy in the head with a vicious impact.

Judy flew into a rage and screamed at the sobbing Liza to go to her room. Liza ran downstairs. Later, when Vincente came to console her, Liza tried to apologize profusely, but her voice always choked with tears.

A few moments later, Judy entered Liza's room. Mother and daughter rushed into each other's arms and after a prolonged embrace, Judy and Liza talked. It was their first real "woman-to-woman talk." Judy explained the art and business of moviemaking to Liza. How difficult it could be; how strenuous it always was. When she realized her daughter was

While Judy was going through her mental crises, Vincente became Liza's oasis of stability. The daddy-daughter duo would spend days at amusement parks (Liza loved the rides). As Liza grew older, Vincente dressed her up and took her on the town. In December of 1958, a twelve-year-old Liza attended the premiere of Vincente's film Some Came Running, *where she first met one of the film's stars, Shirley MacLaine. Today, Liza and Shirley are still close.*

perplexed, Judy tried more common ground: she compared her work to running a race. Liza now understood. "When I come home from work," Judy told Liza, "I'm sometimes a little nervous. And today, I took everything out on you. That was unfair."

From that moment on, the communication system—albeit a strange one—was developed between Judy and Liza. During her troubled times at M-G-M, whenever Judy couldn't cope, and Vincente or Carleton Alsop weren't around, Judy would sit Liza down and "play" therapy. She would scream and rant about M-G-M; how mean they were to her; how could they do this to a star? Little Liza, barely four or five years old, would sit there and nod. "Tsk-tsk, Mamma, tsk-tsk." Liza played Judy's psychiatrist. This went on for years. It was some of Judy's best acting.

One incident, in 1960, solidified their relationship even more. Liza was living with Judy in London, attending Miss Dickson and Miss Wolf's School for Young Ladies, where she was studying French. One day after school, Liza walked into

her mother's suite at the Surrey Hotel and witnessed a doctor injecting her mother in the buttocks. "Oh, no!" Liza exclaimed, fleeing the room. "Not again!"

The incident forced Judy to tell Liza—for the first time—the truth about her narcotics problem. "When I was at M-G-M," she told her daughter, "I'd be wide awake after work, so I was given a pill." Judy explained how, after years of taking pills (she fumbled over the word "pills"), "I kind of need them to feel better." Injections, she explained, were just another kind of pill.

Liza was silent. She had known her mother was plagued by drug problems for a long time, and now she was finally being told first-hand. Liza looked at her mother with a sympathetic gaze and walked out of the room.

Still, other incidents in Liza and Judy's lives are not without humor. After Judy told Liza the "facts of life," she promised her daughter that they would celebrate Liza's first period with a toast of sherry. When the big day came, however, there was no liquor to be found. Sid Luft, in an attempt to keep his wife sober, had hidden it. Yet Judy kept her promise—she and Liza did toast each other, but with cooking wine!

Judy and Vincente Divorce

June Allyson was pregnant, so M-G-M wanted Judy to replace her in *Royal Wedding*. The film would finally reunite Judy and Fred Astaire, and was to start filming the first week of June, 1950, less than three weeks after Judy completed *Summer Stock*. But Judy could not deal with the pressures, and on Saturday, June 17, 1950, Judy was fired from *Royal Wedding*. Jane Powell later replaced Judy.

Judy handled the suspension very poorly. Two days later, on Monday, June 19, Judy was talking with Vincente and her secretary, Myrtle Tully. Suddenly—Vincente claims it was about half past six in the evening—Judy ran into the bathroom screaming, "I want to die!" Vincente and Myrtle heard breaking glass, rushed to the bathroom door and Vincente, using a chair, broke in. There, in a crying heap, he found his wife, her throat cut with the jagged glass. Luckily, the wound was superficial and, like Judy's previous suicide attempt, no stitches were required.

Seven years later, Judy wrote about the incident in *McCall's* magazine. "I was a nervous wreck, jumpy and irritable from sleeping too little. All I could see ahead was my confusion and I wanted to black out the future as well as the past. I wanted to hurt the people who had hurt me. I just didn't want to live anymore. Now that I look back on it, I realize my foolish attempt to kill myself was little more than a desperate effort to get people I loved to say they loved me. I wanted more than anything in the world to be assured. Well, when I saw the horrified faces of Vincente and my secretary, Tully, at least I was reassured. I knew in my heart what a fool I was."

Still, suicide attempts are dire calls for help and again, Judy had to be hospitalized. "We bundled Judy up, put her on the floor of the car and drove her to the house on Sunset," explains Vincente, "where the doctor was waiting." Myrtle had called the doctor in advance and advised him to go to Ten Thousand Sunset to avoid the clamoring press. As for Liza, she didn't learn the truth for years. She thought Mama was just not "feeling well"—again.

Shortly after her suicide attempt, Judy told Vincente she was leaving for good. She had had several drinks before she could do this. Like the pieces of glass that Judy used to cut herself, the Minnelli marriage was jagged, transparent and shattered. The love was gone.

By December 7, 1950, Judy and Vincente were officially separated and Judy rented Marlene Dietrich's old apartment on Sweetzer Avenue, not far from the Evansview and Sunset homes.

Liza lived with her bachelor father. "Liza's well-being would be better served if she had one stable parent," Vincente said at the time, "living apart from his mate rather than having two emotionally wounded parents living together." Three days before Christmas, Judy was off to vacation in Manhattan. "Judy kissed Liza goodbye, gave me a friendly hug and walked out. Our life together," Vincente says, "was over."

On March 19, 1951, after Judy returned to the coast (in New York she had met Michael Sidney Luft, the man who would become her third husband), Judy's divorce suit against Vincente came before Superior Judge William R. McKay. Judy told Judge McKay that Vincente "lacked interest in me, my career, my friends, everything. He shut himself out of my life."

Judy was granted custody of Liza with one provision: the child must spend half the year with her father. Vincente gave Judy the Evansview Drive house, a beach house in Malibu and promised to pay Judy $500 a week in child support for every week Liza was with her mother. He also vowed to pay Liza's medical bills. That was all Vincente could really afford—at the time of the divorce settlement, he and Judy were almost penniless. Whatever money did not go to pay Judy's enormous hospital and doctor bills went to pay for her drug habit.

After their divorce and through Judy's three subsequent marriages, Vincente and Judy remained close. She would often ask him for his opinion on certain matters, especially if they were business related. "We stayed close," Vincente says, "not just for Liza's sake, but because we also respected each other."

When Liza speaks about her parents' divorce, her comments emerge with a fresh-air quality—her choice of words breezy and almost comforting. "Both my parents were terrific about the divorce," Liza says. "They kept all the struggle from me. They never bad-mouthed each other and I never had a problem visiting Daddy if I wanted to."

And though Vincente claims "the divorce didn't seem to throw her," Liza admits her parents' split-up did affect her thinking. "I don't have dreams of white picket fences anymore," she says, "because I found out they're uncomfortable to sit on."

Papa Sid

Liza and Michael Sidney Luft—he preferred Sid to Mike—had their first meeting in April, 1951, during the time Judy was playing at the London Palladium. Liza was only five years old, and was used to hours of undisciplined pleasure with her father, Vincente. She did not want to go to London. Vincente felt he knew better.

"[Judy and Liza] had been apart far too long," he recalls, "and though I selfishly wanted Liza to myself, now was the time she should be with Judy—during the period of one of her mother's greatest triumphs." Vincente took Liza to New York City and put her on a plane to London. "This way Liza, who has lived through so many of Judy's down periods," Vincente adds, "could begin to understand her mother's staggering talent. Liza would also know that, though her parents couldn't live together any longer, her father would always be a Judy Garland fan."

The Palladium concert, arranged by Luft, was a personal triumph for Judy, so stupendous that she toured Scotland, England and Wales with her show. The audiences loved her. Once again, Judy was on top.

It took Liza a long time to get accustomed to Sid Luft, but during her mother's sensational tour, she began calling him "Uncle Sid." One day, Judy asked Liza to call him "Papa Sid." She agreed.

Liza can still remember her mother's and stepfather's faces as she murmured the phrase—faces locked with smiles of pleasure and joy—and several times thereafter, Sid Luft became Liza's "Papa Sid." Liza would continue to be friendly with Luft until November, 1978, when Sid auctioned off about five hundred pieces of Judy's belongings. The incident severed their relationship. Liza now refers to Luft as "litigious."

Judy actually asked Liza's permission to marry Sid Luft. When Liza answered with a defiant "Why? What about Daddy?" Judy told her it was so she could give Liza a baby brother or sister. That idea thrilled Liza and she consented. What didn't thrill Liza was how she heard about the wedding news.

It was June 11, 1952. Liza spent the day with her father and, as a treat, she would be spending the night. Shortly after dinner, Liza and Vincente were watching the six o'clock news. Suddenly, the television flashed with an announcement that Judy Garland had secretly wed Sid Luft on a ranch near Hollister, California, three days earlier—the news broke only after an inquisitive reporter for *The Hollister Evening Free Lance* noticed Luft's name on the register.

Liza was crushed. How could Mama marry without telling me? she thought. Liza wallowed in self-pity, but for only a few minutes. Then she shrugged off the event, went into Vincente's kitchen and found comfort in a frozen ice cream bar.

Recalling that day, Liza has said, "I realized from that point on that it was none of my business when and who Mama married." When Judy married her fourth husband, an aspiring actor named Mark Herron, in Las Vegas on November 14, 1965, Liza could not make the ceremony. She phoned Judy. "Mama," she said, "I promise I'll make the next one." Judy roared at the thought.

Sid Luft thus became the new mentor in Judy's life. In the early to mid-1940s, he had been a test pilot who later got involved in show business—exactly how is still questionable. Luft had married second-rate actress Lynn Bari—they were divorced in 1950—and produced third-rate movies. Now, he was producing the Hollywood comeback of Judy Garland by starring her in a remake of *A Star is Born*. That previous winter, Judy, again "bankable," played an unprecedented nineteen weeks at New York's legendary Palace Theater.

Liza did not understand Luft. At times, he did not seem to know how to be a husband to Judy; he was away on business trips too often, too long. (When Judy and Luft were married, their fights, sometimes induced by vast amounts of alcohol, exceeded those Judy had had with Minnelli in volume. Often, they were so loud, neighbors would summon the police.) Rumors that Luft was connected with what is now called the Mafia were rampant. Police once found a .38 caliber revolver in the trunk of his car. One day, in a blatant burst of chutzpah, Liza asked Luft what he did for a living. His reported answer: "I'm in the suit business, Liza. I sue people." From that moment on, Liza, as young as she was, began to understand Luft for the enigmatic man he was.

When she married Luft, Judy was four months pregnant with her second child. To avoid any complications, doctors admitted her to St. John's Hospital three weeks before the expected delivery date. On November 21, 1952, Lorna Luft—Judy's second daughter, was born through Caesarean section. She named Lorna for two reasons. Sid's mother's name was Leonora, and Judy loved Francis Farmer's portrayal of Lorna Moon in Clifford Odets' play, *Golden Boy*.

Lorna weighed in at 6 pounds, 4 ounces, a blue-eyed blond

with a vivacious cry. And though Judy was delighted at having another girl—"Lorna's birth was the only bright spot in the first year of my marriage," she often said—she fell into a postpartum depression a few days after giving birth. The depression was so severe that Judy sliced her throat with a razor several days after leaving the hospital.

Judy, Sid, Liza, Liza's governess Cozy, and Judy's secretary Myrtle Tully settled into the Lufts' lavish Tudor home at One Forty Four South Mapleton Drive in Holmby Hills. Liza did not mind living with Judy and Sid. She was close enough to her father's house; even more important, she was close to M-G-M, where she often went so she could watch Fred Astaire and Cyd Charisse rehearsing numbers from her father's film *The Band Wagon.*

"I was delighted that we had Liza as a frequent visitor," Vincente says. "She was quite the young lady now and I was glad that I could see her maturing in those areas where life with Judy hadn't already cast her as a near-adult. Judy was

often doting with Liza," he adds, "but there were times when the neglect was inevitable."

At the studio, Liza would carefully study Cyd Charisse's movements—Liza's mini-musicals had ended, but the dancer still offered her insight—and Liza would often practice with Cyd at the ballet bar. "I was delighted that Liza was taking an interest in my work," her father says, "and that she was showing signs of inheriting her mother's talents."

During this time, Liza became Judy's "protector." With "Papa Sid" away so often, Liza served as Judy's daughter, mother, father and psychiatrist. As Vincente recalls, "Liza was only seven, but onerous responsibilities were already being delegated to her. In many ways, Liza played mother to Judy's daughter."

One incident stands out. Sid Luft and Lynn Bari had one child, John, who was eighteen months younger than Liza. The boy, who was living with Sid at that time, was prone to sudden, violent tantrums and, because the children's nurses couldn't always handle him, the responsibility became Liza's. One night, Judy was loudly fighting with Lorna's nurse, then she flew out of the house in a rage.

The nurse followed and Liza was left alone to baby a crying John. Is he sick? Liza wondered. Should I feed him? Using her intuition, Liza was able to bring John's fervor under control. The next day, however, she admonished her mother and asked to be shown some proper baby care techniques—just in case there should be a repeat performance. Liza was able to "take charge"—even then.

Since early childhood, Liza says, "I worried about Mama. She would put too much trust in somebody, then they'd do something slight and she'd take it as a slap in the face. Mama and I talked a lot; the thing I tried to get through to her was that none of it really mattered. Yet I never saw Mama in a situation she couldn't handle—even if she were having a tantrum or hysterically crying. When she'd get in a temper, it was frightening because she'd yell a lot and I'd freeze. Now I avoid people who are screaming at all costs," adds Liza. "My eyes glaze over when someone begins to yell and my mind retreats back to someplace else so they can't get through to me."

Judy wasn't the only Hollywood star who sought out Liza's youthful advice: Marilyn Monroe was another. The blonde bombshell was a good friend of Judy's and she would often be a guest at Judy's parties. "Mama always invited Marilyn," Liza recalls, "because Mama was very adamant about how rottenly people treated Marilyn. Marilyn talked to me a lot. I remember why—because no one else talked to her. When I was about ten, we were really good friends. She used to tell me how lonely she was. I used to tell her she had to talk to people and let them know she didn't want anything from them."

Liza insists that many of Judy's suicide attempts were blown out of proportion by the press—if not by Judy herself. "Everything became so exaggerated because Judy was doing it," Liza says. "My mother did everything she wanted to do, including those suicide attempts. They were just silly things to attract attention. Mama really wouldn't have killed herself in a million years. She'd come in, take two aspirins, and say, 'Oh, Liza, I can't take it anymore.' Then she'd run into the bathroom and hold her breath. I'd catch on after awhile, borrow the gardener's hedge clippers, snip a hole in the screen and

crawl into the bathroom." Once inside, Liza would try to comfort her depressed mother.

"Mama's suicide attempts weren't hysteria," Liza adds, "it was acting. I tried to help her over so many pitfalls. Sometimes I could help, but sometimes I couldn't. I just couldn't cope with the legend."

At Judy's first Carnegie Hall show, Liza, Lorna and Joey—then fifteen, eight and six—sat in the first row. As a final encore, Judy introduced her children to her fans. "I would never push my kids into this business," Judy once said. "I would never want them to go through what I went through."

Judy's third child and only son, Joseph Wiley Luft, was born in the early hours of March 29, 1955. He was to be Judy's last child. Shortly after Joey's birth, she had her Fallopian tubes tied. Like Liza and Lorna, Joey—as he would always be called—was born through Caesarean section. But this time something went wrong. The premature baby's left lung would not open, and doctors, fearing the worst, gave Joey a 50-50 chance for survival.

This was supposed to have been a happy time for Judy. *A Star is Born* was finally released and Judy not only received rave reviews, but in two days she might even win her first Academy Award. Judy would not let the news about her newborn son upset her. She told all her friends Joey would not die. "I just won't accept it," she said—and even phoned Liza. She called Liza to inform her that she now had a baby brother. "They tell me Joey's going to die, but he's not going to, Liza. I promise you that. I won't let him." Liza was only nine years old and today she claims she will never forget the urgency in Judy's voice as she vowed to save her new baby's life.

Judy kept her promise. A little more than twenty-four hours after Joey's birth, the baby's lung opened. That same day—March 30, 1955—Judy watched the Academy Awards from her hospital bed; the room had been wired so that Master of Ceremonies Bob Hope could, if her name were announced, speak with Judy. He never did; Grace Kelly won for her role in *The Country Girl*. Judy would have to wait six years, until *Judgment at Nuremberg* was released in 1961 to be nominated for another Oscar. Again, she would lose—this time to Rita Moreno for *West Side Story*.

Judy was deeply hurt by the loss. How could Hollywood, the town that recently embraced her after her bravura performance in *A Star is Born*, cast their ballots against her? It was Sid Luft who saved the day. "Fuck the Academy Awards, baby," he told his wife. "You've got your Oscar in the incubator."

✻ ✻ ✻

Joey became Judy's precious, breathing prize. She was proud of both Liza and Lorna, but Joey was the son whom God delivered to take Judy's mind away from her troubles; he was

Liza and Lorna, looking more like twins than half sisters, got another taste of Judy's "business" when they earnestly watched a screening of The Wizard of Oz *at a CBS studio. Liza was ten years old; Lorna, four.*

the son who would, perhaps, carry on the Luft-Garland legacy. This son became Judy's reason to live. Judy would often pick up Joey, cradling his lithe body in her arms, lullabying with her soft voice. More often than not, Judy would cry as she held Joey. That's how much she loved her son.

Liza understood her mother's loving obsession with Joey. She was nine years old and, after all she had seen, read and heard, felt she and her mother had a better, differently defined relationship. Joey may be kissed more often than I am, Liza thought, but I was here first. And she was accustomed to siblings by then. She already had a stepbrother. And of course, sister Lorna. While Judy was pregnant with Lorna, Liza had appeared with other celebrity children on *Art Link-*

letter's House Party. Art asked little Liza what she wanted, a baby sister or brother. "A sister!" Liza had insisted. "Boys are too messy!"

Joey's presence was tougher for Lorna to deal with. One day, she climbed into her brother's crib and scratched his face. When Joey screamed, Judy ran into the nursery, caught Lorna and beat her severely. From that day on, Lorna realized she came second in her mother's affection—after Joey, but before Liza.

One summer Liza was sent to summer camp in the mountains, 90 miles from Los Angeles. The camp counselor at the time remembers that, for the entire two months Liza was there, Vincente drove up every weekend in his Cadillac. But Judy only came twice. The counselor also recalls that Liza would cry herself to sleep every night. Being away all summer from the Luft household, where she had real rivals for her mother's affection, must have made her feel all the more out of place—as if she were an intruder. She had tried to gain her half brother's and half sister's affection by smothering them with love, but it didn't work. Lorna's first recollection of Liza takes shape when she was twelve. She has "blocked out" the first eleven years of her life; that is, her early recollections of Liza. Liza must have threatened Lorna's world, where only Mama Judy, Papa Sid and brother Joey mattered.

Today, however, Liza and Lorna are close—even though Liza's hatred for Lorna's father, Sid, is intense. Liza supports Lorna's show biz yearnings and insists her talents are underrated. "Lorna's voice is much better than mine," Liza says, "and it's a shame she has to compete against Mama and me. And what a beauty! I got a Dago mouth and Dago nose, but Lorna is a real beaut; her skin is milky and translucent."

When Lorna starred as Peppermint Patty in the off-Broadway musical *Snoopy* in early 1983, Liza attended opening night. She hoped her presence—which was recorded by several photographers—would increase box-office ticket sales, but it didn't. Liza is also close to Joey Luft, who maintains the lowest profile of the three children. He is said to be a drummer and prefers quiet evenings at home with his friends. He does not visit the discos which his sisters often frequent. And unlike Lorna and Liza, Joey has never spoken to the press about his life with Judy.

Learning To Survive

Ray Bolger, the actor who played the scarecrow in *The Wizard of Oz*, was one of Judy's more understanding friends. His face lights up when he speaks about Garland. But mention Liza Minnelli, and Bolger's face changes; his smile becomes a frown. Ray Bolger is an iconoclast.

"I loved Judy Garland," he says, "but don't ask me about Liza Minnelli. I don't love [her]. I don't even *like* her. All I can say is that the relationship between Judy and Liza was not a normal one."

Bolger refuses to elaborate on his comments, but the many "episodes" that took place in the months before Judy's divorce (and all the years following it) certainly help explain his words. For instance, when Judy had no money—her suspensions and mounting psychiatric bills drained much of her resources—she would teach Liza certain "games" to play, illegal activities to save money. In her 1957 *McCall's* article, Judy wrote:

"When my marriage to Vincente was over, Liza and I moved into a seven-room suite at the Beverly Hills Hotel. When we had been there a few weeks and they started asking about the bill, I packed a couple of suitcases and dashed down to the desk. I told them I had just been called to New York and would they save my suite for me? It was a big bluff, which they never thought to question. [Liza and I] flew to New York and did the same thing at the St. Regis Hotel. I knew it was crazy, but it was the first real fling I'd had in my life."

Such "flings" would happen often in Liza's early life. There would be times—and this would also happen later to Lorna Luft—when Judy would wake up Liza in the wee hours of the morning so they could sneak out to a different apartment without paying the back rent. Liza and Judy would wear many layers of clothing so they could (unbeknownst to the management) walk away with most of their belongings.

"People ask me why I moved around so much when I was young," Liza says. "It's probably because Mama was so broke and owed money to the landlords."

When the "quick getaways" took place at hotels (always first-class ones; that was Judy's style), Judy and Liza would leave their empty luggage as a deterrent. Although Liza looks back on these times as humorous ones, there were times she and Judy got caught—and one can only imagine the psychological pain Liza suffered when police and hotel officials burst into their room, demanding the overdue rent.

Later on, similar events occurred when Judy, who had shortly before left Sid Luft, was living in London. Luft would "try and steal us kids," Liza recalls. A despondent Judy would phone detectives, who would play poker as they staked out the kitchen waiting for the "robber" Sid Luft. "Those were the times when Mama was down in the dumps," Liza recalls, "and I'd say, 'Come on, Mama, let's go to the park and ride the roller coaster.'"

❧ ❧ ❧

"One day I was making tuna salad in the kitchen," Liza remembers, "and I lashed out at Mama. 'You're so full of sympathy and self-pity,' I told her. 'Why don't you stop it?' Mama drew herself up and said, 'Liza, sympathy is my business.' That was her way of survival. That's what I learned from Mama—survival."

Judy taught Liza well. When all else fails, "win 'em over" with a tug of the heart strings. Use sympathy. If you can't make them laugh, make them cry.

And Liza did. Today, Liza is a millionaire and it is hard to imagine her groveling for food. But in the early fifties, when she was living with her mother and they were broke, that is exactly what she supposedly did. Stories abound that Judy would "lock" Liza out of their living quarters and the poor tot—most likely with tears streaming down her face—would beg store owners and neighbors for food. It always worked— "How could Judy do this to her child?" people would think— and Liza would run back home and share her free stash with her mother.

Yet, Judy also taught Liza manners. Shirley Herz, a Broadway press agent, remembers. In early 1961, Herz was doing the publicity on the Broadway show *Do, Re, Mi* when, one day, she got word that Judy Garland and Frank Sinatra were going to be in the audience that night. Eager to meet the stars, Herz went backstage after the performance. "As I walked down the alleyway to the stage door," she recalls, "I heard two voices. One said, 'But why, Mama?' The other answered, 'Because it's rude. If you go see a show, you must go back and say hello, even if you don't know anyone in the cast.' Later," Herz explains, "I realized what had happened. Sinatra had decided not to go backstage and Judy was explaining to Liza why they were. She was teaching Liza to be gracious and polite." Since then, Liza tries to go backstage to meet the cast after she sees a show. Judy taught her well.

If Liza is disturbed by some memories of her mother, she is not telling. And she is not telling a psychiatrist either. "I'm not putting psychiatry down," she says, "but there are doors I don't want opened. I don't want to find out if I have serpents on my brain. If I go to a shrink, he might tell me things I hadn't thought of. I may not like them and I might not wake up tomorrow. I don't want to get lost wandering through the labyrinths of all the roles I play." Liza claims she has never been to a psychiatrist: "I'd rather cook," she says.

Although Liza insists she "doesn't have time to get depressed," she does have severe anxiety attacks. "I hate them!" she says. "My hands get ice-cold and I get palpitations. I become so aware that my body is so vulnerable that I just can't stop. I try to get up and put on a record and dance. I tell myself, 'Liza, you're only having a willy. Don't be silly. You're not going to die, you ass, it's not a heart attack. Soon you'll be perfectly all right.' But it really gets panicky," Liza adds. "That's why I never make fun of loonies. Madness is a dark pit."

PART TWO

Taking Off

Liza's childhood memories and many of her more adult memories are apocryphal. Some have been so altered, so exaggerated, so stretched with pathos and dramatic precision that they now only serve to win the sympathy of the reader and to preserve the image of her mother.

Judy was also a master of hyperbole. "Mama would always change her stories to suit the company," Liza says. "I would hear one story maybe twenty-nine different ways and I asked her once which one I was supposed to believe. Mama told me, 'Whichever one you like the best, whichever one made you laugh, believe that one.'"

One of Liza's favorite tall tales describes how, as a thirteen-year-old, she would drive Lorna and Joey to school because "the family chauffeur was always too drunk." It seems Liza has always had a talent for embellishing the truth. And why not? "After all," she says, "reality is something you've simply got to rise above."

Liza began to rise above her mother's world while still a little girl. Excluding her cameo in *In the Good Old Summertime*, Liza's first real, big show business appearance came in 1956, when she was ten years old. Judy was appearing at New York's Palace Theater (her first engagement there since her 1951 triumph), and, on a Saturday night towards the end of the run, "Mama called me up to the stage and while she sang "Swanee," I danced," Liza recalls. Liza was actually lifted onstage by Rock Hudson. "I thought it was just terrific for me to be able to kick my legs that way. I remember hearing the waves of applause washing over us. I also remember wondering if my panties showed!"

For her professionalism, the theater manager gave Liza a five dollar bill — her first "paycheck" — which she later had framed. Later, in an effort to make the public think she had a great relationship with Sid Luft, Liza claimed he gave her the five dollar bonus.

One of Liza's greatest stage roles was in The Diary of Anne Frank. *Not only did the fifteen-year-old star in the title role, but she was also responsible for some cast members' makeup. When the school took the show to Israel, Liza spent her free time roaming the countryside. Liza and* Anne Frank *cast member "Buffy" Thalheimer were roommates for the Israeli tour. Today, they no longer speak to each other. "The only time I was really depressed in my career," confesses Liza, "was when I didn't get to do Anne Frank on film." The role went to Millie Perkins.*

When Judy played the Palace for a third time in 1967, Liza joined her mother onstage again and sang "Cabaret." As Liza was returning to her seat, Judy murmured, "Liza, you've been marvelous all your life." Liza was anything but marvelous when, in December, 1956, she co-hosted (with Bert Lahr) a television screening of her mother's film *The Wizard of Oz.* It was a gawky and undistinguished appearance; the same fate her November 14, 1958 appearance on *The Jack Paar Show* would suffer.

Yet, the next year, something happened to Liza which only solidified her show business yearnings. She had attended a party at Lee Gershwin's house with her father, when guest Gene Kelly asked the thirteen-year-old Liza to sing with him. She did—and did so well that Kelly asked Liza to also appear with him on his CBS special. He wanted Liza to join him in "For Me and My Gal," the song that he and Judy introduced to film audiences in 1942. Vincente recalls, "I told Gene we should ask Judy if it was all right. She quickly consented."

Pontiac Star Parade's *The Gene Kelly Show* aired live on April 24, 1959. Gene Kelly remembers the day. "We were in front of this big audience and I was scared for Liza," he says. "I thought she was a sweet, gawky kid but was going to blow it. I was so concerned that *I* almost blew it. But Liza? She was

cool and calm." Watching the show's footage today, Liza appears confident and secure. Unlike her previous television appearances, Liza struts her stuff with the best of them. But the public didn't warm up to Liza. She was a mere curiosity and, despite the show's publicity blitz, her appearance with Gene Kelly was forgotten soon after it aired. The following January, Liza sang "Over the Rainbow" on *The Hedda Hopper Showcase.* Her appearance was a total disaster and, luckily, Liza has never attempted to sing her mother's song again.

Liza claims her big show-business break came at age sixteen, when her mother threw her out. She may have been rising above Judy's realm of reality, but she wasn't rising above fabrication. "Mama went on a kick now and then," Liza says, "where she used to kick me out of the house. I'd usually stand outside the door, and pretty soon, Mama would open it and we'd fall into each other's arms, crying and carrying on. But one day when she did it, I took her up on it. I had my plane fare and $100 hidden in my socks. And I've never taken a penny since."

The truth is quite different. In early 1961, soon after she and Sid Luft separated, Judy moved to New York City and sublet an apartment in The Dakota. While she was preparing for her now legendary Carnegie Hall concert, Lorna and Joey were attending public school. Liza was enrolled in the School of Performing Arts (which later became known as the *Fame* school), and she was attending the theater almost every night. One of her favorite shows was the musical *Bye, Bye, Birdie,* which Liza would later claim influenced her decision to go into show business. "I saw all those kids running around and having a fabulous time onstage," she said, "and I wanted to be a part of it."

While at school, Liza also fell in love with one of her classmates, actor Robert Mariano. The teenager had a small role in the chorus of *Birdie*, and Liza idolized him. The romance quickly ended when Liza met another classmate, Marvin Hamlisch, with whom she became fast friends.

Marvin was at the School of Performing Arts for the same reason Liza was—to nurture his talents and, hopefully, catch someone's eye and "make it big." But no one was around those days, so Liza and Marvin decided to go it alone. Together they cut a demonstration record—Liza sang, Marvin played piano—but the demo was a big flop; not one record producer was interested. Today, Liza and Marvin are still close. "Marvin is the best there is," Liza says. "He's $33\frac{1}{3}$, when everyone else is 78."

The regimen at the School of Performing Arts was not an easy one for Liza to follow. She had always loathed school—"I loved English but hated math," she says—and she longed to perform, not study. Her only big moment came when she joined other classmates and sang "Steam Heat," from the Broadway musical *The Pajama Game*, for patients at Harlem Veteran's Hospital. Like "steam heat," the experience vanished into thin air, and Liza's work went unnoticed.

That summer, Liza spent her time apprenticing at the Melody Tent Theater in Hyannis Port, Massachusetts. She and Judy were living across from John F. Kennedy's "summer" White House. Judy loved the idea. She and Kennedy were friends; he often spoke to Judy on the phone and asked her to sing the last few bars of "Over the Rainbow." Judy always did.

For fifteen dollars a week, Liza painted scenery, struck sets, ran lunch orders and even performed. She appeared in the choruses of *Flower Drum Song* and *Wish You Were Here*. When the theater decided to put on *Take Me Along*, they took Liza along and cast her in the role of Marie Macomber. It was an important role, and Liza got to sing "I Would Die."

She invited Judy to attend the opening night of *Take Me Along*. Judy never made it. As she would do again and again in the future, Judy would not appear on Liza's opening nights. She wasn't being rude; she just did not want to steal the attention away from the real star those nights, her daughter. When Judy finally did see *Take Me Along*, she witnessed more than Liza's musical abilities. Liza had taken up smoking Marlboros, and Judy was forced to realize that little Liza wasn't so little anymore.

Vincente remembers Liza's "debut" that summer. "Liza hadn't told Judy and I how serious she was about a show business career," he says, "but we both agreed it was a good way for Liza to spend the summer. Judy and I were both very excited about our daughter's appearance. And Liza was, of course, marvelous. I was delighted that Liza had done us proud."

Liza's work at Melody Tent was also important because it won her an agent; a major sign she was "on her way." The agent, Stephanie "Stevie" Phillips, now a producer for Universal Pictures, Westward Productions, remained with Liza for many years. But today, Phillips will say very little about the Liza she remembers. "She is a very dear friend of mine," Phillips says, "and I cannot hurt her by mentioning past incidents. Yet Liza was probably the only kid who had an agent while she did summer stock. Of course, I wasn't really an agent and Liza wasn't really an actress."

In September, 1961, Judy moved Liza, Lorna and Joey to a sprawling, red-brick house in Scarsdale, New York. Scarsdale lies 20 miles north of Manhattan in Westchester County; it is a posh, elite community that likes to maintain its aloof atmosphere.

When the news hit the townsfolk that Judy Garland, *an actress*—who, dear Lordie, took *pills!*—was living among them, many people resented the intrusion. Actually, the house Judy rented at One Cornell Street is in the town of Mamaroneck and seconds away from New Rochelle, the birthplace of Sid Luft. From that house, the center of Scarsdale is approximately five minutes away by car.

"I Found Our Anna!"

Robert P. Haseltine has been teaching speech and drama at Scarsdale High School since 1958. In 1961, he toured Europe with the Scarsdale High School Dramatics Club's production of *Our Town*. It was there that the seed of *The Diary of Anne Frank* was planted.

"After John Hemmerly [the drama department chairman] and I visited the Frank house in Amsterdam," Haseltine recalls, "we wanted to do the play at school the next season. But we could not find a suitable girl to play the lead, and opted to do *The Madwoman of Chaillot* instead." However, after the school year had begun, Hemmerly called his associate into his office. "Bob," he cried, "I found our Anna!"

Haseltine insists that Hemmerly (who died in 1963) did not know who the parents of the girl he had just cast as Anne Frank were. "It was only after John mentioned Liza's name to another teacher," Bob explains, "that John found out about Judy and Vincente."

Haseltine, the technical director of *Anne Frank*, remembers Liza's dedication to the play. "She worked very hard," he says, "and always knew her lines. She was never a problem. Oh, she could play the devil—she loved playing practical jokes on the cast—but Liza always acted like a lady in front of me. Sometimes after a run-through, she'd come up to me and ask, 'Uncle Bob, how was I?'"

Liza also sought the acting advice of her father. "There were all these long speeches in the play, speeches from the diary," Liza recalls, "and one day, when I was visiting Daddy, I asked him, 'Will you help me?' He told me to listen to the director. I told Daddy he was weasling out."

The Diary of Anne Frank opened in the Scarsdale High School auditorium on December 8, 1961, at 8:30 P.M. Opening night was sold out—all 1,400 seats—and Haseltine still recalls "people calling up asking what night Judy would be there. It seemed," he adds, "that some people were more interested in seeing Judy than Anne Frank!"

Judy came opening night and cried throughout the show. She was genuinely moved by her daughter's portrayal of Anne and, later, when she went backstage to hug Liza, said, "My God! I've got an annuity!"

Nettie Breines, reviewing the production for *The Scarsdale Inquirer*, said, "There were glowing performances, but there are no stars in this educational theater. The players, after seven weeks of co-curricular, after-school study with their creative director, John Hemmerly, achieved a glistening polish." Breines called Liza's Anne "vibrant," then ended her review by making a statement about her fellow Scarsdale citizens: "Many devoted people did not come to the play because many of its anguished episodes came right out of the lives of their relatives and friends."

The Diary of Anne Frank was so well-received that a wealthy Scarsdale matron and patron of the arts, Mrs. Murray Silverstone, decided to underwrite a trip for the cast to perform the show in Israel (Murray Silverstone was, at the time, president of Twentieth Century-Fox International, and his wife was a sponsor of the International Cultural Center for Youth in Jerusalem). It was said that Judy, working in England, funded some of the trip so Liza could be near her. Mrs. Silverstone insists this is not true.

Liza joined the cast in Athens. She had been visiting her mother in England and left there for Greece on July 3. Haseltine remembers that when Liza stepped off the plane, "she was protected by this big hulk of a bodyguard" (today, Liza still maintains several bodyguards; during the run of *The Act*, a burly black man protected her every move).

The Scarsdale High School Dramatics Club performed *The Diary of Anne Frank* in Israel for one month, always receiving lavish praise. They were later asked to do the show in Tel Aviv at the Hebrew University. In her spare time, Liza and the other classmates would perform two other works, *Impromptu*, and a reading of Carl Sandburg's *The People Yes*, in the hinterlands, "because," explains Haseltine, "they required no scenery." Mrs. Silverstone made a ten-minute 16 mm color film of the trip, documenting Liza's offstage activities there. The film boasts a happy Liza amid the country's celebrated ruins. Liza has never seen the film.

After their *Anne Frank* tour was completed, the group of youngsters toured Rome and Florence. It was here that an event took place which marked for Haseltine Liza's emergence as a star. "Liza and I were sitting across from each other in an old train car," he recalls, "when I asked her for a favor. 'What is it? Uncle Bob,' she asked. I asked her if she would sing for me. I wanted her to do 'Born in a Trunk' from Judy's film *A Star is Born*, but I was reluctant to ask. After all, I knew Liza wanted her own identity and to ask her to do a song that was

her mother's, well, I wasn't sure if it was right. But she sang it. There we were, somewhere between Florence and Rome, on an early pastoral morning, with Liza leaning out one window singing her heart out to the hills of Italy. As I watched the wind blow her hair, I knew from that moment on that this dumpy sixteen-year-old girl would be a big star."

Years later, in 1976, Haseltine and his family tried to visit Liza backstage after her performance at the Westchester Premier Theater in Tarrytown, New York. She refused to see them. "Lydia Cornell [another of Scarsdale High's famous alumni] quotes me in magazine interviews," sighs Haseltine. "I guess Liza has no time for her Uncle Bob."

One of Liza's best friends during these times was Elizabeth Thalheimer. "Buffy"—as Elizabeth is still called by Haseltine—appeared as Miep in *The Diary of Anne Frank*, and she and Liza got along famously. Perhaps it was their diverse backgrounds—Elizabeth came from a proper, monied Scarsdale family—that blended them together. Scarsdale High School in 1962 was an extension of familial discipline and both Liza and Liz were rebellious. When they got together, rules were not something they paid much attention to.

Buffy was Liza's roommate during the tour of *Anne Frank*. They tagged along after each other, ate together, and gossiped together. Liza told her friend about her strange childhood; Buffy relished Liza's stories, and she supplied Liza with chatter about her "proper" Scarsdale upbringing. They were buddies—or so they hoped—for life.

Today, Elizabeth Thalheimer leads a quiet Manhattan existence. She is married to Ilja Wachs, the dean of Bronxville's Sarah Lawrence College (often called one of the stuffiest colleges in America) and doesn't like to talk about Liza. "We lived together for several months," she says, "but there are things I don't want to talk about. I'd feel funny revealing things about Liza. The things I could talk about might hurt her. Why bring them up?" One can only speculate that some of what Elizabeth won't talk about is how much Liza hated Scarsdale. "I couldn't find anybody who was as bright as I was," Liza recalls. "Kids there just weren't into adult conversations and nobody would talk to me."

To rid herself of her homesickness, Liza would often sneak away from Scarsdale. She recalls one such time. "I went to the headmistress and told her there was a family crisis in London," Liza says. "There really wasn't any, and God! how I

acted! I told her I *had* to leave that day, right away, and I must have been superb because she let me go. I went to a travel agent, charged a ticket and flew to London by myself. I walked around, met a hippie friend of mine, then flew back to New York—all in one day!"

Then, in February, 1962, Liza dropped by the set of Judy's film *A Child is Waiting*. The film concerned mentally retarded children (Judy played their teacher); and each day she was there, Liza would spend hours playing with the children. Judy, on the other hand, had more trouble. The children reminded her of her days at Boston's Peter Bent Brigham Hospital, when she didn't have Liza with her. Liza's mini-vacations soon came to a close, and she returned to Scarsdale.

Liza's former classmates insist Judy's daughter was messy and unkempt—"a slob with power" was how one female Scarsdale graduate put it. Except for a rare few, no one seemed to like her, including the school board. Is Liza the most famous ex-pupil of Scarsdale High School? No. Explains Bob Hasel-

tine, "She was here for such a short time [not even one year] that the officials don't recognize her as a former student."

At the end of the ten-week *Anne Frank* tour, Liza visited Judy in England on the set of her film *I Could Go On Singing*. It was to be Judy's last film. Her mother had given up the Scarsdale house, and Liza easily put the town behind her.

Best Foot Forward

For Liza, 1962 was a busy year. She was sixteen years old and, she hoped, on the verge of a show business breakthrough. She knew *Anne Frank* was a solid beginning. But what was next? The feature-length cartoon *Journey Back to Oz* was. Originally titled *Return to Oz*, the film was an animated sequel to Judy's classic, *The Wizard of Oz*. Liza supplied the film with the voice of Dorothy (who else?); Milton Berle was the Cowardly Lion, Mickey Rooney was the Scarecrow and Danny Thomas was the Tin Man.

Journey Back to Oz was such a bad film—the few who saw

Liza was dating dancer Tracy Everitt (opposite, left) when she won a role in the 1963 off-Broadway revival of Best Foot Forward. *During one of the show's first rehearsals, Liza and cast member Ronald Walken (opposite, right) danced up a storm — until Liza tripped and broke her leg. Still, she kept on rehearsing (above, right) and even appeared on Jack Paar's show promoting* Best Foot. *Judy arranged the TV appearance and urged Liza to show the audience her cast. Thus, Liza redefined the show biz adage, "Break a Leg."*

it called it "exploitative animation"—that even Judy's own "endorsement" couldn't save it. The film disappeared soon after it was completed and did not get a nationwide release until 1974, twelve years after it was made! In 1980, the soundtrack was sold through television advertising and quickly bought up by collectors.

In the fall of 1962, Liza was taking special courses at the Sorbonne in Paris. Liza finally got to see the Paris her father had so vividly described to her as a child. It should have been an exciting time for her, but Liza was bored. She wanted more. She wanted to quit school to pursue a career in show business. "I knew what I wanted to do," she recalls, "and I had it out with myself." Liza also confronted Judy, who was giving her difficulty about going into show business. How well Judy knew the heartaches it could bring. She was afraid history would repeat itself.

Liza claims she prepared Judy by sending her mother a telegram from Paris reading, "Dear Mama, I'm coming home. I want to talk to you." This, however, is not true.

What really happened was that, one day, after speaking with Judy on the phone, Liza decided to leave the Sorbonne

and fly back to California. "I enjoyed the Sorbonne," she says, "despite the fact that I didn't get much schooling done there. However, I did learn French, which later was helpful for my concerts. I was usually ahead in my studies anyway, because I had private tutors because we moved around so much." Liza actually never graduated from any high school.

On her way to California, Liza stopped in New York, where she met with her father, who was in town on business. At breakfast, Liza, sitting opposite Vincente, with little hesitation, expressed herself. "I want to quit school, come back to New York and go on the stage," Liza told him. "I'll start from the bottom." Vincente responded slowly. "Yes," he said, "I think it's about time. You have so much energy you might as well start using it." Liza added, "But I've got to *tell* Mama." Vincente was supportive. "Just tell her what you told me."

Judy was seated in front of her makeup vanity when Liza decided to break the news. When Judy gently nodded, Liza nervously began. "I think it's really time, Daddy is all for it, I really want to study," she gushed. "Mama, I want to be really good." Before she could say another word, Judy interrupted her daughter. "I think it's wonderful," she said, glancing away from the mirror. "If that's what you really want to do, OK, go ahead. But remember, I'm your best example of what *not* to do. And no more money from me—ever again. You're on your own, baby."

The comment, brought on by Judy's maternal jealousy, stung Liza. Judy was going through rough times—her career was in a lull and her marriage to Sid Luft was about to disintegrate—and she resented the independence Liza was demonstrating.

Judy's words were intimidating. But Judy could fool no one—especially Liza. As long as Liza was able to provide herself with money for food and rent, Judy would see to it that Liza somehow always had enough money to pay for vocal lessons, acting classes and other career necessities. Judy would not let Liza down; her bark was meaner than her bite.

Liza Minnelli arrived in New York City with few personal belongings. She had $100 in savings, the five dollar bill she had earned from her Palace "debut," and a few sachels of clothing. She also had her name—and her parents' reputation. It was 1962 and Liza was determined to make it big.

At sixteen, Liza was far from beautiful. But she had charisma and charm. Those qualities, combined with her sense of flair and her abundance of energy, earned Liza modeling assignments for *Seventeen* magazine. She also modeled for several other magazines. Even after Liza scored her big success with *Best Foot Forward*, she continued to model for the exposure. One of her biggest coups was a five-page color spread in the May 29, 1955, issue of *TV Guide*. The fashions Liza modeled there are icons of the sixties—fabric-covered buttons, kick-pleated skirts, wide-lapeled jackets, and a stark bouffant hairstyle by Kenneth. The article, entitled "The Liza Minnelli Look," shows a poised, assured young woman. It was clear, even in 1965, that Liza knew how to work in front of a camera—even a still one.

With the money she earned from modeling, she was able to pay the rent on her small Manhattan apartment. She studied acting at the noted Herbert Berghof Studio and studied voice with David Soren Collyer. They were Liza's first singing lessons other than the spontaneous lessons Judy "taught" her as a child; and, for Liza, husky-voiced Collyer was the best teacher she could find. Collyer has since given voice lessons to Lorna Luft.

Liza's career in New York took off when she put her best foot forward and auditioned for a role in the revival of the 1941 Broadway musical *Best Foot Forward*. Liza arrived for the audition nearly thirty minutes late. She thought she had missed her chance, but the producer, Arthur Whitelaw, and director, Danny Daniels, were eagerly waiting to see the talents of "Judy's daughter." Liza sang two songs, "The Way You Look Tonight" and "They Can't Take That Away From Me." Despite her nervousness, she was a booming success—no one took anything away from her—and Liza won a role which paid less than forty dollars a week.

"When I called Mama to tell her," Liza remembers, "you should have heard her. She was so great! *She* got so nervous and started telling *me* to relax and remember my poise and not to get nervous. She was funny—and a nervous wreck!"

Winning the third lead in an off-Broadway musical (she played Ethel Hofflinger, the role Victoria Schools created in 1941) was an important coup for Liza. She was, at seventeen, finally given the chance to demonstrate her acting *and* singing *and* dancing abilities to the public, to her parents, but most of all, to herself.

Liza determined to make a name for herself—on her credentials only—yet Liza also witnessed many equally talented performers fall by the wayside. It took more than talent to make it; it took confidence, resolution and the ability to bounce back when rejected. "It wasn't my great talent that got me my first few jobs," Liza confesses. "It was simply my mother's name and the curiosity factor." It was important for Liza to prove that while Judy Garland's and Vincente Minnelli's names may open some doors, it was she who would never let them shut. *Best Foot Forward*, Liza felt, was the best way to start.

Liza took the show's title literally, put her best foot forward, and broke it! During a dance rehearsal, she tripped over a loose piece of floor boarding, breaking her left leg. The accident forced the producers to change the March 27 opening night, and a depressed Liza spent her convalescence wobbling about the streets of Manhattan in a cast. Liza brought new meaning to the phrase, "break a leg."

Jack Paar was a close friend of Judy Garland. The television host first had Liza on his show in 1958. Five years later, on March 15, she was again a guest. What Liza did not know was that her mother had asked Paar for the favor. She felt it would ease Liza's pre-opening jitters and give *Best Foot Forward* some extra, nationwide publicity. Judy was no fool.

In hopes of getting an honest audience reaction, Paar introduced Liza as "Dyju Langard," the "Armenian discovery." The fictitious name was an anagram for Judy Garland. Liza was nervous, but propped on a stool she sang well, her cast exposed to the world. Judy told Liza to make sure the audience saw her cast. Remember, in time of need, use sympathy. The ovation Liza received—before Paar revealed her true identity—was usually given to the best. That night, "Dyju Langard" had made it.

Rex Reed first met Liza in 1962, when he was working as a press agent for her first off-Broadway show, *Best Foot Forward.* Today, the entertainment writer claims he doesn't remember much of those early days. What he does remember, however, is Liza.

"When I first met her backstage," he says, "Liza was trembling with the same kind of sensitivity her mother had. I could tell Liza was her mother's daughter and that this gawkish girl with so much vulnerability was going to do something wonderful with her life."

Over the years, Reed got to know Liza "very well. I don't know what is going to happen to her in the future," he adds, "but she's someone who desperately needs roots in her life. She needs someone to go home to at night; someone to be there so that she doesn't have to sleep with the lights on like she always used to do."

⌘ ⌘ ⌘

Best Foot Forward opened at the Stage 73 Theater on April 2, 1963. It was a momentous occasion in the history of off-Broadway theater. People jammed the streets. The show had long been sold out, and police were forced to put up barricades. The theater was small, and all 172 seats were filled, except three, in the second row, front, reserved for Judy Garland, Lorna Luft and Joey Luft. Those seats were empty.

Liza was not furious that Judy missed her prestigious opening night. Instead she was nervous. Had something happened? Was Mama in an accident?

At intermission, Liza rushed to the backstage telephone and called her mother at the Plaza Hotel. Judy was sleeping. "Mama, are you all right?" Liza queried. Judy answered that she was all right. "Oh," Judy murmured, "the opening was *tonight*. But I thought it was *tomorrow* night." Suddenly, Liza realized that her mother had purposely missed the opening to avoid taking the limelight. Cheerfully, Liza said, "Oh, well, Mama, you can come tomorrow."

Judy did. "I cried and cried because I was so proud of my baby," Judy later recalled after seeing a performance of *Best Foot Forward*. "Liza had worked so hard and done it all alone. And you know, Liza's the first one of us to do this. I never had a Broadway show."

Critics had a hard time reviewing Liza's performance. Her foot was still in its cast, and Liza had to "walk through" her dance routines. Still, most reviewers noted her infectious charm.

"Liza is great! Liza sparkles!" said Robert Coleman of the *New York Mirror*.

"We dig a rising star, Liza Minnelli," declared James Davis of the New York *Daily News*. "*Best Foot Forward* is worth seeing if only to remember back some day to having witnessed a Broadway star in her professional debut."

Some found comparisons to Judy irresistible.

Wrote George Oppenheimer in *Newsday*: "Young Miss Minnelli, barely out of school, cannot belt out a song the way her mother does, but I feel fairly confident that that will come too. In other respects, Liza resembles Judy, not only in appearance and mannerisms, but in that intangible quality of vulnerability. You want to get up on the stage, take her in your arms and tell her how good she is."

And Walter Kerr, then writing for the *New York Herald Tribune*, said: "Liza Minnelli is certainly appealing, and would be even if she wasn't Judy Garland's daughter, with something of her mother's faintly scratched tremolo clinging to her—and with that fading half-laugh that trickles away after lines. She is easy and confident and accomplished and winning and also, I would think, a person."

Along with other cast members (one of whom was Christopher Walken, who later made a name for himself in *The Deerhunter*), Liza sang several numbers in *Best Foot Forward*. But just before the final curtain fell, she sang a long solo, "You Are For Loving." The ballad became alive in Liza's embrace, a turbulent torch of honest heartache. "You Are For Loving" was released by Cadence as a single. It was Liza's first professional record and sold almost 500,000 copies. (Ironically, that single has outsold just about all of Liza's subsequent recordings. Liza live may be a powerhouse, but on record, she seems to fizzle. None of her Capitol, A & M or CBS albums have gone gold.)

"You Are For Loving" was written by Hugh Martin and Ralph Blane, the same team who wrote Judy's songs in *Meet Me in St. Louis*. Martin Gottfried, then writing for *Women's*

Wear Daily, remembers the song. "About five minutes before the final curtain, Liza Minnelli stands alone on the stage singing a new song called 'You Are For Loving.' If you close your eyes you would swear it was the young Judy Garland, and if you keep your eyes open, you will still have those chills running through you. It is a lovely song with Miss Minnelli singing it. Nothing else in the show can match those few minutes for sheer intensity of talent." Shortly after *Best Foot Forward* opened, Liza sang "You Are For Loving" on *The Ed Sullivan Show*. She insists she was "terrrible. I was scared knock-kneed and it showed!"

Her work in *Best Foot Forward* was so well received that theater historian Daniel Blum, editor of the prestigious *Theatre World*, gave Liza one of twelve "Promising Personality Awards." Magazines were running frequent articles and profiles on the new star, and the headlines often reflected her famous mother. *Saturday Evening Post*: "Momma's Girl: Judy Garland's Daughter." *Look*: "Liza Minnelli: Judy's Daughter Bows In." *Senior Scholastic*: "Second Generation, Garland Style."

Since Liza was getting more attention than any other cast member (no one received star billing), the producers and press agents of *Best Foot Forward* encouraged her to take part in extracurricular promotional activities. Liza was asked to appear on several radio and television shows—Judy usually "secretly" arranged these—and on May Day, Liza even made a personal appearance at the now defunct Arnold Constable department store. Sometimes after a late night on the town, Liza would crash at co-star Paula Wayne's apartment.

The results of these events, however, did not always help. Liza would frequently miss performances, and the producers, knowing most people came to see Judy's daughter, were forced to give refunds. Sixteen years later, when Liza was starring on Broadway in *The Act*, the same thing happened. The public outcry then, however, bordered on outrage.

Liza Returns to L.A. for Judy

The real reason Liza left *Best Foot Forward* after just four months was her mother's selfishness. Judy was preparing her own CBS-TV series and was depressed by the marital problems she was still having with Sid Luft.

One day she called Liza. "Come back here, darling," she said. "I miss you." Liza: "Oh, no, Mama, I really can't." In truth, Liza really couldn't, she had signed a contract.

At the time Judy phoned, Liza was dating Broadway gypsy Tracy Everitt, one of the dancers in *Best Foot Forward*. Liza couldn't leave the show for another reason: she was in love and refused to allow her relationship with Tracy to be threatened by her departure.

So Judy schemed. She put a call in to Everitt, told him she needed one extra dancer for her series and asked him if he wanted the job. Everitt jumped at the chance and raced to California. Liza, her heart thumping ardently, quickly followed. Liza was replaced in *Best Foot Forward*, but the show couldn't keep its footing. *Best Foot Forward* closed on October 13, 1963, after a run of 244 performances.

Back with her mother in California and basking comfortably in Tracy Everitt's affection, Liza set out to find work. In September of that year, she had signed a three-year personal contract with Creative Management Associates, New York's prestigious talent agency. Liza appeared on several television shows: On June 3, she performed on *The Tonight Show*; twenty-nine days later, on July 2, she was on *Talent Scouts With Merv Griffin*. On October 27, Liza made an appearance on the NBC special, *April in Paris Ball*.

But the real ball got rolling when Liza, at Judy's request, guested on two of her mother's shows. *The Judy Garland Show*, which aired on Sunday nights, was taped in advance, and Judy usually had problems getting through the shows. She was often nervous on the set; again she was drinking and suffering emotionally. Judy kept a stable of "friends" around her to ease the stress she felt during the tapings. Singer Mel Tormé, who would write her special material, and comedian Jerry Van Dyke, who became a series regular, were two of those friends (Judy's series was pitted against NBC's popular *Bonanza* and after thirteen weeks her show was cancelled).

Liza's first appearance was aired on November 17, 1963, eleven days before Thanksgiving. She and Judy sang eight songs—"Bob White," "Together," "Let Me Entertain You," "Two Lost Souls," "I Will Come Back," "Bye Bye Baby," "The Best is Yet to Come" and "We Could Make Such Beautiful Music Together"—and there seemed to be harmony between mother and daughter.

Liza's second appearance with her mother was aired on December 22, *The Garland Christmas Show*, but this time the limelight was not all hers. Lorna and Joey Luft teamed with Judy and Liza to sing "Consider Yourself" (from the Broadway musical *Oliver!*), and Liza sang "Sleigh Bells" with her mother and special guest Jack Jones. The entire cast, including Jerry Van Dyke and Liza's invited boyfriend Tracy

Elliott Gould and Liza (left) became fast friends when they starred together in a tour of the musical The Fantasticks. *"Liza," says Gould, "is a star."*

Everitt, performed "Deck the Halls."

If Judy and Liza were close most of their lives, they were never closer than in the summer of 1963. It was a good time for Liza; although she regretted leaving *Best Foot Forward*, her relationship with Judy (and Tracy, for that matter) was reaching its zenith. For the first time in her life, Liza felt comfortable questioning her mother about her past. Liza asked Judy: Had she and Mickey Rooney really had an affair? And what about Tyrone Power? Was Mama ever in love with him?

Judy answered Liza truthfully. For the first time in her life she felt connected with her own flesh and blood. Judy laughed about the Power query and said Rooney was "my best pal. He treated me like a boyfriend." Mickey Rooney has this to say about Judy: "I loved her and tried so many times to help her. She was super—one of a kind—and I sorely miss her." Whenever she wasn't taping, Judy would converse with Liza for hours. Judy at forty-one and Liza at seventeen were now the best of friends.

During this time, Judy also began to acknowledge Liza's show business ambitions. At home, she would sit her daughter down and teach her the rudiments of singing. Judy explained to Liza that singing was more than vocal sounds; it was beyond acting, it was a precise science. "You never lose the thought behind the word," Judy told Liza, "you are *not* just singing a note. Just because you're holding a note, don't think that the emotion of the word is over."

Judy would demonstrate in song; one can imagine the scene: Judy, her arms quivering upward, her ripe lips enveloping the lyrics, surges of energy vibrating through the room, while Liza, sweet Liza, sat on the floor of the den, listening, *really listening*, to the legend behind the woman she called "Mama."

Liza also found, during these months, an acting coach in her mother—someone far superior than her professor-mentor at Herbert Berghof's studio. One day, Liza was up for a small role in the medical series *Ben Casey* (a role she did not get).

She was to play a young girl who had an abortion. The scene was short; three lines for her, and three for the actor playing her doctor.

"I sort of gingerly took the script to Mama and said, 'Mama, help me,'" Liza recalls. Judy took the script, and sitting on the floor of her bathroom, studied the scene.

"Mama asked me to read my lines as well as the doctor's," Liza says. "His line was 'Are you sorry?' I read it and Mama said, 'All right, he's a doctor, but how *dare* he intrude on you, how *dare* he ask you that, how *dare* you be in the hospital, how *dare* he be there, if only you had married the father, if only he had loved you. Now, are you sorry?'"

Liza continues. "All I had to say was 'No.' It came out right because Mama taught me the right thoughts. Then she said, 'Read his lines again, and this time, you're going to concentrate on not crying. Your baby is dead, your life is ruined, but you're a strong girl and *you are not going to cry!*' That time," Liza concludes, "my 'No' came out even better."

Judy was teaching her daughter to become the girl she was portraying; to feel her anguish, to feel her hurt, to feel her humiliation. Judy was teaching Liza more than acting that day, she was teaching her Life. "If there is a way I act," Liza says, "then that's it. And I learned it all one day by sitting on a bathroom floor."

Carnival

Judy was prone to illnesses in addition to her mental breakdowns. She suffered severe bouts of kidney attacks. "Having children is a pleasure compared to those," she once quipped, and in 1960 she was hospitalized with a diseased liver. She had unknowingly contracted hepatitis a few years earlier. A doctor took one look at her liver and told Judy she would be a semi-invalid the rest of her life. She proved him wrong.

Liza inherited Judy's kidney ailments. In November, 1963, soon after she finished taping the Garland Christmas gala, Liza woke up in excruciating pain. "My fever was raging and my legs felt like wet noodles," she remembers. The agony was so intense she had grave difficulty getting out of bed. Liza was rushed to the hospital where, after three days of constant testing, the doctors found that she had kidney stones. Some years later, Liza would be told that she also suffers from scoliosis—curvature of the spine. It is a chronic condition, aggravated more when she remains idle. "Nobody is gonna touch my back!" she insists. But Liza sees a chiropractor on a regular basis.

Liza recuperated slowly. Judy, when not taping her series, would fly to Liza's side and offer encouragement. Several weeks after she was better (but not fully recovered), Liza flew to New York. She had heard about a winter stock tour of the Broadway musical *Carnival* and wanted the lead role. Once in Manhattan, Liza—now much slimmer—signed with the show. *Carnival* was based on the M-G-M film *Lili* and Liza would play Lili, a wide-eyed urchin who takes a job with a circus. Anna Maria Alberghetti had originated the role on Broadway.

Nearly eight weeks after her first kidney stone attack, Liza suffered another—so serious that, again, she was forced to be hospitalized. Judy demanded she return to California to recover. "You're not well enough," she told Liza. Liza refused—she stood up for herself—and plunged into *Carnival*. Judy's reaction: "Over my dead body!"

Judy put a call in to the press, informing them her daughter was no longer in the show. Liza retaliated: "Yes I am!" she screamed at confused reporters. Each day, Judy would phone the *Carnival* crew (the stock tour was beginning at the Paper Mill Playhouse in Millburn, New Jersey) and carry on like a madwoman.

"Judy was always pulling some new hysterical stunt," says Pat Hipp, the woman who worked as the show's press agent, "so I didn't know from one day to the next if we had a show. One day, Judy's lawyer called to say Judy was pulling Liza out of *Carnival*. Then he'd call back and refute the story. It was all very crazy! And poor Liza—such a nervous, *nervous* wreck. Judy was putting her through hell, but she was determined to do the show."

Today, Pat Hipp is an effusive woman who furnishes her stories with great details. She is entertaining to listen to.

"The first time I met Liza," she recalls, "she was sitting in an office, near the switchboard. She was wearing jeans and had lots and lots of long hair. She was also crying—Judy had just called her and was giving her another hard time. I took one look and wanted to wrap my arms around her."

Later that day, Hipp caught Liza in a dress rehearsal. "I was standing in back of the house as she was singing 'Love Makes the World Go Round.' Liza knocked me over because she was so brilliant! So divine! So magnificent! Her voice was absolute magic; my breath stopped. I honestly cannot even tell you who else was in the show. All I remember is Liza. Yet, even with all the aggravation she had to put up with," Hipp adds, "Liza always remained the professional. She was never late and always rehearsed diligently."

Carnival opened as planned to a sold-out audience of nearly twelve hundred. Judy was not among the opening-nighters, though Liza claims her mother sent her a case of champagne. In fact, Judy never saw Liza perform *Carnival*. However, soon after Liza returned home from the stock tour, Judy told Liza, "You know, that was the first time you defied me, and it infuriated me. But God, how I admired you for doing it!" Liza was speechless. "Vincente Minnelli had persuaded Judy to let Liza go," Hipp explains. "Just as easily as Judy had started the trouble, she ended it. If it weren't for Liza's dad, the show may not have gone on."

Carnival was a resounding success. Mike McKay, reviewing the show for Long Island's *Newsday*, wrote, "The comparisons to Judy Garland are inevitable—the tremulous voice, the respect for the lyric, the wide eyes, the clenching hands, the eyebrows never still. Yet, by the time Liza sings her second number, 'Yes, My Heart,' the applause belongs to her alone; from that point on, forget to make comparisons."

The final results of *Carnival* may have been a carnival for Liza (she was exceptionally proud of the reviews), but her next two ventures were not. Shortly after *Carnival* closed, Liza starred opposite veteran actor Chester Morris in a production of the comedy *Time Out For Ginger* at the Bucks County Playhouse in New Hope, Pennsylvania. The reviews Liza received paled in comparison with those from *Carnival* and what Liza most remembers of the event was the overbearing smell of Morris's breath.

Later that same year, Liza's agent, Stevie Phillips, got her a small role on the NBC series *Mr. Broadway*. In the "Nightingale for Sale" episode, Liza appeared as Minnie, an aspiring opera singer with underworld connections. The show aired on October 24, 1964, and was soon forgotten.

The Fantasticks

Between *Time Out for Ginger* and *Mr. Broadway*, Liza toured in a production of *The Fantasticks*, which was being produced by Laurence Feldman, one of the co-producers of *Carnival*.

Liza chose to star in *The Fantasticks* because she needed the money. She was living well above her means and was shocked one day to find that she was in debt for thousands of dollars and on the verge of bankruptcy.

"The lights in my apartment went out," Liza recalls, "and I figured, oh well, it's a power failure. So I went down to the deli to buy some food, and the owner said, 'I'm sorry, Miss Minnelli, your credit isn't good anymore.' The next morning I found out my electric bill hadn't been paid. It was like a sledgehammer coming down on my head. I couldn't believe this was happening to me. I was so distraught that I went to Cartier's and bought a watch!"

Liza's lawyer settled her bills, and soon after Liza hired Martin Bregman as her financial manager. "I've got this thing about being solvent," Liza adds with a smile. "I now know how much I've got—to the dime."

Liza had another financial close call in 1974 when she discovered that she was defrauded of $230,000 by the Homestake Productions Company of Tulsa, Oklahoma—the company declared bankruptcy. Liza wasn't the only one out of cash: her friend Candice Bergen and Martin Bregman were also victims.

In *The Fantasticks*, Liza played The Girl, and Elliott Gould, then married to Barbra Streisand, played The Boy. Today, Gould has fond memories of his superstar friend. When he speaks about her, he injects his conversation with nouns like "doll" and "angel" and "baby," endearments he says he reserves only for Liza. "After all," he smiles, "I *am* her big brother."

"I first met Liza when her mother was cutting a record in a Manhattan studio," says Gould. "Liza was all manic and wild and unbelievable. She always had her heart 'out there.' A while later, Liza's agent asked me to do *The Fantasticks*, and I jumped at the chance. We had only two weeks to rehearse—I remember Liza's dad stopping by the Sullivan Street Theater to catch us—but they were two fun-filled weeks. But what really turned me on, and I later told this to Barbra, was that Liza wasn't selfish. She was as interested in *my* work as she was hers."

The Fantasticks opened at the Westport Country Playhouse in Westport, Connecticut, to lavish reviews, and two weeks were added to the original eight-week tour. Audiences loved the simple plot; even more, they loved Liza as she crooned the show's melodic songs.

Towards the end of the stock tour, a macabre event took place that was so wild Gould remembers every detail of it. He should. He helped save Liza's life.

"We were performing in Ontario, Canada, one night and had stopped at a roadhouse about eighty miles from the highway," Gould says. "We were all having fun, drinking and eating. Suddenly, Liza jumped on stage and began singing; I think it was 'Big Spender' or 'Someone to Watch Over Me.' Some guys started getting rowdy, so I told Liza to get down, I wanted to split. Well, two guys started following us — one had gray eyes and a gray T-shirt on — harrassing us and eventually sideswiping our car. Luckily, no one was hurt. Michael Mann [a cast member, who introduced Gould to Liza] called the cops and it seems the gray guy was wanted because he had been in an auto accident and killed someone. It was the eyes that gave him away. Anyway, we all got dragged into court — me, Liza, the others in this small Canadian courthouse — but I begged the police to let us go. We didn't want to testify; we wanted to go home. The cops said fine. As I was driving off, I noticed a red car following us. Then, there were fourteen other red cars . . . something right out of a B-movie. It was pretty scary. Finally, I pulled into a restaurant, told Liza to have a *long* lunch and I called the highway patrol. But they didn't do a fucking thing. I decided to handle it myself. I went up to the gray guy and said, 'Look, we're actors, outsiders, and we don't want any trouble. How about if, tomorrow, I get us a police escort out of town? Then you'll be free to rob a bank. No cops!' The gray guy grinned and nodded. And that," Gould finishes with a smack of his lips, "is the entire story, every detail of it, exactly as it happened!"

Later that night, to celebrate their safe recovery, Gould drove Michael Mann and Liza to a graveyard. "We were all laughing pretty hard," Gould recalls. "I guess none of us realized we could have ended up there."

Liza's work on *The Fantasticks* was fantastic, but cannot compare with what took place that November. It was an event that would turn her life — and Judy's — around.

Judy and Liza at the Palladium

In September, 1964, Judy was living in the Chelsea section of London, preparing for her upcoming Palladium engagement. One day, Liza's first album, *Liza! Liza!*, arrived in the mail. Judy listened to the record — one of Liza's songs was "Try to Remember" from *The Fantasticks* — and was overwhelmed. "Where did she get that voice?" she asked no one in particular. "My God, she must have worked her little ass off!"

Judy immediately called Liza in the United States. "How would you like to sing with me at the Palladium?" she asked. Liza was thrown by the idea; could Mama really mean this? After what she did to me in *Carnival*! Liza politely turned her mother down. "Oh, no, Mama," she cried. "It's too much, Judy and her kid. Why don't you just do it yourself?"

Judy would not take "no" for an answer. She called the press and announced that both she *and* Liza would be per-

In this rare photo, Liza and Judy are shown rehearsing their 1964 London Palladium concert engagement. The shows went well until Judy, apparently miffed by the audience reaction to Liza, pushed her daughter offstage.

forming at the Palladium on November 8. Tickets went on sale and the concert was sold out in a matter of hours. Tickets for the show were in such demand that another performance was added. Liza got the call the next morning. Judy: "We're sold out! Isn't it great?" The next day Liza could only agree.

Liza solicited the help of her former classmate, Marvin Hamlisch, to prepare her song arrangements (Liza was still close to Marvin; she recorded his song "The Travelin' Life" on *Liza! Liza!*). If Liza was going to appear on a co-starring bill with her mother for the first time, then she wanted to do it right. Marvin, she knew, could help.

Liza flew to London on September 9, 1964. Judy and Mark Herron, Judy's new husband, met her at the airport. The concert was sixty days away.

Judy wanted to introduce Liza to the audience in the way she knew best, through song. She thought she would simply sing, "Liza . . . . Liza."

Mark Herron disagreed with the idea. How could Judy do that? This was an important event for Liza — "the big time." Herron suggested a more honorable introduction: "Ladies and gentlemen, Liza Minnelli." Judy finally agreed.

On Sunday, November 8, the London Palladium was packed to the rafters with the black-tie crowd. Even the stand-

Even at a young age, Liza knew the value of publicity. She got herself invited to the chicest parties (Judy's name helped open doors) and was photographed with the chicest celebrities. No one seemed to mind Liza's undistinguished clothes. Trini Lopez took time from his busy career to pose with Liza (above, left). At the Twelfth Annual April in Paris Ball, held in Manhattan, actress Lisa Kirk, Frank Sinatra, Junior and French film hearthrob Jean-Pierre Aumont flanked the seventeen-year-old Liza (below). Across the ocean from the Paris Ball, Liza dropped by the set of her mother's last film, I Could Go On Singing. With Liza are Ronald Neame, the film's director, the film's costar Gregory Phillips and Liza's smiling friend, Kate Manning (opposite). Kate is the "hippie" friend Liza visited in London during her spontaneous sabbatical from Scarsdale High School.

ing room space along the back wall was filled. Some of the audience wondered if the fire laws had been violated. They had never seen such a bevy of people.

The overture included the tunes "Over the Rainbow," "The Man that Got Away," "Smile," "Liza" and "Never Will I Marry." Judy made her entrance singing "The Man that Got Away," one of her theme songs from *A Star is Born*. The audience loved it; they were welcoming home their goddess. Liza was then introduced (Herron's words worked perfectly), and Liza sang "The Travelin' Life." The British loved her too; they were accepting a new talent into their hearts.

Liza sang a total of eight numbers; Judy sang ten. They sang twelve numbers together. One highlight was the tune "Hello, Dolly," with a change in the lyrics. "Hello, Mama, Well hello, Mama, You're still growing...You're still crowing ...You're still going strong." The audiences roared.

In October of 1965, Capitol released a two-disc album of the concert entitled *Judy Garland and Liza Minnelli "Live" at the London Palladium*. The record sold well (eight years later, at the height of Minnelli mania, Capitol rereleased the album on a single disc, this time selling poorly). The BBC also broadcast an hour-long taping of the show on December 9. Liza was furious with it: "They cut most of the numbers," she sighs, "and left in all the applause and hugging."

The Palladium shows did not go on without problems. The most significant one was Judy's jealousy over the reaction Liza received from the audience. Although Judy requested—no, demanded—Liza's participation in the show, Judy could not deal with the results.

One of Liza's big numbers was a jazzy version of Connie Francis's classic, "Who's Sorry Now?" The ovation Liza received was genuine—the British are known to applaud only when you're good and that night Liza was *very* good—and Judy watched in bewilderment.

She often stepped on Liza's lines during the show and, at times, seemed to deliberately try to upstage (and upset) her. This was especially noticeable as mother and daughter sang "Chicago." There are some people who insist, during one part of the show, that Judy actually pushed Liza offstage.

Liza remembers Judy's antics. "When I was a little girl and I jumped on stage to dance while Mama sang," Liza says, "it was an unrehearsed, amateurish and spontaneous thing. But at the Palladium, Mama realized that she had a grown-up daughter and that I wasn't a kid anymore. I'm sure this happens with almost every mother and daughter. It happened to my mother in front of eight thousand people. Mama became very competitive with me. I wasn't Liza, but another woman in the same spotlight."

Liza does admit that the Palladium experience prepared her for life. "Working with Mama," she says simply, "was something else. After that terrifying experience, I was never afraid to perform with anyone else again." Liza never did appear with Judy in a concert setting again. In fact, for years she searched for a film for the two of them to make together, but nothing ever came through. Some good did come out of the London experience. "Immediately after the Palladium show," Liza says, "Mama's competitiveness disappeared. She then fell into a period of unparalleled motherhood."

Judy Meets Peter Allen

Judy did not "drift" or "fall" into anything throughout her life. She was a talented, vulnerable and manipulative woman, whose actions often belied the truth. The London concerts are a perfect example.

In late May, 1964, while vacationing in Hong Kong, Judy dropped into the Starlight Room of the Mandarin Hotel one night. Mark Herron had gone there several nights before and had seen a singing duo called The Allen Brothers. He recommended them to Judy.

Judy loved the brothers. Actually, Peter and Chris Allen were not related; Chris's surname was Bell. They purposely fooled the public as a way of attracting more attention. She found Chris reserved and erudite; Peter was funny and charming—and single.

After she arrived back in London (this was shortly before she called Liza about sharing the Palladium bill), Judy began booking the Allen Brothers in London nightclubs. She later used them as her opening act, and in the back of Judy's mind was one thought: to see Liza and Peter get together.

"I have met the most divine boy," Judy told Liza shortly after she arrived in London. "You two have the same crazy sense of humor." Judy introduced her daughter to Peter and the two hit it off immediately. Liza and Peter would often pop into London nightclubs, meeting the likes of such notables as Noel Coward, Rosalind Russell, Rex Harrison and Peter Sellers. The latter would come to play a very important part in Liza's life. They would party with Judy and Mark Herron and dine in exclusive Chelsea pubs. Liza and Peter, it seemed, were falling in love.

A little more than one month after they met, Peter, Liza, Judy and Mark Herron were dining in Trader Vic's London restaurant. Peter turned to Liza and asked her to "go steady" (Judy was in the bathroom and missed the event). When Liza asked if that meant they were engaged, Peter nodded. Liza smiled demurely, and Peter gave her a small diamond ring he used to wear on his pinky. When Judy finally heard the news, she sobbed. Her plan had worked!

Years later, Liza would recall that day in Trader Vic's. "We were pretty high on those exotic drinks they make," she said. "I was also scared and uncertain."

Liza and Peter did not marry for nearly two and a half years after they met. Their engagement was long and protracted. "Liza was too busy to marry right away," Peter says. "Her career was taking off, so I said, fine, I'll wait." He did. And Liza, the day after her engagement, flew to New York to audition for a new Broadway show.

Flora, the Red Menace

Fred Ebb first met Liza Minnelli towards the end of her run

As a child, Liza was cherubic and chubby. As an adolescent, she was gawky and chubby. As she blossomed into womanhood, Liza could look either soft and feminine—like she did with George Hamilton at a CBS party (opposite, left)—or she could look hard and garish, as she did when she showed up at Jack Jones' nightclub opening (opposite, right). Both photos show Liza pre-Halston, when her taste in clothes was primitive. After Liza opened on Broadway in Flora, the Red Menace, she managed to appear more stylish—thanks to Fred Ebb's mentorship and the presence of Judy and Vincente.

in Best Foot Forward. "I remember this shy and awkward girl coming into the room," he recalls. "She looked awful. Everything was a little soiled and a little torn, just like Raggedy Ann. Liza just sat there staring at me. So I stared back."

Ebb liked what he saw. In Best Foot Forward, he had witnessed a girl with talent and determination; a gawky innocence that could easily be transformed into sexy magnetism. Ebb knew Liza would go far.

The lyricist played Liza a few songs from Flora, the Red Menace, a Broadway musical for which he and his partner John Kander were writing the music. Liza listened, a smile ripening on her face. Would you like to play Flora? Ebb asked. Liza nodded, Yes! At that moment, Ebb knew no one else would do—Liza Minnelli was Flora, the Red Menace.

Ebb began working with Liza, molding her style of singing, encouraging her to use the reservoir of talent that he knew lay

deep within; talent that Liza left untapped. Liza listened feverishly to her new friend and later, at the London Palladium with her mother, Liza would discover how helpful Ebb really was.

Fred Ebb and Liza became the closest of friends. He became her mentor and confidant; she became his devoted pupil. They were lovers—without sex. "Fred is the only person I've ever loved and trusted," Liza has said. "He knows me better than anyone else. He is to me what Roger Edens [Judy's music mentor] was to Mama. He makes me decide to be a little better than I've ever been before. He reminds me that I'm not great unless I'm great. I guess you can say we're joined at the hip."

Ebb urged Liza to sing his compositions, and on her first album, Liza recorded two Kander and Ebb tunes, "If I Were in Your Shoes" and "Maybe This Time." The latter became one of Liza's standards—she sang it in *Cabaret*—but contrary to popular belief, "Maybe This Time" was not written for Liza. Kander and Ebb originally wrote it for comedienne Kaye Ballard.

Two other songs, "Liza with a Z" and "Exactly Like Me," were written by Ebb for Liza. To her fans, these songs *are* Liza. Since she introduced "Liza With a Z" at the Empire Room of Manhattan's Waldorf-Astoria in 1968, it has become one of her standards; and she first sang "Exactly Like Me" to New York audiences during her 1974 Winter Garden stint.

Liza also learned a lot of English from Ebb. During the mid 1970s, Ebb—to help Liza compensate for her lack of formal education—taught Liza three new vocabulary words each week. Liza would write them on her left foot in magic marker and then learn them by staring at her limb while she was resting in bed. Liza's method of self-study was unusual, but it worked. Today, Liza will liven up her conversation with words that sometimes perplex the listener.

Liza began auditioning for *Flora, the Red Menace* at the time she was preparing for her Palladium concerts with Judy. She commuted back and forth from London to New York to see how the show was progressing. "I wanted to do *Flora* so badly that I just kept auditioning," Liza recalls. "I just kept going back until they couldn't get rid of me."

Ebb and Kander wanted Liza to star in *Flora*, but George Abbott, one of the show's authors and the play's director, believed Liza was wrong for the part. He originally wanted singer Eydie Gorme for the role. He thought Liza's first audition would be a waste of time and publicly said so. "She's not right for Flora," he explained at the time. "She's not what I have in mind and I don't think she'll be able to carry it."

Liza refused to be daunted by Abbott's criticisms. "*Flora* was something I really wanted," she recalls about those trying times. "I persevered—I hounded Fred Ebb and George Abbott—until I got it." Finally, with no one else on the horizon, Abbott relented and gave Liza the role. She threw herself into rehearsals, positive that this, her first Broadway role, would bring her stardom. Abbott was amazed by his star's energy and, after rehearsals were underway, commented, "I've never seen anyone take direction that fast since Helen Hayes."

Liza later "repaid" Abbott when she appeared as a special guest in *George Abbott...A Celebration*. The one-night show, held on Sunday, May 2, 1976, at Manhattan's Shubert

When Flora, the Red Menace *opened on Broadway in 1965, the reviews didn't exactly tickle Liza pink. In hopes of increasing ticket sales, Liza made appearances on* The Ed Sullivan Show. *The show's backers hoped to capitalize on Liza's famous lineage. Though no one in* Flora *received star billing, producers hoped Liza's name above the title would draw crowds. It didn't. Even the cast album, which Liza and the cast recorded in May (center), failed to help the show. Today,* Flora, the Red Menace *is but a memory for Liza and the show's director, George Abbott (right).*

Theater, saluted Abbott's countless contributions to the theater world.

Almost two years later, on November 12, 1978, Liza would repay two other friends: John Kander and Fred Ebb when she appeared in *Sing Happy!* at Avery Fisher Hall. Liza sang several Kander-Ebb songs, but the evening's highlight was the rousing production number she performed with Chita Rivera and Gwen Verdon.

Abbott was not the only one impressed by Liza's energy. Mary Bryant, the press agent for *Flora*, was another. It was the first time Bryant was associated with a Hal Prince show (Prince produced *Flora*); today, Bryant and Prince—one of the musical theater's best innovators—still work together, most recently on *Evita* and *Merrily We Roll Along*. Sitting in her cluttered midtown Manhattan office, Bryant, who strongly resembles Shelley Winters, fondly remembers the Liza Minnelli she knew in the mid-sixties.

"Liza was an effervescent girl who always reminded me of her father," she says. "And boy, what legs! Just like her mother! I used to take her on interviews—*everyone* wanted her—and she'd say to me, 'Do I *have* to talk about Mama?' But our out-of-town reviews were far from great, so I told Liza she should do anything she could to sell the show, even if it meant mentioning Judy."

"One time," Bryant continues, "a photographer wanted some special pictures, so he asked Liza if she could tap dance. She said yes. Now, Liza didn't know *how* to tap dance, but she said yes because she knew she could do *anything*. And you know what? She pulled it off perfectly! But difficult? Liza? Never. She was super in *Flora*; a great talent."

Liza celebrated her nineteenth birthday during the rehearsals of *Flora*. Abbott brought her a big birthday cake and the cast and crew helped Liza celebrate. The party was a far cry from the ones her father used to throw for her, but for Liza, this one was just as important.

Shortly into the previews of the show, theater artist Al Hirschfeld drew his first caricature of Liza. Bryant still can recall Liza's reaction. "She was furious, absolutely livid," she says. "Liza felt Al drew her nose much bigger than it was, and she was very offended. It took her days to realize that to be drawn by Hirschfeld was an honor." Since then, Liza has been immortalized at least six more times by Hirschfeld. She has never complained again.

Flora, the Red Menace opened in try-outs on Saturday, April 3, 1965, at the Shubert Theater in New Haven, Connecticut. Most of the reviews were favorable, although nothing special; eleven days later, on Wednesday, April 14, a slightly revised *Flora* opened at the Colonial Theater in Boston. Again, the musical garnered favorable responses and audiences flocked to see "Judy's daughter." In the show, Liza played Flora Meszaros, an extroverted young commercial artist who joins the Young Communist League at the suggestion of her boyfriend. Bob Dishy co-starred as Liza's beau, and after the show, the two would often go out to dinner. They were close friends only, but their evenings sometimes ran long and Liza would drag herself into the apartment she shared with actress Tanya Everitt on West Fifty-fifth Street.

Flora, the Red Menace opened on Broadway at 7:20 P.M. at the Alvin Theater on Tuesday, May 11. The opening night

had long been sold out and most of the patrons were wondering the same thing: Would Judy and Vincente appear?

Both did and found their daughter's performance captivating. Even though two of Liza's biggest numbers were cut during try-outs, she nevertheless brought down the house with a song titled "Sing Happy." If the name has a familiar ring to it, think of "Get Happy," Judy's rousing number, from *Summer Stock*. Judy and Vincente joined the many celebrities at the cast party, and Liza beamed with pride. She was, now, a Broadway star. After the show, Judy hugged Liza and whispered, "You are standing in stardust."

Then the reviews came in. Though they were not extremely harsh, they were not the glowing notices *Flora* needed to sustain a healthy run. *Time* dubbed Liza: "A star-to-be with an arresting presence that occupies the stage," and Howard Taubman of *The New York Times* wrote, "Liza's voice is not yet distinctive, but she can belt out the climactic tones." Norman Nadel, in the *New York World-Telegram & Sun*, wrote, "Miss Minnelli has established, beyond a shadow of a doubt, that she is no second edition Judy."

But Liza forgot the praise she received when she read what *Newsweek* said about her: "Liza Minnelli is engaging, but far from accomplished; and it is unpleasant to see her rushed into a big Broadway show at nineteen, as though she were another Barbra Streisand. But Miss Minnelli lacks Miss Streisand's equipment. Her voice is thin, her movements stiff, her presence wobbly and uncertain." (Streisand had wowed the critics with her portrayal of Fanny Brice in *Funny Girl* thirteen months before *Flora* opened.)

"To say the least," Fred Ebb now recalls, "*Flora* was a disaster. It just did not work. The book was sort of strange and the score sounded like a series of revue numbers because it wasn't connected by the strength of the libretto."

Hal Prince has also commented on the demise of the show. "By the time we previewed in New York," he says, "I began to believe we had a hit. But the reviews on Broadway were awful and they needn't have been." As for Liza, Prince says, "She had a voice that reminded you of her mother, intelligence about character and, best of all for me, she moved wonderfully."

Flora, the Red Menace closed on Saturday, July 24, 1965, after eighty-seven performances. The show lost $381,000 of its $400,000 investment. The cast still recorded an album on May 9 on the RCA Victor label; today, an original pressing of the record is highly sought after by collectors of Minnelli memorabilia.

On Sunday, June 13, 1965, Liza won an Antoinette Perry Award as Best Actress in a Musical for her role as Flora. At the time, Liza became the youngest female recipient of a Tony. It would be her first Tony Award; two others—one for *Liza*, the other for *The Act*—would follow. Liza's competition in 1965 was Nancy Dussault for *Bajour*, Elizabeth Allen for *Do I Hear a Waltz?* and Inga Swenson for *Baker Street*; all noted performers in equally dismal shows.

Although Judy never publicly commented on Liza's Tony Award (it was one of the few honors Judy had never won), the following incident is an indication of her feelings. Shortly after Liza won, Judy was in California, playing Monopoly with a friend. At one point, the man commented that, although Liza was good in the show, he felt she didn't deserve the Tony Award. Judy poured a drink over his head and kicked him out of her house.

Fred Ebb: "She's an Assertion of Life"

After *Flora* closed, a dejected Liza was persuaded by Ebb to devote her time and energy to developing a nightclub act. Ebb had originally planned to write a new musical for Liza, *Tomato Pie*, but the idea never ripened. Once again, Liza listened to Ebb and readied herself for her September, 1965, engagement at the Blue Room of the Shoreham Hotel in Washington, D.C. It was a smashing success—the engagement broke all existing attendance records.

Liza sang eighteen songs—everything from "Too Marvelous" to "Gypsy in My Soul" to "Everybody Loves My Baby." Ebb had written Liza a special number, "Songs I Taught My Mother," which the audience loved, and Liza's finale was the showstopping "Sing Happy" from *Flora, the Red Menace*.

Liza had two male dancers with her, Neil Schwartz and Robert Fitch, but from beginning to end, the show's star was Liza Minnelli. Although Halston was not yet her designer, her costumes were still special: a short gown embellished with red sequins and white beads, a blue chiffon dancing dress and a stunning white dress that Liza wore for "Sing Happy."

The audience's reaction dazzled Liza; the reviews turned that astonishment into reality. "Her songs, dances and patter are magnificent," said one usually stoic D.C. critic, "and they are written to make the most out of her remarkable talent and personality." *Variety* noted that Liza's standing ova-

Fred Ebb, more than anyone else, is responsible for perfecting the Liza Minnelli persona. They first met in the early 1960s—and have been linked ever since. "Liza never stops," explains Fred. "She has a rage to live."

tions "were unusual in the huge, sophisticated Blue Room." Liza was a winner, she knew it, Judy and Vincente knew it, and Fred Ebb knew it. His pupil had learned well.

"I'm not a star yet," Liza said in response to her newly found acclaim, "but I'm on my way. It's kind of an advantage that my mother is Judy Garland. I know why people come and see me; I hear them talking in the lobby. They expect a carbon copy—or they expect me to be no good. Originality is one thing they don't expect."

※ ※ ※

Fred Ebb is not a handsome man; some might even describe the songwriter as ordinary. But Ebb is extraordinary when he speaks about his love, Liza.

"She is the constant woman in my life and I am the constant man in hers," he says. "There is no reason at all why Liza and I shouldn't have been lovers. I guess we just knew too much about each other. Plus there were just too many other guys in her life."

Ebb understands Liza's need for companionship. "Like her mother," he explains, "Liza can't be alone easily, and she knows this. In every situation she's in, she always looks for a person, usually masculine, to depend on, to be close to. She has a deep need for complete trust and that can be quite scary. But the essential thing about Liza is that she's an assertion of

A twenty-one-year-old Liza, sans makeup, goes through pre-taping tests in this rare photo, taken behind the scenes of the NBC special Kraft Music Hall's Give My Regards to Broadway *(above, left). Two years earlier, Liza joined Paul Anka and Dionne Warwick (bottom) for a song fest on the TV show* Hullabaloo. *When Liza guested on her mother's ill-fated CBS show, the camera caught her in an act of daughterly concern. "Liza was often a mother to Judy," one of Liza's friends once remarked. This photo expresses that best.*

life. She went through crazy, sordid things with her mother that I *still* find hard to believe. One push either way would have made her crazy," Ebb adds, "but somehow—between her father's calming influence, her mother's love of life and marvelous sense of humor and Liza's own talent—she came out of it. It still amazes me sometimes."

Ebb continues: "When Liza first started out in *Flora*, she was afraid to open her mouth. Eight out of ten ideas from her were terrible. It got to be a standing joke and her fingernails were chewed up to her elbows. You know, feature by feature, Liza's *not* beautiful. But the whole is greater than the sum of her parts and when she shines, she's devastating. But the real secret of Liza's appeal? She flatters an audience. She really cares for them; she makes people want to look after her. She's everybody's kid sister; every guy's dependent girl. Liza's never idle. She never stops. She just has a rage to live."

☙ ☙ ☙

Shortly after her Blue Room engagement, Liza filmed *The Dangerous Christmas of Little Red Riding Hood.* The ABC musical special also starred Cyril Ritchard, Vic Damone and The Animals, a popular sixties pop group. Liza played Lillian Hood to Ritchard's Lone T. Wolf—the show was a spoof of the classic children's fairy tale—but the special, which aired November 28, 1965, was execrable. (Liza did, however, eventually record the Jule Styne-Bob Merrill-Robert Emmett score.) According to *The New York Times*, performing in *The Dangerous Christmas*, "Liza Minnelli brought an earnest sincerity to her singing and playing, but her limited resources in both were a handicap in raising the program to a tuneful lark."

Liza was tuneful, however, when she debuted her nightclub act in Manhattan in early 1966. She knew that although the D.C. bigwigs loved her, New York was the only city where she would learn what the critics *really* thought. After all, Liza thought, New York is the city to make or break me.

Liza's Manhattan nightclub premiere, held on February 9, 1966, at the Persian Room of the elite Plaza Hotel, was an instant success. Her program was more streamlined than it had been in Washington; even her clothes were changed to more sexy ones: a black, no-back gown, form-fitting tights and a pale blue dress with a Peter Pan collar. Again, Liza knocked the critics dead.

Some of the best praise came from Dennis Cunningham,

then writing for the *New York World-Telegram & Sun.* His February 10 review was effusive: "Liza Minnelli proved she could sock the stuffing out of a song, dance beautifully for a singer—even pretty well for a dancer—and turn on that built-in spotlight that is the *sine qua non* of the cabaret performer."

Even with the rave reviews, Liza did receive some negative criticism; ironically, it was again from *Newsweek*, the magazine that had panned her performance in *Flora, the Red Menace*: "Nineteen-year-old Liza Minnelli's song-and-dance act at New York's Persian Room is, on the surface, flawless: smooth, quick-paced and high-stepping. She has a pleasant voice, in spite of a need to take refuge from high notes in shouts. But all the slick Las Vegas arrangements couldn't get her to sing "He's My Guy" or "They Wouldn't Believe Me" as if she meant it. A girl has to have lived a little to sing about the seamy sides of life and love."

Soon after her Persian Room stint, Liza toured with her act. In May, 1966, she performed at London's Talk of the Town, and a little while later, she gave a command performance before Prince Rainier and and the late Princess Grace of Monaco.

When she returned to the United States, Liza performed at Los Angeles's Coconut Grove. It was here that French singer Charles Aznavour caught Liza's act. He arranged for her to perform at the Olympia Music Hall in Paris and has never regretted the decision. The French loved Liza, comparing her to their own Edith Piaf. "She pulls songs out of the heart," said one critic.

Charles Aznavour will never forget the Liza Minnelli he first met back in 1966. "Liza is versatile, sad, funny, over-doing," he says in clipped English. "She's a personality and a child of this century. I can count on two hands the great performers in America, and Liza Minnelli is one of them. The rest? Mere shadows of her." Aznavour and Minnelli would, eight years later, perform on stage together. Their concert, *Love From A to Z*, was filmed at the Rainbow Theater in London and aired to American audiences on April 30, 1974. In response to the rumors that he had a romantic affair with Liza, Aznavour merely says, "What we had was better than romance."

Shortly after she returned from Europe, Liza toured in a summer stock production of *The Pajama Game.* It was a successful tour, and again Liza demonstrated her singing and dancing—talents she had honed since her *Carnival* days. In December, she recorded a third album for Capitol, *There is a Time.* Several selections from the record were released as singles, most notably "I (Who Have Nothing)." The album sold

moderately well and was named Best Album of the Year by *Hi-Fi/Stereo Review* magazine.

Charlie Bubbles

Throughout her life, Judy would try to get Liza work; more often than not, Liza was unaware of her mother's meddling. *Charlie Bubbles* was one such case.

Judy was a close friend of Michael Medwin, the British actor who was producing the film. Medwin had signed actor Albert Finney as both star and director; Billie Whitelaw, a noted English actress, was to play Finney's wife. One role had yet to be cast: Eliza, an intelligent American girl who is Bubbles's worshipful secretary and, later, his mistress. Judy asked Medwin to let Liza test for the role. He agreed.

Liza recalls that she was in Las Vegas when a call came from Finney. "I didn't ask why he called," she says. "I figured if Albert Finney wants to see you, you go." When she found out why the actor wanted to see her, Liza was delighted. The fact that Judy got her the audition was unimportant to Liza;

she was going to be in the movies—*that* was important.

Liza felt the first audition, held in California, went poorly. She was too eager for the role and it showed. Finney had Liza reread her lines over and over—"You have a face that registers everything," he told her. "It's not veiled enough. Do half of what you're doing."—then dismissed her. Disgruntled, Liza went back to her nightclub work.

A few weeks later, Liza received a second call from Finney. The role of Eliza was hers; could she be in London in two weeks to start production?

Charlie Bubbles was a pleasurable experience for Liza, and Finney was a joy to work with. "All the time we were making the film," she gushes, "he never lost his temper once." It was also, excluding *In the Good Old Summertime*, her first film role; certainly it was her first plum.

Vincente recalls his daughter's association with the film. "Liza wrote me a serio-comic letter in which she told of her imagined terrors," he says. "I immediately wrote back: 'I know your own intuition and good taste will carry you through. The

Liza's resemblance to Judy began at an early age. While she was carving out her niche at M-G-M, Judy posed as a pilgrim (opposite, left). Liza, publicizing her appearance on The Arthur Godfrey Thanksgiving Day Show *(opposite, right), struck a similar pose. Most critics gobbled up Liza's lovemaking scenes opposite Albert Finney in* Charlie Bubbles *(below). The film marked Liza's first featured role—which Judy helped her win.*

only advice I can think of is "Don't press." Remember that you register so strongly and so easily that you can project any emotion from ecstasy to anger and still be in control. I am delighted that you are doing this picture, and I think it's a marvelous break for you. I feel absolutely sure that you'll be fresh and great and appealing and something completely new.'"

Liza received fourth billing, even though her role was no more than an extended cameo. In the film, Liza has a love-making scene with Finney and is seen in only her bra and panties. On screen, Liza comes off with the right amount of polished naïveté and awkwardness. During the filming, however, Liza was embarrassed by her apparel—or lack of it. Because of the love-making scene, gossip magazines tried to romantically link Liza with Finney. *Photoplay*, for instance, ran one article, its headline blaring, "Why Finney Wanted Liza Minnelli." Nothing had gone on between them. But the film did make it clear that Liza was no longer the pudgy teenager of days gone by. She had developed into a mature, buxom, young woman.

Charlie Bubbles was released in the United States in January–February, 1968. Medwin, the film's producer, hoped the American release would beef up interest when the film was released in England. Most of the film's reviews were favorable (both in America and England); *Charlie Bubbles* was even named by many critics as one of the Top Ten Films of 1968.

Liza's American reviews were, for the most part, fair. Renata Adler in *The New York Times* said, "Liza Minnelli does [her] part wide-eyed and with her voice pitched to set the teeth on edge."

"She is a trifle cloying," said *Variety*.

But *Newsweek* loved Liza's work. In his review, Joseph Morgenstern wrote, "Every single performance in the film has a life of its own, and several leave you drunk with delight and desperate for just one more scene [including] Liza Minnelli."

Although the British press was amazed by Liza's portrayal—*Monthly Film Bulletin* said, "there is a beautifully caricatured performance by Liza Minnelli"—the movie did not win the audiences it needed to survive. And for a while, Liza's cinematic career bubble had burst.

Liza Marries Peter Allen

Soon after Liza returned to New York from filming *Charlie*

On March 3, 1967, Liza May Minnelli became Liza May Minnelli Allen. Judy beamed with motherly pride after she witnessed Liza's simple ceremony (opposite). Liza and Peter appear
in a domestic setting (opposite, far right). "Liza convinced me
to go into songwriting," Peter remembers. "She had just come
back from making her first film with Albert Finney [Charlie
Bubbles], and Finney's son's name was Simon. 'I love that
name,' Liza said to me, 'write me a song called "Simon."' So I
sat down and made the whole thing up!"

Bubbles, she decided it was time to marry Peter Allen. While Liza was quickly zooming to the top, things were slower for Peter. He was playing in small, predominantly gay clubs, tinkering with songwriting and opening for Judy's nightclub act. He was watching his fiancée's ascent and learning to deal with what would later be deemed the "Mr. Liza Minnelli syndrome"—marriage to a celebrity.

Vincente Minnelli did not want his daughter to marry Peter Allen. "She was just twenty years old. They were both quite young," he says, "and I thought she should wait. They were both also on the brink of professional careers and I knew that the survival rate of such marriages was infinitesimally small. And yet, marriage to Peter was, I knew, something Liza wanted very much. My eventual consent—if one can call it that," Vincente adds, "was one more request of Liza's I could not refuse." Denise Gilagante Minnelli, Liza's stepmother at the time, did not approve of the marriage and refused to attend the wedding. "She was totally honest about it," Vincente explains. "Liza understood."

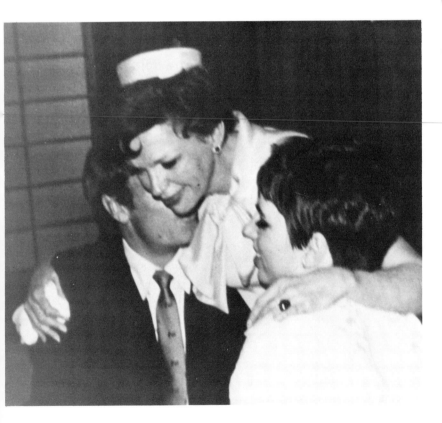

When Peter found out how Vincente felt, he contacted him. "Peter wrote me a respectful letter in which he tried to dispel my reservations about his marriage to Liza," Vincente recalls. "I was impressed that he was so tradition-bound that he felt he had to ask for Liza's hand."

Liza and Peter arrived at Manhattan's Muncipal Hall on February 2, 1967, to obtain their marriage license. They were, of course, badgered by the press for comments. Liza told them the truth—or a near facsimile of it. "Peter and I have been engaged for two years," she quipped, "and it's taken us that long to get down here."

The wedding was held eleven days later, on March 3, nine days before Liza's twenty-first birthday, at the home of Liza's agent, Stevie Phillips. Liza wore a simple white dress which properly set off her new, short hairstyle. Peter had convinced her to shed her long tresses for the more "mod" look.

Like Judy's wedding to Vincente, Liza and Peter's was a small affair. Friends Pamela Reinhardt and Paul Jasmen were, respectively, the maid of honor and best man. Judy arrived on Vincente's arm. New York City Judge Joseph A. Macchia performed the ritual; a few minutes after Liza and Peter exchanged brief vows they left to celebrate at an extravagant party in the apartment of Martin Bregman, Liza's business manager.

Liza told Judy she wanted an old Irish linen tablecloth as a wedding gift, but Judy could not afford one. She was so broke during this time that a sheriff's attachment had been placed on her house. She owed the state and federal governments more than $400,000 and she was more than $100,000 in personal debt. Judy, however, would not let Liza down. She borrowed some money from her maid and butler and rushed into Beverly Hills to buy the tablecloth at Maison Blanche. She was about to purchase an eighty-eight dollar one when the saleswoman told her she still had an active account in the shop. "I do?" Judy exclaimed. She beamed and charged a more expensive cloth.

Liza and Peter settled into domesticity. He answered the mail, paid the bills and, according to Liza, "kept me from going off the deep end over little things." He even wrote her a song, "Simon," which Liza recorded on her album *Come Saturday Morning*. It became the only "sincere" gift he ever gave her. Liza and Peter lived in Liza's three-room apartment on East Fifty-seventh Street in Manhattan; the apartment was small, but homey. Often, Lorna and Joey would camp out there; it seems that Judy was so severely depressed during that time that she often locked her children out of their rooms.

Liza comments, "Our house became a haven for them when Mama was in a bad mood. They needed help and peace, and Peter and I were there to help. And since Joey was only twelve, he needed a man around the house. Peter was that man."

It was hard for Peter Allen to deal with his wife's burgeoning success. Although they appeared together on stage and television—Peter and Chris Bell opened Liza's nightclub act and they won kudos for their *Tonight Show* appearances—it was Liza's career, and not Peter's, that was profitable.

In January, 1968, Liza opened to enthusiastic crowds at the Empire Room of the Waldorf-Astoria in New York. Joel Grey, Ethel Merman, Dionne Warwick and Ed Sullivan were some of the first nighters. Judy didn't attend until a few nights later. When she did, however, Liza called upon her mother to sing with her, just as Judy had called Liza years earlier at the Palace. The duo sang "When the Saints Go Marching In," then Judy sang "Liza," while Liza sat in awe at Judy's feet. The audience gave mother and daughter an ovation loud enough for Judy to begin crying. It was the last time Judy and Liza would publicly sing together. Judy was dead fifteen months later.

The Sterile Cuckoo

Liza first read John Nichols' novel, *The Sterile Cuckoo*, in

1965. "A friend had told me how much she enjoyed the story," Liza remembers, "so when I saw the book in an airport newsstand, I bought it. I read it straight through that night. It was a strange feeling, but I felt a deep understanding and sympathy for Pookie Adams, the lead character. It was like the same things that happened to her happened to me not very long ago. I knew that if a film was made of *The Sterile Cuckoo*, I would play it."

Liza checked with the book's publishers and learned that the film rights were owned by Alan Pakula and Robert Mulligan. "I went to their office and told them that when they decided to make the film, I was the one who should play Pookie. I did the same thing to them that I did to Fred Ebb and George Abbott for *Flora, the Red Menace*.

Liza was already demonstrating her tenacity. She knew she could bring the right amount of compassion and humor to the role—why, it even seemed she fit Nichols's description of Pookie: "a skinny, scrubby-haired, dark-eyed, pale girl, with a thin-lipped sarcastic, almost smiling mouth."

Pakula, like Fred Ebb before him, was startled and impressed. No longer a gawky and chubby adolescent, Liza displayed exactly what Pakula's Pookie would be, and he wanted her for the role. "I couldn't separate Liza from Pookie," Pakula says. "She had such a passion for the character, a kind of wild, passionate enthusiasm."

The top honchos at National General Pictures, the firm that would finance and distribute *The Sterile Cuckoo*, said, Liza Minnelli? No. An actress with no acting ability (they dismissed *Charlie Bubbles*) for the lead in our film? They all but laughed Pakula out of Hollywood. Instead, they suggested Patty Duke, or better yet, Elizabeth Hartman, the young actress who had just won an Oscar nomination for her performance as the blind girl in *A Patch of Blue*. Pakula stood firm. Either *The Sterile Cuckoo* would be made with Liza Minnelli as its star or it wouldn't be made. N.G.P. didn't back down and cancelled the film.

It took Liza three years to finally win the role of Pookie Adams. In March, 1968, Liza was playing in Las Vegas when she received a phone call from Pakula. He explained that he

Judy and Vincente were both instrumental in teaching Liza how to act. Judy taught Liza the importance of emotion; Vincente stressed the importance of words. When Liza finally won the role of Pookie Adams in The Sterile Cuckoo, *her father often helped with her lines. It obviously worked: the performance garnered Liza her first Academy Award nomination.*

The climactic telephone scene from The Sterile Cuckoo *(top) was shot on Friday the thirteenth. But for Liza, it was all good luck. The scene is a study in Minnelli mannerisms and ranks as one of her most powerful film sequences. Liza's* Cuckoo *costar was twenty-one-year-old Wendell Burton (left), then a political science major at Sonoma State College. The film was Burton's screen debut and he made no grave mistake. Instead, he delivered a memorable performance. The Sterile Cuckoo brought blessings to Liza's career— (above) a publicity still of Liza dancing with a nun is proof! "Girls went up to the casting office in kooky clothes and biting their nails," Liza recalls, "trying to be Pookie. But I knew all along who Pookie really was—Me."*

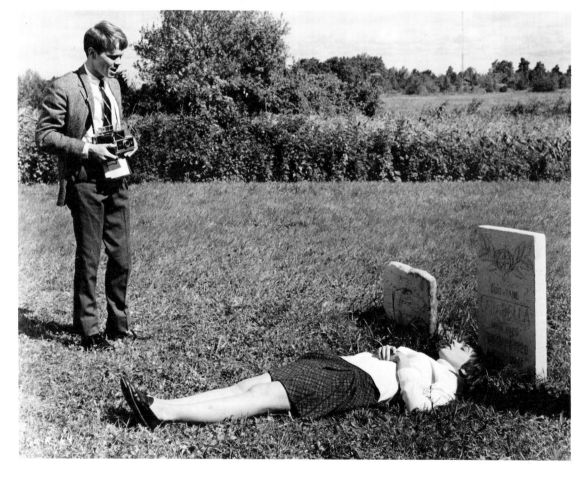

had backing for *The Sterile Cuckoo* from Paramount and asked her to come to Los Angeles to audition. Several days later, on March 11, the day before her twenty-second birthday, Liza flew to L.A. and tested for the role of Pookie Adams. She stayed with her father and waited for the results. But they didn't come, so Liza resumed her concert career. She performed at various theaters and clubs throughout the country and guested on various television shows, including the 1968 Tony and Grammy Awards. Summer had come and still no word from Pakula—or Paramount.

The Paramount people were not sure if they wanted Liza for the role. They were disappointed with her *Charlie Bubbles* performance; many felt the film was too high brow and that there was no evidence Liza could carry off the comedy involved in *Cuckoo*. Still, Pakula would not relent. "Liza was the only person I seriously considered for the role," he says, "despite pressure from the studio for a more established figure." Pakula was, in fact, so overwhelmed by Liza that he once remarked that if he had to cast his film *Inside Daisy Clover* all over again, he would choose Liza Minnelli for the Natalie Wood role. He insisted the film would have come out better.

Finally, with the agreement that they could hold rein on

future Pakula pictures (*The Sterile Cuckoo* was to be his directorial debut), Paramount, in July, 1968, gave the OK. Liza Minnelli could star as Pookie Adams.

There was, however, one slight hitch. Liza was offered the lead role in the Burt Bacharach-Hal David Broadway play *Promises, Promises*. The show was a musical remake of *The Apartment* (Liza would play Shirley MacLaine's part) and Liza was about to sign the contract. The deliberation took only a few seconds: no to *Promises, Promises*, yes to *The Sterile Cuckoo*. The play, with Jill O'Hara in the lead, later became a big hit. Lorna Luft replaced O'Hara toward the end of the run.

Judy did not think Liza should make *The Sterile Cuckoo*. She felt Pookie Adams was "weird and unsympathetic." Why take something like that, she asked Liza, when you could be wowing Broadway audiences? Liza had given her mother similar advice when Judy was up for the role of Helen Lawson in *Valley of the Dolls*. "I don't think it's a good role for you, Mama," Liza explained, knowing that film audiences would think the has-been show biz drunk, Lawson, was a slightly disguised version of Judy. "There's no doubt you can do it brilliantly," Liza added, "but do you think the public would like to see you in that role?" Shortly after, Judy was fired and replaced by Susan Hayward.

The Sterile Cuckoo began filming in September, 1968, on the 815-acre campus of Hamilton College in Hamilton, New York. Pakula chose Hamilton because the novel was based there, and he felt the college's quiet charm would lend proper ambience to the film. In fact, Pakula had Alvin Sargent revise parts of his script so that certain scenes between Liza and Wendell Burton, her co-star, could be shot in a "camperdown" elm, a nineteenth-century tree that was one of Hamilton's more cherished landmarks. The rest of the film was shot in Vernon Center, New York, and at the Paramount lot in Hollywood, California.

Filming went smoothly and Liza recalls an event that still makes her laugh. During the production, Pakula recruited high school and college students to appear as extras in the film. But Liza did not get along with all of them; they were too "Scarsdale" for her.

"One was a minister's daughter," Liza remembers, "and she collected antiques. Another was an artist, the snobby type and all that. One day, they asked me about myself. I told them my father was a pimp and all sorts of awful things!"

Pakula was glad he stuck with his decision to use Liza. "I

never saw anybody get more joy out of working," he says, "and it became contagious. Liza was always on time and always prepared. I remember one scene where we had great difficulty. I was trying to explain what I wanted and I talked a lot, possibly more than I should have. After a while, Liza got up and said, 'OK, let's try it!' She did, and it was right."

The most memorable scene in *The Sterile Cuckoo* is Pookie's five-minute climactic telephone call to her boyfriend, Jerry Payne. The scene was filmed early on the very first day of shooting—a sudden rainstorm cancelled the exterior shots that were supposed to be filmed—and it was all shot in one take.

"I couldn't believe that would happen," Pakula says, "but it did." When Liza finished, the film's crew broke into applause. "They were absolutely stunned," Pakula adds. "They didn't know from Liza Minnelli. They knew from Judy Garland, but they didn't know Liza."

Stuffed into a telephone booth, the scene finds Liza talking and babbling and crying for the entire monologue; on screen, the scene reeks of brilliance, and it is one of the longest telephone scenes in film history.

"We had yakked it out in rehearsals," Liza recalls, "but I didn't know how to work it. I was scared to death, but right before I stepped in front of the cameras, it hit me like a rock and I just did it."

Some of the scene's impact comes from a lesson Vincente taught Liza when she was young. "I gave Liza exercises to read," he recalls, "and told her to take the unimportant words away until she had mental images in her mind." Liza picks up the rest of the story: "In the telephone scene, there's a line where I have to say, 'I didn't have a sandwich with my father.' I used that lesson Daddy taught me and made the most important word 'sandwich.' That lesson was very, very, very important."

Liza was afraid that people who saw that scene would think that she drew the emotion she used for it from events in her own life. "They're going to say, 'Poor girl, she's acting her own life,'" Liza said after the filming. "But that girl isn't me! My parents didn't play that scene; Hollywood didn't play that scene, *I* played that scene. *Me!* My ability played that scene!"

When *The Sterile Cuckoo* was released in late 1969, Liza received rave reviews. "Liza's just about perfect!" exclaimed Pauline Kael in her review in *The New Yorker*. "Her sad, quizzical persona—the gangling body and the features that look too big for the little face—are ideal equipment for the

The transformation of Liza Minnelli into Junie Moon. Though Liza all but dismisses the film, Tell Me That You Love Me, Junie Moon *is a prime example of Hollywood makeup wizardry. When the film opens, Junie Moon appears as a sweet and nubile lass (top); during a date with her psychotic boyfriend, Junie Moon gets battery acid poured on her face. She is rushed to a hospital, and when the bandages come off, the new Junie Moon emerges (opposite, top right). It took makeup genius Charles Schram nearly two hours to apply Liza's scar tissue. Liza prepared for the film's most crucial scene—in which Junie Moon sees her scarred face for the first time—by locking herself in a room and telling ghost stories.* Junie Moon *received great publicity after director Otto Preminger was sued by a woman who claimed Liza's nude cemetery scene took place on her husband's grave (bottom). Liza insists she was not entirely nude; still, it looks a bit cheeky.*

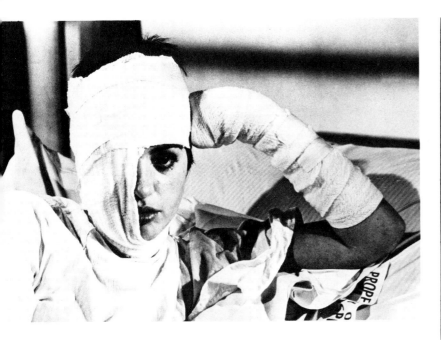

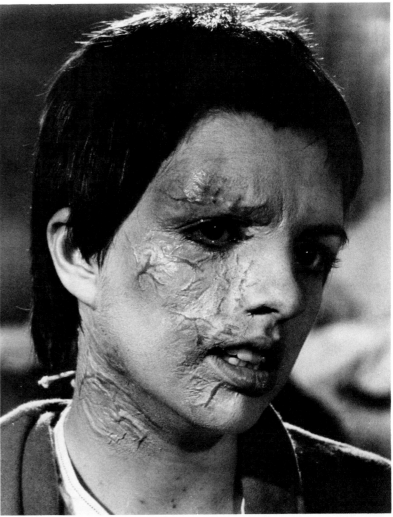

role. She's very funny and is probably going to be acclaimed as a great actress."

Charles Champlin of the *Los Angeles Times* hailed Liza as "warm, sad-looking, serious-funny, touching and beguiling." Rex Reed, critiquing the film for *Holiday* magazine, also gushed: "Liza is wonderful as Pookie Adams. She plays her to the hilt with awkward horn-rimmed glasses, eyes like chocolate jawbreakers, a twitchy nose like a bunny with hay fever and a funny hee-haw laugh that crashes through your heart like a flash of sun on a foggy day. It's the kind of performance that breaks hearts and wins Oscars."

Although Liza did not win an Oscar that year, she was awarded Italy's David Di Donatello Award as the year's best foreign actress.

Liza was pleased with her work, even though she was unsure of her final Pookie Adams characterization. "If I had been more cautious," she now says, "I could have made Pookie more appealing to the audience. But I liked her too much. She improvises life, and I sympathized with her."

The most prophetic comment, however, came from author Christopher Isherwood, the man responsible for immortalizing Sally Bowles in print in his *Berlin Stories*. "You know," he said to a friend after he had seen a screening of *The Sterile Cuckoo*, "that girl Liza is a lot like Sally."

Tell Me That You Love Me, Junie Moon

Otto Preminger was in the process of casting his new film *Tell Me That You Love Me, Junie Moon* when he stumbled across

Liza claims she doesn't smoke as much as she used to; perhaps she remembers the ad campaign she did for the American Cancer Society in the late 1960s.

a work print of *The Sterile Cuckoo*. The film had not yet been released, but Preminger was amazed by what he saw. He was in awe of Liza's performance and knew she would be perfect as Junie Moon.

"Liza had a strange Chaplinesque humor that came through her eyes and body," Preminger says. "She had the qualities of a star."

Preminger wanted Liza to sign a long-term contract with him; the Austrian director wanted to nurture Liza's film career with his direction and guidance. Liza refused to sign anything and announced that she would play Junie Moon as a one-shot deal only—and for $50,000, double her *Sterile Cuckoo* salary.

Preminger fumed. "Tell Miss Minnelli that there are many brilliant young actresses dying to play this part," he informed Liza's agent, Stevie Phillips. Liza was told of Otto's threat and still wouldn't budge. She had a taste of glory from *The Sterile Cuckoo* and knew she now had the upper hand. Finally, Preminger gave in—he had had enough of the Minnelli determination—and cast Liza as Junie Moon. And she was paid $50,000. Liza had forgotten that she had met Preminger once before. He attended Judy's thirty-first birthday party at Ira and Lee Gershwin's house. Liza was then seven.

Rehearsals for *Junie Moon* were to begin that summer. Liza had spent the previous months perfecting her nightclub act in Puerto Rico, Los Angeles, New York, Las Vegas and Miami. Except for a television special she had taped in Paris, she had not been in front of a camera since *The Sterile Cuckoo* wrapped production.

Liza immersed herself in her work. In *Junie Moon*, Liza played a woman who is horribly disfigured after a boyfriend pours battery acid on her face. In the hospital where she is recovering, she meets two other misfits, Arthur (Ken Howard) and Warren (Robert Moore), and the threesome decide to live together.

Marjorie Kellogg had adapted the screenplay from her own critically acclaimed novel, and Liza was touched by the script's poignancy. She prepared for her role by meeting with Kellogg (who was also a social worker) and discussing cases similar to those of Junie Moon. Liza also visited hospitals where she talked with disfigured women, learning how they coped with their grotesqueness. It was not an easy task.

"For the duration of the film," Liza says, "Junie Moon and I were the same person. I felt what she felt; but I felt it as Junie Moon, not as Liza Minnelli, the actress."

When the film was finally underway, it took hours for Charles Schram to apply the hideous scar makeup. "I got too used to how it looked," Liza says. "So before the scene where I see my face for the first time and cry with shock, I went into a room by myself and told myself every ghost story I could think of. I scared the bejesus out of me! Funny way to make a living, isn't it?"

Liza spent the weekend of June 20 in Southampton, Long Island. She was there with Peter Allen and his sister, relaxing and putting the final touches on her Junie Moon characterization. It was a warm, lazy weekend. The phone call came on Sunday morning, June 22. Peter answered it; Deanna Wenble, Liza's secretary, was calling. They talked briefly; then Peter, his face void of his usual smile, rushed into the bedroom. "Darling, you better wake up," he said, shaking Liza. "I've got something to tell you."

End of the Rainbow

Mickey Deans, Judy's fifth and last husband, found the body. Judy was naked, her head resting on her hands, sitting on the toilet in the locked bathroom of their small cottage on Cadgogan Lane in London. Judy always locked the bathroom door; it was a habit she acquired as a youngster at M-G-M.

Deans woke up in the middle of the night to discover that Judy was not in bed. His intuition told him something was wrong. When Judy did not answer Deans' frantic calls, he climbed up to a rear section of the roof and peered into the bathroom window. Inside, he found the lifeless body of the woman he had married less than three months before.

Deans pried open the window and grabbed at Judy's body. It was stiff; rigor mortis had set in. "I noticed that her skin was discolored with a red and bluish tinge," Deans recalls, "and that Judy's face was dreadfully distorted. Blood came from her nose and mouth, and the air escaping from her mouth sounded like a low moan."

Judy Garland died on June 22, 1969, the victim of a stormy life, grave misunderstandings and, according to the final autopsy report, "an incautious self-overdose" of Seconals.

She had celebrated her birthday just eleven days before—she was forty-seven.

When Liza first heard the news, she was stunned. Surely, she thought, there must be some mistake—it must be Daddy who is dead. After all, how can Mama—who has survived so much—be gone? When the truth sank in, Liza went outside, sat on the Southampton grass and cried hysterically for less than five minutes. It was, some say, the last time she ever cried for Judy.

The Funeral

At first, the older woman tried to get her younger companion to talk, but as the sleek, black limousine maneuvered onto the airport runway, few words were spoken. Instead, everything was done with a nod of the head, a glance of the eye, a touch of the hand. The two women were in quiet mourning, their silence an expression of immense loss. It was very early in the morning and only sounds of birds and chirping crickets—and the car's overworked air conditioning—could be heard.

The limousine finally reached its destination and pulled into the small courtyard alongside the International Arrivals Building at New York's Kennedy Airport. Almost at once, a small bevy of security guards surrounded the car; close enough to offer protection from the group of more than three dozen reporters, but not close enough to interrupt the women's privacy.

A few moments later, at 12:55 A.M. the TWA Star Stream jet landed. The doors opened and two men departed: the widower, pale and drawn, his red eyes hidden from view by the dark sunglasses he wore, and his friend, the reverend who just three months before officiated at the wedding of the woman they had come to bury.

The men walked behind the jet, quietly watching as airline personnel lowered the plain brown coffin—covered in burlap and fastened with heavy rope—into the waiting gray hearse.

Liza greeted Mickey Deans and his companion, the Reverend Peter Delaney. "The sight of Liza in her dark floppy hat, so like the hats that Judy wore, and looking incredibly like Judy at the moment, made me flinch," recalls Deans. He said nothing to the clamoring newsmen. He left it to Liza.

"I think Mama was just like a flower that blooms, gives joy to the world, then wilts away," she said. "She had lived eighty lives in one and yet, I thought she would outlive us all." Then Liza slipped into the limousine, beside Kay Thompson, Mickey Deans and Reverend Delaney.

The car sped off into the late morning, falling in line behind one of the few other cars on the road—the hearse.

Upon Judy's death, Liza carried out her role as the dutiful daughter. She called her father, then Lorna and Joey to tell

Liza, Lorna Luft and Mickey Deans leave the Frank E. Campbell Funeral Home in New York after saying goodbye to Judy. Even in death, Judy is protected by Liza. In 1976, Liza sued the National Lampoon for $8 million, after the magazine printed a fictional letter in its June issue. The so-called letter was a cartoon, showing a puppy leaning into a toilet, with a caption alluding to Judy's drug overdose "in the crapper." Liza felt the cartoon defamed her character and that it presented an inaccurate portrait of her relationship with Judy. Liza settled out of court. In September, 1977, the Lampoon—in lieu of a retraction—printed a letter Liza wrote to them, in which she expressed her anger toward the magazine. Liza was also given a headline on the cover announcing the letter inside, and a promise that the magazine would not print her name—or her mother's—for eight years.

them the news. She told Mickey Deans, now a man made senseless by his wife's sudden death, "I'll handle everything." And she did—with few tears and an uncanny sense of pride.

"I wasn't going to panic or run away from the truth," Liza says. "Instead, I just pulled myself together for the funeral." Liza wanted to follow all of her mother's wishes. Judy loathed the idea of being buried in a coffin and often voiced strong opinions about being cremated. Mickey Deans, however, refused to cremate Judy and appealed to Liza.

Sid Luft also appealed to Liza; he insisted that Judy be properly buried in California. Liza agreed with both men. She would not cremate Mama; she would bury her, but not in the ground. And not in California. "Mama hated California," Liza told Sid. Judy would be buried in a mausoleum.

Judy was interred in a simple marble crypt at Ferncliff, a sprawling mausoleum/cemetery in Hartsdale, New York. The story surrounding her burial is strange. When Judy's body was taken to Ferncliff, it was placed in a receiving vault in the mausoleum's basement. It seemed no one wanted to pay for the $3,000 crypt. Liza thought Mickey Deans should pay; Mickey thought Liza should. This bickering went on for months.

Then, on November 4, 1970—more than a year *after* she died—Judy Garland was finally buried. Though rumors persist that Frank Sinatra paid the burial costs, Judy's crypt is, according to Ferncliff's official records, owned by Liza Minnelli. It is also one of the most visited crypts at Ferncliff; Joan Crawford, Jackie "Moms" Mabley, Diana Sands, Basil Rathbone and Paul Robeson are the others.

Judy and Liza sometimes kidded about death. But what Judy never realized was that death was not a subject Liza found appetizing; the thought of Mama leaving for good was unthinkable. "When I die," Judy often quipped, "the fags will fly the flag half-mast on Fire Island." Today, Liza can smile at the joke. But in June, 1969, nothing had her smiling.

Kay Thompson had given Judy a bracelet upon Liza's birth. Judy often let Liza wear it. "It was good luck," Judy said, and she told Liza that she wanted to wear it when she died. Liza found the bracelet and promised herself that she would give it to the mortician.

Liza remembered that her mother wanted well-known

Hollywood makeup artist Gene Hibbs to do her up when she died. "He'll make me look perfect," she said. But Eva Gabor, then starring in her television series *Green Acres*, would not permit Hibbs, who was then her makeup man, to go to New York. Liza finally asked Charles Schram, the man responsible for Judy's makeup in *The Wizard of Oz* (and Liza's scar makeup in *Tell Me That You Love Me, Junie Moon*) to do the task, and he agreed. James Mason, Judy's co-star in *A Star is Born*, would deliver the eulogy.

At Kay Thompson's suggestion, Liza picked the Frank E. Campbell Funeral Home on Madison Avenue for the public viewing. Kay chose an unobtrusive mahogany casket with a light blue velvet interior.

Liza hated the mahogany. "The coffin must be white," she demanded. The funeral director interrupted, telling Liza they had no white coffins. "At M-G-M," snapped Thompson, "we'd get a spray gun and *paint* it white!" Judy had a white coffin.

Liza insisted no one wear black—she wanted the funeral to be a "gay occasion"—and she wore, despite the unbearable heat, a plain navy blue wool suit and a wide-brimmed, black velvet hat. Liza ordered thousands of flowers: a blanket of yellow roses draped the glass-topped coffin (Liza was afraid fans would tear at Judy if the coffin were unprotected), and countless yellow and white chrysanthemums dominated the room.

On the first day of public viewing, Liza and Lorna visited the funeral home early. It was a draining and emotionally challenging experience. Liza looked at Judy. The woman she knew as Mama was now a gaunt, 97-pound corpse, dressed in her high-necked, gray chiffon wedding dress, a brocaded, silver, pearl-studded belt around her tiny waist, silver slippers on her feet, her white-gloved hands resting on a small white Bible.

Liza quietly walked up to the coffin. Trembling, she forced herself to look at her mother. Judy seemed to be smiling—later, Liza would recall how perfectly straight her mother's lipstick was applied—and Liza felt a sad serenity.

"Mama," Liza whispered, "you look beautiful."

PART THREE

Stardom

Otto Preminger was willing to give Liza a reprieve from the filming of *Tell Me That You Love Me, Junie Moon*. The director thought she would need, or at least want, time to grieve. Liza vehemently rejected the idea; work, she knew, was the answer to her depression, and shortly after she returned from visiting her father in California (Vincente did not attend Judy's funeral), Liza plunged back into *Junie Moon*. It was not a good idea.

The production of *Junie Moon* did not go smoothly. Liza, dealing with the lingering trauma of her mother's death, was unusually curt to visiting interviewers. One day, while shooting on the Paramount lot, Liza suffered an agonizing kidney stone attack and was rushed to the hospital. Otto sat by and waited the six hours for her release.

Liza also had extreme difficulties with Preminger. The tyrannical director, whose reputation precedes him to this day, was demanding of Liza, and Kay Thompson (who had won the role of the eccentric Miss Gregory through Liza's influence) was often their middle-man sounding board. Liza missed the spontaneity of Alan Pakula and the friendliness he had brought to the set of *The Sterile Cuckoo*.

When Liza describes Otto, she is adamant. "His theory is that the actor is hired to act, and he must be ready at all times," she says. "He wants the work immediately—and perfectly. You get the impression with Otto that you don't have time to ask questions, and you come in and don't ask. If you do it wrong, you get yelled at. It's like teachers. There are some who correct you by saying, 'It would be better this way,' and others would just say, '*That's* wrong!' Otto is the latter."

The most interesting (if somewhat macabre) and highly-publicized incident during the filming of *Junie Moon* occurred in Quincy, Massachusetts. Junie Moon goes on a date, is taken to a local

In the late 1960s, Liza was accused of having an extramarital affair with Australian Prime Minister John Gorton (left). To counterattack the tale, Liza interrupted rehearsals for a Miami Beach concert engagement and held a press conference. Liza called the story "a pack of lies," and vehemently defended Gorton and his country. Liza threatened to sue the perpetrators of the rumor; she never did. The Gorton-Minnelli "relationship" ended, but was never forgotten.

cemetery and told to strip. As she is taking off her clothes, her psychotic boyfriend (played with crisp brilliance by Ben Piazza) tries to sexually arouse himself by muttering dirty words. Junie Moon laughs. She is beaten senseless by her date, and as she is writhing on the ground, he then matter-of-factly pours battery acid on her face. As this happens, Liza emits some of the most horrifying screams ever heard on the motion picture screen (the writhing scene was later deleted by British film censors). The scene was actually filmed in the Blue Hills Cemetery in Quincy.

Without realizing it, Preminger had violated an 1880s Massachusetts statute stating that anyone creating a graveyard nuisance is guilty of a misdemeanor. That was just the beginning. Not only did a woman file action against Preminger (she claimed the scene took place upon her deceased husband's grave), but Liza was cited in public court for appearing nude

in the cemetery. The press had a holiday with the news. Preminger received lots of free publicity for the film; he hoped the news would cause a stir at the box office, but it didn't.

"I was not nude," Liza claims, recalling the incident. "I had the front part of a bathing suit pasted on top and bottom, and they only shot my back, which was about as sexy as a dog. It was night and the shot was beautifully lit. The only reason we shot it in a cemetery was so that Otto could protect me and keep the lookers out. Then, the next thing I know," Liza adds, "a little old lady and her lawyer—truly a formidable combination—claim I was dancing on her husband's grave! I wanted to write her a letter and say it wasn't like anything she thought. Besides, if she had only looked back on my life those past few months, she would have known I could not do anything like that."

Junie Moon was released in July, 1970. Most critics did not like it; many felt the 113-minute movie was 112 minutes too long. Paul D. Zimmerman, writing for *Newsweek*, said: "How many times will the public want to see Pookie Adams?"

Still, some critics liked the film and praised Liza's dramatic efforts. Ann Guardino, in *The New York Daily News*, wrote: "Liza rates an Oscar in this Four-Star drama." In *Newsday*, Joseph Gelmis wrote: "Liza Minnelli's struggle gives this film a perverse appeal that is both grotesque and very touching." Liz Smith, then writing for *Cosmopolitan* magazine, called Liza "brilliant."

Ken Howard, one of Liza's *Junie Moon* co-stars, recalls Liza's total professionalism. "Liza's mother died while we were making the film," he says, "but Liza held herself together beautifully and was always her cheerful, pleasant self. She's a very 'up' gal who's nice to everybody."

Soon after *Junie Moon* was in nationwide release, Liza was being interviewed by a reporter. He asked her what she had learned from working with Otto Preminger. Liza's answer was summed up in one line: "Never to make another movie with him." She never has.

Liza & Peter Divorce

Peter Allen was suffering terribly from his wife's success. *The Sterile Cuckoo* and *Tell Me That You Love Me, Junie Moon* had made her a movie star and now, more than ever, Liza was an object of public adulation. Peter, on the other hand, was little more than an object of public curiosity.

On April 8, 1971, the day after the Oscar telecast, Liza announced that she and Peter were separating. It did not shock Peter (he had expected it for awhile), but it did shock him to hear what some Minnelli detractors were saying. In reply to the stories that Liza left him because he was made jealous by her Oscar nomination, he said, "That's crazy. Yet Liza must have gone to the awards with some seeds of doubt in her mind that I might object to her winning an Oscar. Those are the kind of people who put all the pressure on us."

Liza, at first, claimed her marital split-up was because of obligatory Hollywood reasons. "It was just due to the pressures of trying to be a Super-everything," she told the press. "It had nothing to do with the Oscar or the motorcycle accident." Some insisted Liza was more than just chummy with Tony Bill, whom she was with in the cycle crash one week before the Oscars, and Peter knew this.

"I hated Peter's friends and he disliked mine," Liza says. Peter's companions were usually pretty young men and Liza found their flamboyance distasteful. "Marriage to Peter was miserable—*horrible!* When we got married," Liza adds, "we were equal in terms of career success. Then we started playing 'A Star is Born.' I went up and he went down. Peter almost broke up when I started making it big. As a matter of fact, the competition nearly killed us both. That's when I said that after Peter, I would never marry another entertainer. Ever, ever."

In 1981, Peter and Liza were asked to perform at a Carnegie Hall benefit for the Nyack, New York, Tappan Zee Playhouse. She had appeared there in *The Fantasticks*. Negotiations went on steadily until Liza finally backed out. "She just couldn't deal with the fact that Peter, at the time, was a much bigger star than she was," explains Linn Tanzmann, who, in 1983, handled some of Peter's press affairs.

Peter did get back together with Liza on February 14, 1981 —Valentine's Day—at the taping of *The Night of 100 Stars*. At the post-show ball, Liza and Peter reluctantly danced for photographers. It was a gesture of good will for the cameras.

Today, Peter Allen is no longer close to Liza. He rarely likes to speak of her. "It's all so boring," he sighs, as if he were speaking about a long, forgotten past.

"Liza and I aren't friends," he says. "Friends are people I can call on the phone, like Carol Bayer Sager and Marvin Hamlisch. I can't call Liza."

Since the late seventies, Peter Allen has achieved stardom as a singer-songwriter. It is a status that has come after years of hard work. "I began to take my career really seriously the day Liza and I split," he explains. "It was also the day Chris [Bell] and I split." Today, Chris Bell is a pilot in the Midwest. "Liza and I knew the marriage wasn't working—she was going off in one direction and I was going off in another." Peter's slight smile tightens. "The day Liza left me . . . well, it was like a weight being lifted off my shoulders."

The demise of a loveless marriage always brings relief. It is possible that Liza never loved Peter. She was in love with love and her scenes of domesticity were nothing but vignettes. "We were two kids playing at life," says Liza. On the other hand, Peter felt a brotherly responsibility toward the girl he was manipulated into marrying. If Peter rejected Liza, he rejected Judy, and he could not afford such guilt.

The Liza Minnelli-Peter Allen marriage was an exercise in convenience. They never had children—some say the marriage was never consummated—because Liza claimed "we were too immature."

Liza won her first Academy Award as Best Actress for her brilliant portrayal of Sally Bowles in Bob Fosse's homage to divine decadence, Cabaret. The John Kander-Fred Ebb songs, intricately woven into the plot, proved once and for all that Liza with a Z meant Liza with Zest. The spotlight is on Liza as she sings "Mein Herr" (opposite, left). Cabaret costar Michael York, who played bisexual Brian Roberts, enjoyed splendor in the grass with a thoughtful Sally (left). Liza and Joel Grey gave audiences their money's worth when they sang "Money, Money" (bottom, left). Liza's live-in lover during the filming of Cabaret was Rex Kramer. Here, Rex shoots Liza on a kitchen set that was not used in the film's final print (bottom, right).

As Liza's fame grew, so did the stories about her extramarital affairs. One of the first to be published—indeed, it nearly created an international scandal—occurred in Sydney, Australia, in June, 1968. Liza was appearing for three weeks at the Chequers Club, and one night the Australian Prime Minister, John Gorton, went backstage to meet Liza.

The innocuous encounter was blown into worldwide headlines: it was rumored that Liza and Gorton were having an affair in Bali and Canberra; Liza supposedly admitted to this in an exclusive "tell-all" article for *Private Eye* magazine.

When Liza returned to the United States to prepare for her nightclub act in Miami Beach's Deauville Hotel, she was met by inquiring reporters. "The rumors are vicious lies," she said. "The entire story is untrue and ridiculous. I am appalled at such irresponsible statements that have no foundation in fact. I've never written any article; why, I don't even have the time to write letters! And I've never been to Bali! Somebody is just trying to pin some kind of rap on Gorton, and his record is spotless."

Liza also came to the defense of her husband's country. "I love Australia and cannot believe that people would tolerate such a dishonest way of attacking someone. I cannot imagine that anyone would believe anything so absurd. I am going to sue whoever is causing trouble for my husband's country. They must be pretty desperate for a little scandal to use." Liza never did sue.

Yet some people referred to the "little scandal" loudly. Albert James, who was then Gorton's opposition party leader, demanded that the Australian House of Representatives look into the rumor. They refused, and the matter was soon dropped.

If Peter Allen heard the story about Liza's "affair" with Gorton, he shrugged the whole thing off. He learned early on not to let anything like this bother him; the only man he was unsure of was Fred Ebb. Liza explains, "I'm sure Peter misunderstood my devotion to Fred, just as I distrusted his coterie of acquaintances."

Liza easily dismisses the Gorton episode of her life. "I was in Sydney doing my act, and after the show one night," she says, "they came running up, saying that the Prime Minister and his party would like to come backstage and meet me. I said, 'Sure.' Suddenly, there were about ten people in the room. Gorton and I talked maybe five minutes at most. He

said he and his mates sure enjoyed getting away from the office and seeing the act and I must come back to Australia and it's cheerio and everybody's off. He was a really nice guy. Then," Liza adds, "time passes and I get a call in the middle of the night and the newspapers are printing stories that I had an affair with the Prime Minister and had written an article about it and that the CIA was paying me $50,000 to kill the story! I mean, it was *hysterical!*"

John Gorton was just one man Liza was linked with. In December, 1969, while she was performing at the Olympia Music Hall in Paris, Liza supposedly played offstage as well— with singer Charles Aznavour and playboy jet-setter Baron Alexis de Rede, nicknamed "The Red Baron," who named a race horse after Liza; and with two sexy French film stars, Jean Claude Brially and Jean Pierre Cassel. But, back in the United States, she had already met Rex Kramer.

Rex Kulbeth changed his name to Rex Kramer in hopes of making it big in show business. Primarily a drummer, he was also a singer and dancer and had his own rock band, Bojangles, also known as The Wire Band. A native of Smackover, Arkansas, Kramer had the boyish charm of an imp and the uneven good looks of a rogue. He was more at home in his Tweety Bird and Sylvester T-shirts than in a three-piece suit, and Liza was attracted to his rugged, gentle manner.

Rex Kramer was also married. Liza met Rex in late 1969, just before her engagement at the Olympia. He introduced Liza to rock 'n roll; she liked his suggestions of songs for her to sing. They eventually recorded an album together, *New Feelin'*. It was Liza's third album for A&M and was released in December, 1970. It boasted classic tunes—from "Stormy Weather" to "God Bless the Child" to "Can't Help Lovin' Dat Man"—all performed with a country-pop twang. Needless to say, the album did not do well.

Liza saw a constancy in Rex that her husband, Peter Allen, could not give her. Later, when asked for his comments on Liza's beau, Peter said, "Rex was exactly the opposite of me. He was a country boy who hated the city and loved girls."

In fact, Rex was such a country boy that he spent many idle weeks at his grandparents' farm in Smackover, Arkansas. Whenever Liza wasn't working, she joined him there. "It's what life is all about," Liza said at the time. "Rex's folks grow their own fruits and vegetables and Granny makes black-eyed peas and cornbread! She even calls me Liza May. Down here, nobody even *thinks* of me as Judy Garland's daughter."

When Liza returned from Paris, she signed a contract that

made Bojangles her backup band and, before launching a nationwide concert tour, Liza and Bojangles—with Rex Kramer as leader—opened at the Empire Room of the Waldorf-Astoria on December 2, 1970. The reviews were stupendous. Rex and Liza were in love. And life was beginning to be a cabaret!

Cabaret

Liza had wanted to star in *Cabaret* ever since Fred Ebb told her that he and John Kander were writing the score in late 1965. They began just as *Flora, the Red Menace* was closing. She auditioned for the role of Sally Bowles once (not the dozen or so times she later claimed to the press), but Joe Masteroff, who adapted the John Van Druten play *I Am a Camera* into what became *Cabaret*, insisted that Sally be played by a British actress.

Harold Prince, the producer and director of *Cabaret* on Broadway, recalls, "When we got around to casting Sally Bowles, Kander and Ebb opted for Liza Minnelli, an idea which I summarily rejected. She wasn't British—I'm not sure why that was important to me—and she sang too well; I still think that was a flaw in the film" (Jill Haworth eventually won the Broadway role).

After the release of *The Sterile Cuckoo* and *Tell Me That You Love Me, Junie Moon*, speculation was high that Liza would star in the film version of *Cabaret*. She had been singing the show's title tune in her nightclub act for years, perfecting the notes she would later immortalize on screen. In May, 1970, while Liza was at the Cannes Film Festival (*Junie Moon* was an official entry), she was told that the role of Sally Bowles was hers. Liza would be paid $250,000 for her work.

Liza does a great amount of research as she prepares for a role. As she had turned to hospital patients for *Junie Moon*, she now turned to the Berlin of the thirties for *Cabaret*. Liza saturated herself with the look and feel of Nazi Germany. She studied the music of Kurt Weill, the art of George Grosz and the films of Elisabeth Bergner, one of Germany's most famous leading ladies. Liza was enthralled by the German actress Lya du Putti and set about capturing some of the star's quasi-erotic qualities in her characterization of Sally.

"You know," Liza says, "it was so glamorous in Berlin at that time. The writers were in Paris, but the fun seekers were in Berlin and there was this insatiable quest for joy. But doing research had been a nightmare. The first thing I did when I got to Munich was try to find traces of that whole era. People just did not want to talk about it. I mean, I couldn't even find anyone who admitted being German! They were all Austrians!"

Liza also supplied her own costumes for *Cabaret*. She did not like what Charlotte Flemming, the film's costumer, designed for her. "They made me look like Joe Namath," Liza explains, "with wide Joan Crawford sleeves, padded shoulders and pleats. I said, 'Forget it!' and Gwen Verdon and I hunted all the old antique shops in Paris" (Verdon was married to director Fosse at the time). "I finally ended up with my slinky black dress I wore at the Waldorf in my nightclub act."

Liza liked Sally. "I think she was eternal and that's what attracted me to her. There will always be a Sally Bowles somewhere. I saw her as a reflection of many tragic figures; I think she's the kind of person you look at and say, 'Oh, I remember doing that in *my* life.' You know she's going to say something terrible every minute, but you understand her in a strange, crazy way. I never found Sally admirable," Liza said, "but I do find her understandable. She's really a tramp, selfish and mean, and not just a kook like Holly Golightly; and I've wanted to play her forever."

Liza was, however, unsure how Sally should physically look. Though Christopher Isherwood described her as "very beautiful, with her little dark head, big eyes and finely arched nose," Liza never gave Sally's appearance much thought. Despondent, Liza turned to her father, who offered some help before Liza left for Munich.

"When I told Daddy I was doing *Cabaret*," Liza says, "he asked me, 'What are you going to look like?' I got a blank expression on my face and said, 'I don't know. Sally looks like a kook, but a kook gets boring unless she's specific. What should I look like?' Daddy told me I had to look special, but also like me."

Liza continues: "Three days later, I walked into Daddy's room and on his bed were books and pictures to help me out. I had thought there was only that very high cheek-boned, incredibly sophisticated Dietrich look in the thirties," Liza says, "but then Daddy and I discussed Louise Brooks (the famous twenties actress who wore her hair like a pixie and who, like Sally Bowles, was a curious enigma). He said, 'Yes, she will give you the effect you want.' Oh, Daddy was so helpful."

Vincente was also helpful during the filming of *Cabaret*. "I'd get periodic calls from Liza in Germany," he recalls. "'I don't know if I'm doing it right,' she'd say. 'It seems terribly hard.' I'd ask her, 'How does Bob Fosse feel?' She'd say, 'Well, he's pleased.' Then I asked Liza, 'In the rushes, do you see yourself or somebody else?' Liza: 'I see somebody else.' Me: 'Then you're on the right track.' I had a feeling something extraordinary was happening and I was positive when Liza took me to see a rough cut at the studio. She came through brilliantly!"

Vincente may have offered his daughter help, but Liza also received training from Bob Fosse, the film's director (*Cabaret* marked his second cinematic directorial attempt).

"Bob knew exactly how he wanted the picture to look and sound," Liza says, "but it was rough explaining that to the German engineers. Making *Cabaret* in Germany was a great help to us, but more than that, Bob went through all of the George Grosz and Otto Dix drawings he could find and got the cameraman, Geoffrey Unsworth, to light it exactly that way. Then, to get us in the mood before each scene, he'd play Marlene Dietrich's 'Falling in Love Again!' He strove for authenticity."

And authenticity is what Fosse got—right down to the extras. "We wanted to show the decadence and decay and perverse atmosphere of Berlin," Liza adds. "We even used real drag queens! And the women extras hated us because they had to grow hair under their arms. When we finished shooting, we had a party and everybody gave them razors and soap and they celebrated by shaving!"

Cabaret began shooting in Munich on February, 1971. Liza and Rex Kramer were living in Schwabing, which Liza says "was the artists' bohemian quarter of Munich, much like New York's Greenwich Village." It was, she soon learned, a far cry from Beverly Hills.

"There were swastikas on the walls and riots going on," Liza remembers. "The *Cabaret* company was met with a lot of anti-semitic feelings and insults. We used hidden cameras everywhere to get real German reactions to all the 'Heil Hitlers!' in the film. The older people cringed, but the younger ones loved it. I really couldn't wait to get out of there and go home."

Liza got along well with the film's other stars: Michael York, who played her lover, the bisexual Brian; Joel Grey, who recreated his Tony Award-winning Broadway role as the garish Master of Ceremonies, and Marisa Berenson, the highly touted European model, who helped Liza gain entree to the jet-setting circle she still frequents today.

Liza and Rex spent many nights cavorting in and around Munich. "In Hamburg we went to the dens of sin on the Ree-

Liza in a transparent, décolleté mood was caught by the camera. Although she is known to wear daring and elegant clothing, she is rarely photographed in such candid exposure.

persbahn," she recalls, "where they still had semblances of cabarets going. There were lesbian fights in mud puddles on stage and pornographic shows in which the audiences were invited to participate. No wonder I was a bit uncomfortable the whole time we were there."

Cabaret was hard work for Liza; it was the first film she had made which took her away from the United States for a prolonged period of time. "I worked twelve hours a day for six months," she says, "and I was so sick of Wienerschnitzel!"

Besides Rex, Liza was also kept company by her dog, Ocho. Liza found the stray mutt outside the Club Ocho in San Juan, Puerto Rico, in February, 1969. When Vincente first saw Ocho, he cried, "That's the best imitation of a dog I've ever seen!"

Liza had Ocho's teeth removed in 1973; shortly after, Liza was sued by her former wardrobe mistress, who claimed the dog bit her backstage in Miami, and she was left partially incapacitated. The woman, Rita Stander, sued for $27,700 but was awarded only $7,500. In 1975, Liza "retired" Ocho to a beach house belonging to a Brazilian friend. For awhile, Liza would fly to Rio and visit the dog. Today, Liza never mentions Ocho anymore—one can only assume he is dead.

Minnelli Mania

Liza's payoff in *Cabaret* was worth it. "I always knew *Cabaret* would be a terrific movie," she says. "Of course, I said the same thing about *Tell Me That You Love Me, Junie Moon*, and the less said about that one, the better. But I've always had lots of faith in this one. And one thing's for sure—*Cabaret* is no *Sound of Music*."

Liza was right. When *Cabaret* premiered at Manhattan's Ziegfeld Theater on February 13, 1972, New Yorkers found the perfect valentine. The reviews were raves. Rex Reed in the *New York Daily News* exemplified what most critics felt: "*Cabaret* is dazzling! Sound the trumpets! *Cabaret* strikes gold! It's a cause for rejoicing. Liza Minnelli defines the word 'star!' She has her own inner radiance and the built-in charisma of her mother's own heart-rending magic and that's good enough for me!"

One critic who did not like Liza's performance was Andrew Sarris of New York's *The Village Voice*. In his column, Sarris wrote: "I have endured Miss Minnelli in all of her previous filmic incarnations as the vulnerable ugly duckling and I discover to my shame and sorrow that she has become too conspicuous for my taste. In *Cabaret*, she comes crashing through with all the finesse of a water buffalo in heat."

Sarris's review meant little to Liza—or the rest of the filmgoing public. Two weeks after *Cabaret* opened, Liza's photo graced the covers of both *Newsweek* and *Time*. Simultaneous cover stories rarely happen between the rival news publications. *Time*, perhaps, best summed up Liza's accomplishment when it dubbed her "The New Miss Show Biz."

Still, it wasn't enough. Peter Allen recalls that soon after the cover stories came out, Liza said, "Big deal. Now what?"

Not only did *Cabaret* make just about all the Top Ten Best Film lists that year—it was, without a doubt, Liza's most com-

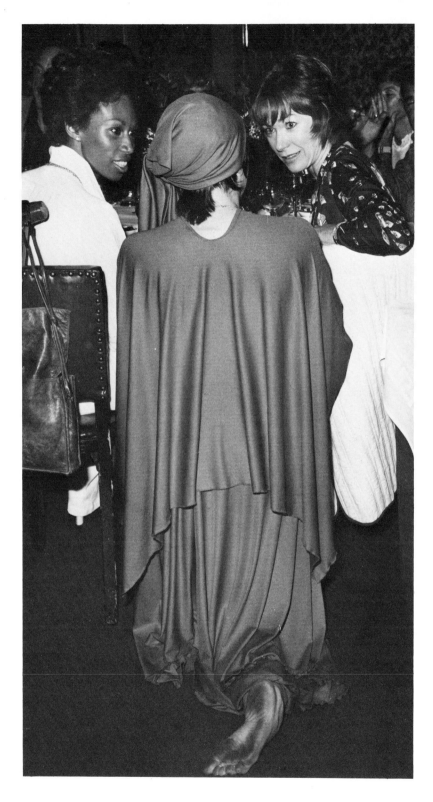

Liza, wrapped in a cocoon of silk: the social butterfly. At a Hollywood fête, Liza flew to the feet of her pals Altovise Davis and Shirley MacLaine (above). Never mind Liza's dirty feet; she was positive no one was looking! Everyone was looking at the surfboard Liza gave to her halfbrother Joey at his nineteenth birthday party, held at the home of Liza's makeup artist friend, Christina Smith, with whom Joey lived for awhile.

mercial vehicle to date—but Liza also started a fashion trend a la Sally Bowles.

In the film, Liza's fingernails are painted a snazzy shade of green (Sally Bowles called the color "divine decadence") and when the film opened in England, green nail polish became the rage among fashion mavens. In the United States, that trend was not as popular.

Young women in the United States and abroad also fashioned their hairstyles after Liza's *Cabaret* look. Gus Lepre had created the "Ella Cinders" look for Liza—her hair was cut very short, with the slightly uneven bangs forming a peak in the middle of the forehead—and Minnelli devotees eagerly aped their idol.

Liza also revived a culinary trend, albeit a short-lived one. To soothe her morning hangovers, Sally drank Prairie Oysters, "a raw egg and Worcestershire sauce, all sort of whooshed together." Some people tried the cure—once.

Cabaret left Liza a full-fledged, 14-karat superstar. Her beaming countenance often appeared on the covers of the chicest fashion magazines. Her name also began appearing on the Best Dressed Women lists, both in the United States and in Europe. It seems that wherever she went, whatever she did, and whoever she did it with, Liza made news. And she was always recognized—if not by her contagious laugh, then by her asterisk eyelashes, made especially for her by Christina Smith. "I know they're kind of outrageous," Liza says, "but I can get away with it."

Almost two years before *Cabaret* premiered, on June 29, 1970, Liza's first television special, *Liza Minnelli*, was aired. Although it wasn't a great artistic achievement—Liza wanted a one-woman show but was forced to have Randy Newman, Anthony Newley and Michael J. Pollard as her guests—it was good enough for NBC to offer her a second one.

On May 31, 1972, Liza taped the special *Liza With a Z* before an invited audience at Manhattan's Lyceum Theater. The show, presented by Singer, aired on September 10, 1972, and won an Emmy Award for Most Outstanding Single Program in the Variety and Popular Music category. Later that same year, Liza was named Female Star of the Year by the National Association of Theater Owners. She also became the only woman to receive the Las Vegas Entertainer of the Year Award for three consecutive years and was twice voted the American Guild of Variety Artists' Entertainer of the Year.

Yes, Liza had now made it, with, as *Time* would say, "fire, air and a touch of anguish." Liza had grown out of Judy's shadow. She was no longer just a star. She was becoming a superstar—she was just twenty-six years old. It was the early seventies, and "Minnelli Mania" had begun.

❧ ❧ ❧

But everything was not the way Liza planned it. Along with her sudden burst of fame came the realization that she was now, more than ever before, a public figure. She had to change her life style drastically—bodyguards hid her from potential kidnappers and her devoted staff kept overzealous fans away—and Liza wasn't comfortable with her new life style. Nor was she comfortable with the reputation *Cabaret* left her with.

"After I did that film," she explains, "everybody started talking about me. They got me mixed up with the role, as if I really were a decadent *femme fatale* like Sally Bowles. Suddenly, I'm reading that I'm dating people I've never heard of before."

One such incident occurred when Liza was in Paris watching an unusal floor show featuring a troupe of men dressed as women. "Their show was really terrific," she explains, "but they weren't doing enough business. So I said, 'Look, why don't you use me? Invite me to a special show and we'll get a bunch of press people to come in and it'll generate some excitement for you.' I helped some terrific artists out and the press turns it into 'Liza's Having an Affair with Brazilian Transvestites!' That stinks!"

Liza's attitude towards her fans also has changed since her

early, struggling days. Once gracious when it came to signing autographs, her *Cabaret* fame helped change that. She is aware that some fans go beyond mere adulation; that some fans are obsessed with her. Today, when Liza enters or leaves a theater's stage door, she demonstrates extreme caution. If she doesn't have the protection of several bodyguards (usually they are black), Liza will either wait for the crowds to thin out or exit through another door. It is rare that a fan can say hello—let alone ask for an autograph.

However, some fans are granted special privileges. Limelight on Liza is a fan club started in 1964 by Nancy Barr, a close friend of Liza's (Liza had asked Nancy to start the club). Fans who have belonged to the club for years are sometimes—exact times are never firm until the last moment—granted the honor of meeting Liza.

"Fans put their hands all over me," Liza says, her voice edged with disgust. "They push me and grab me and touch me with their iron grips. Yet nobody ever touches Barbra Streisand; it's as if she has 'Don't Touch' all over her. But with me," she adds, "they even leave bruise marks on my body. Everyone seems to want a piece of Liza."

Liza is so fearful of her fans that when they clamor to the edge of the stage after a concert, she refuses to shake any outstretched hands. Her fear of being pulled into the crowd is so great that, rather than reach for them, she usually urges her fans to throw flowers *at* her.

Liza, like Judy, also has a very large homosexual following. Liza readily acknowledges this, but sometimes with disdain. In more than one interview, Liza has referred to gay men as "faggots." Liza talks about her gay audience: "Gay men recognize themselves in me and Mama. They often identify with us, especially Mama. They saw a little woman up on stage, calling for a better world, a place where she—and they—would be happier. A place," Liza says, "where they would be understood."

Lawsuit and Exit Rex

One month after *Cabaret* opened, Liza made headlines again. But for a very different reason. Liza was hit with a $556,000 lawsuit by Rex Kramer's wife, Margaret Louise Kulbeth. She charged Liza with stealing her husband away from her and making him abandon their then four-year-old son.

"By the use of her great power, wealth and influence," the lawsuit read, "Liza Minnelli Woolnought [Woolnought is Peter

Allen's real name], an entertainer of worldwide fame, gained the affection of Rex and persuaded and enticed him to abandon the society of his wife and child." The suit also stated that Liza "did knowingly and willfully engage in carnal intercourse with Rex and consorted with him openly."

The press was having a ball. Everyday, Liza's name seemed to be front-page news; the *New York Post* even dubbed Liza a "home wrecker." Liza, of course, denied all charges. "I deny every allegation in the plantiff's petition," she said, "and I was not the pursuer in this matter."

Margaret Louise Kulbeth's lawsuit against Liza Minnelli Woolnought was finally settled out of court—the exact monies paid are said to have been quite large. It did not matter that Liza was losing Rex. She had been growing tired of him for some time—when Liza becomes bored with a man she drops him faster than anyone can imagine—and wanted him out of her life anyway. "I was with Rex a year," she says, "when I realized I wanted my freedom."

During the last few months that she was still attached to Rex, Liza was also dating other men. Much to the chagrin of Rex, she was escorted to the New York premiere of *Cabaret* by *two* men, Desi Arnaz, Senior and Desi Junior. Liza was far from subtle when showing off her new romantic interests, yet she knew she had to officially break clean with Rex.

So Liza devised a plan. She and Deanna Wenble, her longtime secretary, convinced the drummer that there was a new man in Liza's life.

Rex did not take the brushoff well and bad-mouthed Liza to everyone. "She drives herself into the ground," he said at the time. "She just doesn't know how to slow down. Liza can't sleep and has to take downers to get herself together. And her temper tantrums—wow! She'd just rant and rave, then finally collapse in a heap!"

And Liza said, "I knew Rex was only using me, but I worried about him. I was afraid he might do something silly. He said he would only leave me if I was desperately in love with someone else." What Rex didn't know was that there really *was* another man in Liza's life.

Lisa & Desi Arnaz, Junior

Liza first met Desi Arnaz, Junior in June, 1970. She was performing at the Now Grove of the Los Angeles Ambassador Hotel and Desi, then seventeen, arrived at the opening-night party with Liza's pal, Gayle Martin. Liza greeted Desi, but the two soon departed—Liza was busy entertaining Rex and the rest of the well-wishers.

They met again fifteen months later, when Liza returned from Germany. In September, 1971, in Los Angeles, Liza performed at the Greek Theater; Desi went to catch her there. Soon after, he flew to Las Vegas to see Tony Bennett's show. However, when he got there, he caught Liza's closing-night performance instead. The next night Desi took Liza to see Bennett. The magic had begun.

The press immediately picked up on the romance. Gossip magazines ran cover stories: two show biz babies from two show biz families in love, spending time alone at Desi Senior's Del Mar, California, beach home—stories that guaranteed a boost in circulation.

Liza's relationship with Desi was, from the beginning, a strange one. He often referred to her as "my fiancée"; she called him "my husband." One week Liza was telling the

The quintessential Liza (right): Christina Smith's spider eyelashes, Elsa Peretti's sterling silver armband jewelry and Minnelli's no-nail look. "How can people judge me because I bite my nails? Does nail-biting invalidate everything I do and everything I am?" Liza's long time lover, Rex Kramer (left), says yes. When Rex and Liza split in the early seventies, he publicly deemed Liza a pill-popping, insecure neurotic.

press, "I want Desi forever and I'm going to have him." The next week it was, "He's too young for me. He tells me he knows what he wants, but I can't believe it."

People close to Liza never really believed the union would last. There were even times when the romance seemed over: several weeks after they began dating, Liza fulfilled another concert engagement at the Olympia Theater in Paris and Baron Alexis de Rede entered her life again. He threw a lavish opening night party for Liza at his seventeenth-century Île St-Louis townhouse. The intimate dinner later turned into a benefit for the United Jewish Appeal, with such invited guests as Elizabeth Taylor, Richard Burton, Yves St. Laurent and Marisa Berenson contributing to the cause.

Liza remembers the Baron. "When I was with him, I was in the most relaxed atmosphere I had ever been in," she says. "But my God! Our relationship was not as serious as all those people made it sound."

When Liza returned from her Parisian *tête-à-tête*, she found Desi waiting. He escorted her (along with his father) to the February 13 premiere of *Cabaret*. The Desis wore black tie and Liza, looking ravishing, wore wedding-white—including a white chinchilla cape. Photos of the trio graced newspapers and magazines everywhere, and once again, Desi and Liza were an item. To emphasize the fact, they began living together.

It never bothered Liza that Desi was seven years her junior. Though she seemed to gravitate toward older men—men with strong paternal instincts—Liza found a different sense of stability in Desi.

"Desi is really much older than his age," she said at the time. "He understands my need for calmness. He knows I hate abrupt changes of emotion." The age difference between Liza and Desi did not bother Desi's mother, Lucille Ball, either. She was always eager to point out that both her husbands—Desi Arnaz, Senior and Gary Morton—were years younger than she.

Yet Desi had a tarnished reputation among women, especially Patty Duke. The actress still claims that Desi is the father of her son, Sean—the two had a long, involved affair—something that Lucy found hard to tolerate (she later claimed Patty "used" Desi). Desi may have visited Sean the day after his birth, but he never married Patty.

Desi Arnaz, Junior, on Liza Minnelli, 1972: "I just want everyone to know that Liza and I are deeply in love. We feel we've been married all our lives and it would be wonderful if she had my baby. I want her to have my baby—I want her to have *all* my children—and I don't care if we're married or not! Just the picture of Liza pregnant with my child gives me goose pimples!"

Desi may have wanted to father Liza's baby, but not necessarily marry her. At the time Liza was still officially married to Peter Allen. Her divorce was being delayed because of Peter's alien status.

"Liza and I don't see any need for marriage," he said. "We don't need that jazz. We're not going to be bound by that trap—if we fall out of love, we're going to go our own ways. Plain and simple, no bickering, no ugly proceedings. Marriage is unrealistic; they expect you to devote a whole life unselfishly to one person."

But one thing stepped in Desi's permissive way: his mother, Lucy Ball. "Mother doesn't want Liza and me living out of wedlock and she cringes at the idea of our having a child out of wedlock." Desi said. "It's a struggle between what *we* want and what *Mother* wants. We don't know what to do—please ourselves or please Mother."

Liza always got along well with Lucy. They first met when Liza was seven years old and Lucy and Desi were filming Vincente Minnelli's *The Long, Long Trailer*. In fact, when Liza and Desi first began dating, Lucy and her son were not on the best speaking terms. Liza reconciled them. Liza even once gave Lucy a black Halston pantsuit.

"I felt like a mother to Liza before my own children were born," says Lucy, "and I *know* Liza! She took on all the responsibilities long before Judy died. Oh, I love Liza!"

When Liza visited Desi in Tokyo, Japan in the early summer of 1972—he was there filming *Marco*—they exchanged gold rings. He later gave Liza another ring; one boasting a big diamond. They were now officially engaged, but, as Liza told the press, "We're not talking about it."

Some people feel Liza was pressured into the engagement, that she only exchanged rings to keep the pestering press at bay. She never mentioned a marriage date—perhaps she felt the relationship was coming to a end. Desi Senior, however, added more fuel to the fire when he announced that Liza and his son would marry on September 6 at his home in Las Cruces.

On January 19, 1973, Liza threw a surprise party for Desi's twentieth birthday at a nightclub in Los Angeles. It was a joyous evening, later shattered by an incident which, on the sur-

face, seemed harmless. Liza wanted to dance. Desi did not. So she grabbed another man—"I'm an adventurer and I do things spontaneously," she has said—and the following day, Desi's angry reaction made newspaper columns.

Liza did explain: "The night of Desi's birthday, I felt like doing some wild dancing, but Desi—who is more uptight than I am—wouldn't dance. Guys who won't let themselves go irk me. So," she adds, "he sat on the sidelines while I danced with someone else."

Ten days later, on January 29, Liza attended the Golden Globes Ceremonies to pick up her award as Best Actress for her *Cabaret* role. While there, she met another winner—for Most Promising Male Newcomer—Edward Albert, Junior, who was chosen for his work in the film *Butterflies are Free*.

Like Desi, Edward Albert also boasted famous show business lineage (his father is actor Eddie Albert). Liza found Edward dashing and charming despite the fact he was five years younger. And he was willing to accept a relationship without the same demands that Desi made.

"I tend to like older women," Edward explained. "I believe that as a woman matures, she becomes more female." Yet Edward never really had a chance to see Liza ripen; they dated too infrequently and soon their love fizzled.

Then, in mid-May, 1973—just two months after Desi escorted Liza to the Oscars—their romance came screeching to

Liza fell for Edward Albert, Junior (above left), because she found him less demanding than most of her other lovers. That didn't stop Edward from going into hiding when their romance became too public. The Baron Alexis de Rede (above) wined and dined Liza and wooed her with red roses. He even named a racehorse after her.

Liza with three of her loves. French singer and parttime actor Charles Aznavour was captivated by Liza from the first moment he saw her (opposite page). He unofficially took Liza under his tutelage and helped guide her through many of her concert engagements at Olympia Music Hall in Paris. Liza denies any romance, but Aznavour calls Liza "my dear girl" and insists what they had together was "better than romance." Bob Fosse (left) also took Liza under his wing; most notably as he directed her in Cabaret. *"Bob is a real person," says Liza. "It's something you can't put your finger on; you just know he knows what he's doing." Adds Fosse, "I've never seen energy like Liza's from anyone. If I told her to jump into the ocean, she'd say 'OK, I'll try it.'" Liza had a festive time when she attended a carnival in Rio de Janeiro with Brazilian playboy Pedrinho Aquinega (below, left). Liza's pals were sure the romance would peter out; when she announced her engagement to Pedrinho and "retirement" from show business, they knew it was all over.*

a halt. Liza found someone new. Someone *much* older. Someone named Peter Sellers.

The Minnelli-Sellers Romance

On May 11, 1973, Liza opened at the Palladium in England — the same stage she had shared with her mother nearly nine years before. Once again, the British were lavish in their praise of Liza, and all three performances were sold out weeks in advance. One man who attended the trio of shows was Peter Sellers. Then forty-seven years old — and twenty years Liza's senior — the late comedian easily won Liza's affections. Several days after she arrived in London, Liza was announcing her new romance and renouncing her old one.

"It's all very simple," Liza said, "my engagement — Desi's and my relationship — has been deteriorating for some time; pleasantly, luckily. We are no longer engaged. It's all called off."

Liza, laughing and giggling as she spoke to reporters, continued: "I fell in love with this man [Sellers], and I am pleased to say he fell in love with me. I have always been an admirer of his marvelous talent and we both believe in humor and in having good times. Why, we haven't found anything that we disagree on!"

97

Liza and Desi Arnaz, Junior began dating in the early seventies and soon afterward began living together. Desi and Liza even exchanged gold engagement rings. Some insist Liza only accepted hers as a way to temporarily appease her pushy lover. Although Desi was seven years Liza's junior, they looked like a happy show biz couple (opposite). Desi's father, Desi Senior, found Liza amusing —even when she didn't speak in "sign language" (right). Desi's mother, Lucille Ball, loved Liza dearly; they first met in 1953, when Lucy and Desi Senior were filming Vincente Minnelli's The Long, Long Trailer. *In July 1974, Lucy, Liza and Lucy's husband, Gary Morton, dropped in to see Shirley MacLaine's Las Vegas show at the M-G-M Grand (below).*

Desi Junior first heard about Liza's new love as he was watching a television news broadcast, although he had suspected something was wrong. Right after Liza left for London, he told an inquiring reporter, "Something has turned sour since Liza went away."

Later, Liza verified the news with a phone call to Desi. "It all happened so fast," he said. "Liza and Peter dated two or three times, then she told me she loved him! I wish we hadn't broken up. I loved Liza," Desi added. "I still do." To console himself after the breakup, Desi began dating several attractive women, most notably an aspiring actress named Karen Lamm.

Liza returned to the United States, and with the help of godmother Kay Thompson, packed several trunks of clothes. She flew into London's Heathrow Airport on June 4, and was picked up by a disguised Peter Sellers. The actor then took Liza to his home at Eleven Eaton Muse North.

Liza lived with Peter for about five weeks. Then the relationship fell apart. Liza moved into a suite at the Savoy Hotel, and her actions were defended by her father, who told the press that Sellers's apartment was probably "too small."

Soon, Liza admitted the truth and blamed the British press

for the breakup. "We couldn't even go out to dinner without being followed," she says.

The badgering press was only one reason Liza left Sellers. The other reason Liza broke up with the actor was at the advice of noted British psychic Frederic Davies. Davies, in late May, was a guest on the BBC radio show *Today* and he predicted the Minnelli-Sellers romance would not last.

When Liza heard about this from a friend, she contacted the psychic. "She came to my home in mid-June," Davies recalls. "We talked a little and then I read the Tarot cards for her. I told Liza that the romance was ill-fated. She became slightly emotional, and dabbing at her eyes, she confessed that she was thinking of breaking off the romance. All I could tell her," Davies adds, "was that it seemed to be the right course for her. And three days later, on June 20, Liza publicly announced that her romance with Peter Sellers was over."

"It's over," Liza told reporters that June morning, "but Peter is marvelous and we had a lovely, lovely time. Regrets? No, I have none. How can I regret something that was so happy?"

Peter Sellers also met the press. His comments: "It's true, but it was for Liza to say so. We are finished, but it was not my wish."

Liza at the Winter Garden

It would, Liza insisted, be an event never before seen in the history of theater. It would be ninety minutes of song and dance and knock-'em-dead pizzazz. It would be sheer energetic entertainment. There would be no opening act; just Liza, live. It would be her first Broadway one-woman show. It would simply be called *Liza*.

Liza (later, when she recorded the cast album, the show became *Liza at the Winter Garden*) sold out—the entire three-week engagement—within thirty-six hours after tickets went on sale. Within days, scalpers were selling the top-priced $15 tickets for phenomenal profits. The ducats also became collectors' items—Liza's name was misspelled *"Liza Minelli."* "Can you believe it!" Liza shrieked. It is also interesting to note that in January, 1974, some people—including Douglas Watts of the *New York Daily News*—considered the $15 price tag "outrageously high." In 1977, Liza's *The Act* would set another theater precedent with its top-priced $25 ticket.

Liza wanted to be sure that nothing would go wrong with *Liza*. She spent weeks rehearsing for it, and surrounded herself, both on stage and off, with only trusted friends. Jack

The late Peter Sellers (above) was married when he fell in love with Liza in 1973. "At last I've found the sort of woman who will take care of me," Sellers said. For five short weeks, Liza did—until she decided she was tired of Sellers' name, wealth and fame. Liza had a taste of more fame when Henry Kissinger (right) dropped backstage during Liza's Winter Garden stint.

French, who had worked with Liza since 1966, would conduct the twenty-eight-piece orchestra; Deanna Wenble would handle the scores of lighting cues; Marvin Hamlisch would serve as musical coordinator; Fred Ebb would write the show; Nancy Barr would help handle Liza's quick costume changes; and Bob Fosse, whom she was dating at the time, would direct. *Liza* looked like a winner.

New York was also preparing for *Liza*. It would mark Liza's first Manhattan stage appearance since *Flora, the Red Menace*, nine years before. A giant marquee-billboard, emblazoned with red letters screaming "Liza" spanned the top of the Winter Garden Theater, almost running one city block in length. The graphic lettering was done by artist Joe Eula, who dotted the "i" in Liza with a simple, effective drawing of the super-

star. Eula later would also create the advertising motif for *The Act*.

People were buzzing with anticipation, especially since another superstar, Bette Midler, had opened to highly enthusiastic reviews one month earlier. Liza had worried that Bette's act would outshine hers. She bought tickets for the December 23 performance at the Palace Theater—Bette's closing night—and that evening, her fears subsided. Though she loved the Divine Miss M's stinging sense of camp and polished vulgarity, she knew their acts were two separate entities. There was, she knew, no room for comparison.

Liza opened at the Winter Garden Theater on Sunday, January 6, 1974. First-nighters included Betsy Palmer, Dudley Moore, Vincente Minnelli, Lorna and Sid Luft, Kay Thompson, Fred Ebb and John Kander, Bob Fosse, Kitty Carlisle Hart and Ben Vereen.

From the opening "If You Could Read My Mind/Come Back to Me" to "More than You Know" to "A Quiet Thing"

(from *Flora*, a song Liza calls her "favorite") to "Cabaret," Liza was a breathtaking powerhouse of talent.

Each number was highly stylized and vocalized. However, much to the chagrin of the theater aficionados, Liza and her quartet of dancers performed several lip-sync songs, including "A Natural Man." Liza used this *faux pas* of musical theater again—to great critical outcry—when she starred in *The Act*, three years later.

"We decided to lip-sync because we had no other choice," Liza explained. "There were numbers people wanted to *really* see—especially 'Ring Them Bells'—and I just couldn't do that huh-huh, panting kind of singing as I danced."

After the opening night performance, more than 300 people jammed the Rainbow Grill, where Vincente Minnelli, Columbia Records and the Shubert Organization hosted an Italian buffet in Liza's honor. She arrived a bit after 10:30 P.M.—on the arm of her father, and looking every bit the Talk of the Town. Liza wore a fox jacket, wide-brimmed polka-dot

Borsalino hat, and a white tuxedo jacket which hid her black-and-white polka-dot pantsuit. For that occasion, Liza's clothes were designed by Jacques Bellini—not Halston, who also was at the fete. When Liza walked in, she looked mildly startled and exclaimed, "You're all super. Thank you very much!"

The critics loved *Liza*. "Liza makes it seem like summer again," wrote Clive Barnes in *The New York Times*, "and in every respect, *Liza* is a winner. It is probably her nervousness, those stretched-out moments of the spirit, that make Liza's performance so exciting. Her vitality is unusual. It is not the sheer powerhouse drive of some singers, but rather the result of some exciting internal tension. It is compulsive and, for all its ease, a little agonized. She has a voice that can purr, whisper, snarl and roar. But why only three weeks, Miss Minnelli? Stay longer next time."

Anthony Mancini in the *New York Post*: "Liza has a clarion voice and her songs urge us—against the odds—to drink long drafts of life. She carries it off because of her ability to create a bond of instant intimacy. She dances like a colt and most of the time (even with her four dancers), it's just Liza with a Z and alchemy."

Only Douglas Watts of the New York *Daily News* qualified the praise: "Liza proves to be an engaging, but far from magnetic, entertainer. And, for whether or not she and her groomers care to admit it, the image of the plucky Judy Garland is never far off, particularly when, in a velvet suit with knee britches and patent-leather pumps, Liza slams home with 'Mammy.' She unavoidably calls to mind Judy's 'Rock-a-bye Your Baby With a Dixie Melody.' Liza, even with all her tremendous energy and appeal, is not yet a Sinatra or Streisand."

The January 25 performance of *Liza* was videotaped for posterity. Liza agreed to pay half the cost after she, Fred Ebb and John Kander videotaped an interview for the Library of Performing Arts at Manhattan's Lincoln Center on January 14, 1974. It was a special midnight performance; a benefit which raised more than $20,000 for the Actor's Fund. At the end of the show, Liza was presented with an Actor's Fund citation—as a "thank you" for her contributions—from drama critic Clive Barnes. It was a star-studded evening, and Liza was overwhelmed by the applause. One audience member leading the ovation was entertainer Ben Vereen.

Liza & Ben

Liza's introduction to Ben Vereen took place on Memorial Day, 1972. That evening—May 30—Liza, in town to film her television special *Liza with a Z* the next night, attended a performance of the Broadway smash, *Jesus Christ, Superstar* at the Mark Hellinger Theater. Vereen was starring in the pivotal role of Judas, and Liza was impressed by his talents. The fact that he was black did not seem to matter.

"Liza had just done *Cabaret* and I was doing *Jesus Christ* when I met her," Vereen remembers. "She would drop by with Bob Fosse, and she'd help me in my performance by giving me some great advice." Their real relationship, however, did not blossom until 1974.

Liza and Ben would be seen everywhere—kissing, holding hands—yet both would insistently deny there was a romance. Then, in February, 1974, something happened that blew the lid off their secrecy.

Liza and Ben shocked Hollywood moralists when they appeared in a *Newsweek* photograph. It was no ordinary shot: the photo, taken by renowned photographer Francesco Scavullo, showed a bare-chested Vereen protectively holding a nude Liza, his arms encircling her chest.

"It was a great, fantastic photo," Vereen now says. "Liza was in front and I was embracing her. It was in the Robert Redford issue [the actor was on the cover of the February 4 issue], but it was our inside picture that made the big, big sales. As a matter of fact, I still have the original photograph."

During this time, Vereen tagged along wherever Liza performed, and they showed no discretion in their "friendship." Both would attend nightclubs and restaurants looking every inch the lovers people claimed them to be, and when they returned to New York, Vereen, also appearing on Broadway in Bob Fosse's *Pippin*, would often pop backstage to visit Liza

Liza usually embraces a song the same way Judy did, with razor-sharp poignancy and a full vibrato. Even when the song is a spoof—as "Ring Them Bells" was during Liza's Winter Garden run (opposite)—Liza gives her all. Liza also gave her all during her relationship with Ben Vereen (above). Although Liza and Ben both denied they were lovers, they were photographed together, quite bare, by Francesco Scavullo—the photo appeared in Newsweek.

at the Winter Garden. Sometimes he would bring his daughter, whom Liza adored (Vereen was, at the time, married to a white woman).

Liza has never elaborated on her relationship with Vereen. Vereen himself suggests they were never lovers. Others feel differently. Vereen suffered from his involvement with Liza. He was flooded with threatening phone calls and letters from white and black bigots. "It taught me a great lesson about people," Vereen says with a faint grin. "I guess Liza and I gave them something to talk about."

After Liza's triumphant Winter Garden stint, no one could stop talking about her. On January 30, four days after her final *Liza* performance, Liza opened at the Riviera Hotel in Las Vegas. She was now a full-fledged Vegas superstar, reportedly earning close to $150,000 a week. For her Winter Garden performances, Liza earned a reported $300,000; a fair amount since the show grossed approximately $412,000.

Soon after, she performed a week-long engagement in Rio de Janiero, where Liza met the young Brazilian playboy Pedrinho Aquinega, whom the press dubbed "the most beautiful man in Brazil." Halfway through her run there, Liza claimed she fell in love with Aquinega, and promptly announced her "engagement" and planned retirement from show business. No one took her seriously — most people were, by now, used to Liza's transient emotions — and the vapid romance ended as quickly as it had begun. Liza returned to the States alone, where she again saw Ben Vereen. But the Vereen episode did not last much longer.

Liza and Ben did get together again in 1976 when they starred on the NBC special, *The Bell Telephone 100th Anniversary Jubilee*. The show, which aired on March 26, featured Liza and Ben performing a modern gospel-like melody — ironically, Liza sang "I Don't Know How to Love Him" from *Jesus Christ, Superstar*. In the fall of 1982, Liza and Ben also performed on the same bill when they taped the *President's Command Performance* at Washington, D.C.'s Ford Theater. They may no longer be lovers, but their friendship is still strong.

※ ※ ※

Every year since 1951, Harvard University, as a way of promoting its Hasty Pudding Theatricals, has given its Hasty Pudding Trophy Cup to a newsworthy celebrity. In 1974, the all-male club bestowed its "Woman of the Year" award to Liza. She was so overjoyed by the honor that Liza ventured to the Cambridge, Massachusetts, campus and graciously participated in the festivities. Liza rode through the town in a chauffeured 1940 Lincoln convertible, trailed by antique fire engines and hundreds of photographers and fans. Later, after she watched scenes from the original production *Bewitched Banyou*, Liza sang "Cabaret."

"This is the greatest party I've ever been to," she told the wildly enthusiastic crowd. And it was: Liza found herself at ease with the young students. She knew these people liked her work, but they were not the ones necessarily buying her records. Liza knew that to reach them, and to reach the audience she never had, she had to break into the "Top 40" market, the youth market. She knew she had to change her image from an 8 by 10 glossy into someone more accessible; someone young people could relate to.

Liza turned to rock star Alice Cooper. In the early seventies, Alice Cooper *was* rock 'n' roll. His concerts were more spectacle than show — boa constrictors would dart between his legs, electrocutions, hangings and decapitations would be simulated on stage — and the youth of America loved every gory minute. It showed in Cooper's sold-out concerts; it showed in his numerous gold records.

Liza announced that she and Alice (that is, Vincent Damon Furnier) were making an album together. There was also talk that the unlikely duo would do a concert tour together; this was never realized. Alice promoted Liza whenever he appeared on radio and television. It seemed like Liza's new image was working. Not only did she have her original fans (the change was coming about so slowly that none of Liza's diehards were lost), now Liza was scoring with Alice's fans as well.

But when push came to shove, the change did not work. *Muscle of Love*, Alice's 1974 Warner Brothers album, was a flop. Liza recorded background vocals on two of the disc's cuts: "Teenage Lament '74" and "Man With the Golden Gun," but not even her singing helped. The album sold poorly and, today, *Muscle of Love* has muscled its way into cut-out record bins everywhere.

The Cooper incident should have taught Liza a lesson. In the past, whenever she has tried to "change" her image, it has failed. When she wore her hair in a shag in the early seventies, the look did not work. In 1977, Liza recorded *Tropical Nights* for Columbia, but the album, a mix of rock and disco, was a dismal failure and is probably Liza's poorest.

"The greatest gift a man can give a woman is his name," Liza explains. On September 15, 1974, Liza May Minnelli Allen became Liza May Minnelli Allen Haley. The gift lasted nearly four years—before Liza exchanged it for another one, named Gero.

Liza continued to be busy in 1974. In March, she performed at a benefit for actor Jim Stacy, who had lost an arm and leg in a skiing accident. On April 21, she received a second Tony Award; this time it was for *Liza* and "superior concert entertainment on the Broadway stage" (Bette Midler also received one for her Palace engagement).

Nine days later, on April 30, NBC finally aired the special she had filmed with Charles Aznavour in England, *Love From A to Z.* The next month, Liza, escorted by her father, joined some show-biz pals—including Carol Channing, Tony Bennett and Robert Morse—for the benefit *Jule's Friends at the Palace.* A salute to composer Jule Styne, the one-night show held on May 19, 1974, raised money for the American Musical

In Jack, Liza found the maturity—and drive—lacking in Peter Allen. Twelve years older than Liza, Jack gave in to every pet peeve of his wife's, including meeting her at Los Angeles International Airport with her pet dog and pet fur (left). Sometimes life with Liza was eventful: one night, while Jack and Liza were dining in a Japanese restaurant, their waitress spilled a bowl of soup all over Jack. The reason? She was excited seeing Liza in person!

and Dramatic Academy and the National Hemophilia Foundation. Liza sang two Styne songs: "I Guess I'll Have to Hang My Tears to Dry" from *Glad to See You* and "Some People" from *Gypsy.*

Liza and Jack Haley, Junior: A Marriage

Liza Minnelli, daughter of Oz's Dorothy, and Jack Haley, Junior, son of Oz's Tin Woodsman, first met at a Hollywood party for actor George Hamilton in 1960. She was fourteen; and at twenty-seven, Haley, an Air Force veteran, was nearly twice her age. It did not matter.

Liza and Jack pose for a That's Entertainment *publicity shot on a decaying backlot at M-G-M. For the film, Jack amassed more than a quarter of a billion dollars worth of film. When he first approached Liza to narrate the Judy Garland footage, she backed down. But Vincente urged his daughter to meet with Jack. Liza not only found a brilliant filmmaker with a winning personality, but she also won a husband. Now, that's entertainment!*

"I found Jack fascinating and knowledgeable," recalls Liza. "We sat down on a diving board and rapped for hours. He was so, so smart!"

Liza and Jack did not meet each other again until 1974. "Oh, I'd bump into Jack at parties," Liza recalls, "but we never really dated or anything like that. They were purely casual meetings."

Then, in early '74, after her booming success in *Cabaret*, Liza was approached by Haley to film a segment of his movie *That's Entertainment*. It was to be a homage to M-G-M musicals, and Haley wanted Liza to narrate the Judy Garland footage.

At first, she backed off. "Who needed that?" Liza says. "I really couldn't handle all that tribute stuff about Mama, and I hate anything that smacks of exploitation of my family. But my father told me, 'This guy is good and you should at least look at what he's done.' So I went to the studio and when Jack met me," Liza adds, "he said, 'I've got something to show you.' I thought, 'What a con man!' Well, I watched the film for a while, but it was so damn sensitive that I had to have him stop the screening. I was howling like a baby! I knew it was bound to be an emotional experience, but I didn't think I'd be overcome by it."

After the initial screening, Liza asked Haley to walk her around the studio lot. "He helped me out of the private theater," Liza says, "and spent the rest of the day comforting me. Then I went back for more."

After she finished watching all the Garland footage, Liza realized what Jack had done. "The thing that got to me," Liza says, "was that it wasn't camp. Jack didn't end the film with 'Over the Rainbow.' He used 'Get Happy.' The film was done with love. To see someone treat my mother like that and not put her on . . . wow! It was a great tribute to Mama—a eulogy even—and I wanted to be a part of it."

Liza agreed to work on *That's Entertainment*. About six months later, Jack approached Liza to open the 1973 Academy Awards telecast with the specially-written Kander and Ebb number, "Oscar." (He was directing the telecast.)

"Everybody around Liza said, 'No, she's overexposed,'" he recalls, "but I went to Las Vegas where she was working, locked her dressing-room door and described the number to her. She said, 'Okay, okay, I'll do it.'" Liza and Jack's relationship was, at this time, she says, "strictly business."

"When I was little," Liza remembers, "I used to hear about the way Jack was dating some terrific-looking lady and how he had this snappy reputation. I never dreamed that he'd ever look at *me!* What would a talented playboy want with Liza?"

Jack *was* interested and made the first move. While Liza

Lucky Lady was Liza's first film since Cabaret —*and an unlucky one at that. Critics sank the $16 million flick about rumrunning, even though Liza immersed herself in the script (below). Liza hated Guaymas, Mexico (where most of the film was shot) and often found herself ill from the weather and food. Lucky Lady's cigar-chomping ménage à trois —Gene Hackman, Liza and Burt Reynolds (right)—proved to be a poor facsimile of Groucho, Harpo and Chico Marx.*

was performing at Harrah's in Lake Tahoe, he went to consult her about a benefit they were both involved with. After Liza's midnight show, the couple conversed—all night. They repeated this several nights in a row. Then, on April 15, the night after Jack left, Liza collapsed backstage as she was waiting to go on. She had the flu and was subsequently ordered to bed by her doctor. When Jack found out about this, he was riddled with guilt.

"I called Liza," he recalls, "and started yelling at her. 'What are you doing to yourself? I'm worrying about you and want you to start taking care of yourself.'"

Liza remembers that night. "I was angry—how *dare* he talk to me like that?" she says. Moments later, after her anger subsided, Liza saw the reasoning behind Haley's line of fire.

"And that," Haley says simply, "is how it all began."

"For the first three months, I did nothing but pump him for information about himself," explains Liza. "After that, we found out we were having a more interesting time together than apart. There were no fireworks displays, no cymbal crashes. Just a slow and gentle falling in love. It was much better than a wild affair."

Once again, Liza's lover's age—Jack was twelve years her senior—meant little to her. "Jack was so full of life, he left all those young guys around Hollywood at a standstill," she says. "I never really even thought about his age. I just knew that marrying an older man would be the best thing I could do. Older men are more experienced in life, and I felt Jack could give me security to start with. And his eyes—those wonderful blue eyes! I fell in love with those first! I could always tell he had something going on behind them."

Liza moved into Jack's Hollywood hilltop home on Devlin Drive. "It was then," she says, "that I found out what a hell of a bachelor Jack was. I had some very jealous ladies to deal with—I think they came out of the woodwork. And they were all mad at me!"

It was not easy for Jack Haley, Junior to fall in love. The film writer-producer-director was a Hollywood child, and he was used to his unattached freedom. Gossip columnists linked him with every available bachelorette—he had torrid affairs with Jill St. John, Nancy Sinatra and Sue Lyon. There was even a joke around town: "I believe every girl should be engaged to Jack Haley, Junior," quipped *Hollywood Reporter* columnist Hank Grant, "at least once in her lifetime."

Haley admits it was not easy getting close to Liza. "I had seen her in *Cabaret* and in her shows," he says, "and I said to myself, 'My God, how can I keep up with someone with her energy?' But the more I got to know Liza, the closer we became—I realized that she had full control of all her energies—she harnessed it so damned well that none of it was really wasted."

At first, Liza and Jack denied marriage rumors, despite the fact that everywhere they went—from the Sammy Davis Broadway opening in June, 1974, to the five major premieres of *That's Entertainment*—they wore the look of love. "I'm married to my career," Liza told the press. "I have no time for marriage. Jack is merely a friend. Anyway, I'm still married to Peter Allen and that's where the matter rests."

On July 11, shortly after Liza began her romance with Haley, Peter Allen appeared at Manhattan Supreme Court to receive his divorce. The proceedings were brief. Liza did not attend. "When you've been separated longer than you've been married," he told reporters, "it's time to get a divorce."

On June 22, Liza and Jack accepted a special invitation from Prince Rainier and Princess Grace and attended a Monaco charity gala. Then, Liza returned to the United States to fulfill a two-week stint in Las Vegas. A little more than one month later, on August 9, during Liza's concert run in Allentown, Pennsylvania, the couple officially announced their engagement. Liza proudly showed off her ring—a 5-karat marquise-cut emerald surrounded by diamonds. Haley also gave his fiancée a gold and diamond bracelet with this inscription: "I offer you all my worldly goods, my name and my heart." "That ring," Liza says, "was the first real jewel I've ever owned."

Liza remembers how Jack proposed to her. "We were driving along Hollywood's Sunset Boulevard and he just said, 'Let's get married!' I said, 'Okay.' It was as simple as that, but it wasn't impulsive. Both of us had been thinking about it. Both of us knew this was *it*."

Almost one month later, at 3 P.M. on September 15, they married in a private ceremony in the chapel of the First Presbyterian Church in Montecito, California.

Liza wore a yellow silk cardigan pantsuit with a yellow chiffon sleeveless blouse and scarf (all by Halston) and Elsa Peretti jewelry, including a necklace of gold and diamonds. She carried a bouquet of daisies. Her shoes were breathtaking: $400 Beth Levine creations covered with 3,000 ocher-shaded red sequins—and looking very much like those Judy wore in *The Wizard of Oz*.

It was a small ceremony; Liza was given away by her best friend, Fred Ebb; Sammy Davis, Junior, was best man. The ceremony took less than fifteen minutes. Beverly Hills Judge John Griffin officiated. The ceremony ended with Liza's special vow to her new husband: "You multiply my joy, you divide my grief, you are my love, my companion and my dearest friend."

Sammy Davis, Junior recalls the wedding. "I really feel like an uncle to that girl," he says. "I was best man because, after all, Jack and Liza are two of my best buddies. This also made me eligible to be the main shoulder to cry on when they were breaking up. I guess," he sighs, "that's what uncles are for."

On the night of their wedding, Liza and Jack hosted a small, quiet reception at their home. Only a select number of guests—including Gene Kelly and his two children, Yul Brynner, Vincente Minnelli, and Sammy Davis, Junior and his wife Altovise—were invited. The *real* celebration came the following evening.

On Monday, September 16, Sammy Davis, Junior, his wife and Vincente Minnelli threw a wedding reception for the newlyweds at Ciro's, a Hollywood nightclub. It was no small affair. The interior of Ciro's was a throwback to the forties (Liza and Jack later called it "The Celebration"), and the party could have competed with the best movie premieres.

Seven hundred guests were there; the invitation list read like a Beverly Hills phone directory: Alice Cooper, Zsa Zsa Gabor, Gene Kelly, Rita Hayworth, Ava Gardner, Jack Benny, Milton Berle, David Bowie, Warren Beatty, Fred Astaire, Rona Barrett, Lana Turner, Johnny Carson, Sammy Davis, Junior (who sang "Liza"), Peter Lawford, Raquel Welch, Elizabeth Taylor, Goldie Hawn, Rock Hudson, Ann-Margret, George Hamilton and Shirley MacLaine. "It would be easier," quipped Hollywood columnist Joyce Haber, "to name those who *weren't* there." Outside, close to 1,400 uninvited guests —fans and photographers—had gathered to gawk.

Most guests arrived after midnight (ex-Monkee Mickey Dolenz was refused entrance because he wasn't in black tie), nibbled on sugar-coated almonds and imbibed the drinks served by waitresses dressed in 1940s costumes. One guest, Halston, recalls that evening. "I just had enough time to get from the airport to the hotel, shower, shave and put on my tuxedo. I left for New York on a 1 A.M. flight, but it was worth it. Liza's just like my kid sister."

For the festive occasion, Liza wore a Halston-designed strapless black velvet gown and elbow-length white leather gloves. She looked gay throughout the evening, as she danced with her father and accepted obligatory congratulations. "It was a real star party," she remembers.

Just as the party was ending, Liza turned to one guest and said, "This time it's going to work. Listen, I know what I've been through, like older men, like Peter Sellers. Maybe it was all a hunt for emotional security. But with Jack, it's different. He is the man I will live with forever. His is the love of my life. You got to believe me."

Jack was equally in love. "We may have an unconventional marriage," he said, "but we're going to make it work. We both know the pitfalls, and we won't let anything happen to us. Still, Liza and I are *so* close that, well, I keep waiting for something to go wrong."

Four years later, it did.

Unlucky Lady

Liza began filming *Lucky Lady* in February, 1975. It was to be the first film of her two-picture deal with United Artists. She was excited about the movie: "I chose to do it because it was the first script since *Cabaret* that I really liked," she remembers. "And I must have read 400 scripts by then!"

Lucky Lady seemed like it would be a lucky film for Liza. She would receive top billing over co-stars Burt Reynolds and Gene Hackman, and Stanley Donen—most noted for his crowning M-G-M achievement *Singing in the Rain*—would direct. "It was also the first movie that featured three biggies with a woman in the middle!" Liza adds. "I would have done it for anything in the world!"

In the comedy, Liza played Claire Dobie, a floozy, down-on-her-luck, would-be singer with tangerine-colored hair, who becomes rich when she and her two cohorts (Reynolds and Hackman) illegally run booze to the West Coast during Prohibition. Like *Cabaret*, *Lucky Lady* took place in the thirties. Unlike *Cabaret*, *Lucky Lady* had trouble from day one.

For one thing, the press romantically linked Liza with Burt Reynolds. Movie magazines screamed with headlines: "Burt and Liza Are Lovers," "Lucky Lady Liza With Lucky Burt," "Unlucky Jack Haley, Junior." The truth is that Burt *was* having an affair—but with Liza's half-sister, Lorna Luft.

Liza introduced Burt—who had recently ended his long relationship with Dinah Shore—to Lorna. She would visit Burt on the Guaymas, Mexico, set, and the two would quietly slip off to dinner. (The romance fizzled soon after it began, and some say it was all a ploy to start Lorna's career rolling.)

Lorna's relationship with Burt was kept hush-hush until Liza, forced by Haley to announce the truth, broke the news. She defended herself by saying, "I haven't slept with anyone but my husband since I got married." And she also made frequent long-distance telephone calls to calm her spouse.

Then there was the problem of drinking water. There was no purified water for Liza to drink. "We finally did get some," she recalls, "but the Mexicans felt insulted because I wouldn't drink their water. I didn't want them to feel insulted, so I labeled mine 'cleaning fluid.'" The Mexicans did not like the visiting Americans and were, more often than not, quite hostile to them.

Finally, the planned three months of filming turned into six. Donen originally intended to shoot only the sea footage in Guaymas, but bad weather kept the crew and cast there much longer. Donen eventually used the time to shoot interiors.

"Guaymas," Liza recalls with a not-too-sweet smile on her face, "is not 'sort of dreadful.' It was *truly* dreadful! They shot *Catch 22* years before we shot *Lucky Lady* there—there was

The Lucky Lady *crew afloat. Robby Benson (far left) with the trio. One of the major reasons the film flopped was the ending, which director Stanley Donen changed after previewing the film across the country. "If Donen hadn't ruined the film," Reynolds explains, "Liza would have won another Oscar."*

A chunky Liza replaced her pal Gwen Verdon for five weeks in the Broadway musical Chicago, *in 1975. Chita Rivera (bottom corner) costarred. "Liza is amazing," Chita gushes. "She's all gusto, energy, talent and determination."*

nothing to do then, there was nothing for us to do either. It was very difficult for me to keep my energy level up from 6 A.M. to 6 P.M."

Most of *Lucky Lady* was shot on water and Liza, working six days a week, twelve hours a day, suffered from extreme seasickness. One Hollywood columnist reported the sickness as a pregnancy. When Liza heard the news, she laughed: "Everyone wants me pregnant!"

"It seemed as if I was on a boat all day," she recalls. "You know, when you get fifty-five people on a boat that's built for twelve, it's not exactly comfortable. I sat around and watched the tuna burp. There was nowhere to sit. I seemed to spend all my time lying on top of Burt with Gene's head in my lap. At the end of the day, everybody split and headed for their own little corner. We were all going stir-crazy; it was such a torture chamber. We just had to get away from each other."

Jack did whatever he could to help Liza relax. He visited every free weekend. "There was no TV in Guaymas," Liza remembers, "so Jack would put up a bedsheet, set up a 16mm projector and show movies to us." Liza claims she also took up painting: "I had to do *something*!"

Back in the United States, word was out that *Lucky Lady* (the title referred to the 60-foot schooner used in the film) was a dud. Some people quipped that the film stunk—and

not because one film base was located next door to a plant that turned sardine and shrimp rejects into animal feed.

Lucky Lady finally completed shooting, at a cost of $16 million, in Mexico City. Although it previewed across the country soon after, it did not open in New York until Christmas Day. It could have waited. Santa Claus delivered a bomb.

The critics sank *Lucky Lady*. "The film is a manic mess that tries to be all things to all people and ends up offering nothing to anyone," wrote Frank Rich in the *New York Post*. "[There are] a couple of incongruous Kander and Ebb songs that sound like those the team wrote for the equally dreadful *Funny Lady*. And Liza Minnelli—she might as well have been left behind. I've never much admired her in movies, but I think even a fan would agree that she is going to have to stop playing Sally Bowles if she intends to pursue a screen career. As the heroine of *Lucky Lady*, she generates so little eroticism that the film would have made more sense if Reynolds and Hackman fell for each other rather than her. At times, Minnelli's cuteness also makes her seem like the oldest child actor in show business."

Vincent Canby in *The New York Times*: "Miss Minnelli's Claire is neither funny nor sad, but an actress trying like hell to convince you she is. The more she tries, the worse she gets. Miss Minnelli's performance is a mistake in make-believe.

As a payback to her musical mentors John Kander and Fred
Ebb, Liza appeared in Sing Happy!, *a tribute to the songwriting
duo, held on November 12, 1978. Liza sang several of her
Kander-Ebb signatures, but the real audience treat was when
she teamed with Gwen Verdon and Chita Rivera to recreate
magical moments from* Chicago.

Lucky Lady is a misnomer of miscast and mismanaged comedy, an old-fashioned movie made out of new, cheap, synthetic material."

One critic, however, Jack Kroll in *Newsweek*, found Liza's performance riveting. "Minnelli is a born performer and a natural star," he wrote. "In *Lucky Lady*, she's better than she was in *Cabaret*, giving a tighter, harder, funnier, more knowing performance without the quality of yearning vulnerability. As Claire, she creates one of the most sheerly enjoyable female characters in years. [With her] outrageous print dresses, knock-kneed, loose-breasted voluptuousness, her sexy clown's face, Minnelli becomes the thinking man's Betty Boop. She is real fun."

Liza and Burt have publicly blamed director Donen for the film's failure. Donen, under pressure from studio executives, changed the ending of *Lucky Lady* several times. The original ending, shown to preview audiences, had Reynolds and Hackman killed by government agents. The film's final scene showed Liza, some ten years later, married to a rich but boring businessman, reminiscing about her colorful past.

"I always thought the original ending worked," says Alan Ladd, Junior, then head of production at Twentieth Century-Fox. "But Donen directed so well that the audiences didn't want the men to die. We didn't want to alienate any segment of the audience that would have found *Lucky Lady* too violent or too unhappy. People in the Midwest wanted a happy ending, so we changed it."

Liza was in Rome filming *A Matter of Time*, so Donen, Reynolds and Hackman flew to Italy one Saturday afternoon to shoot *Lucky Lady*'s new finale. Donen claims Liza knew what the final result would be. Still, she maintains the film was butchered.

"I was shocked and stunned by what Stanley did to the picture," Liza says. "It was not the same film I set out to make. The ending changed the whole tone of the picture — it was too light, without any real meaning. They cut out all the tender, meaningful scenes — all the film's guts — and now it's just as silly as an old *Road* picture with Crosby, Hope and Lamour."

Reynolds agrees with Liza. "Stanley Donen ruined the picture — it's an abomination! *Lucky Lady* could have been a classic and meant another Oscar for Liza. I'll never work with Donen again." Donen took all the comments in stride. "Liza is an emotional child," he says, "and I told them that if they didn't like it, they could lump it. I made *Lucky Lady* for the

millions of people who paid to see it. Not just to please a couple of actors."

Gene Hackman's stand on *Lucky Lady*? "I saw both Liza and Burt's points of view," he says, "but when it comes down to the final crunch, it's up to the director." The release of *Lucky Lady* was a flop, and Liza's first film failure.

Chicago

Shortly after she completed *Lucky Lady*, Liza received a call from John Kander and Fred Ebb. They were in trouble — rather, their new Broadway musical, *Chicago*, based on a real-life 1924 murder case, was in trouble — and they phoned for some advice. Gwen Verdon, the star of the show, was suddenly hospitalized for a "minor throat ailment." Kander and Ebb were afraid the show would fold unless they found someone else. "We just mentioned to Liza that we were in a spot," recalls Kander, "and she was the first one to come up with a suggestion." The suggestion? That *she* replace her pal Verdon.

Liza flew to New York, caught a performance of *Chicago* and immediately began rehearsals. She would take over the role of Roxie Hart on August 8, 1975, for five weeks. *Chicago* marked Liza's first appearance in a book musical since *Flora, the Red Menace*, one decade earlier.

"Liza did the show out of respect for Kander and Ebb," says Stanley Lebowsky, the show's musical conductor. "She's never forgotten what these men have done for her career. But she also did it for Bob [Fosse, *Chicago*'s director]. He was her dear friend and it was her payback."

Liza made one stipulation for her *Chicago* stint: she was to receive no official billing — although there was a lengthy bio in the show's souvenir program and a giant placard in the theater's lobby — and there would be no advertising. Liza did not want critics reviewing her work: she had learned the role in just six days and was afraid she would fall on her face.

At the time the substitution was announced to the media — tickets for the run sold out in twelve hours — Liza's press agent simply said, "Liza does not want to take the spotlight away from Gwen." But during her five-week run, Liza did manage to outshine her.

One song in *Chicago* — "My Own Best Friend" — was originally performed by both Verdon and her co-star, Chita Rivera. When Liza arrived, the tune became her solo.

The summer of 1975 was a hot and humid one, and Liza on Broadway made the temperature rise even more. Each night, an announcement was made over the loudspeaker of the Forty-sixth Street Theater: "Ladies and gentlemen, at tonight's performance the part of Roxie Hart will be played by Miss Liza Minnelli."

As the announcement was being made, the crowd would hoot and holler, and security guards would run to the edge of the stage to prevent rioting. One night, a man jumped on stage and ran after Liza. To protect her from overzealous fans that gathered at the stage door, the theater's management hired even more guards. But Liza was smart: she usually arrived at the theater very early and left very late. If fans were still waiting, she would don a hat and stroll out of the theater's lobby. Still, she would sometimes get caught—and the chase between star and her public would be on.

Chita Rivera remembers those days. "When Liza came in-

Liza always wanted to work with her father, and her dream came true when Vincente directed her in A Matter of Time. *Liza starred as Nina, a hotel chambermaid who becomes a movie star. When the film was released, Liza's dream turned into a critical nightmare.*

to the show," she says, "everything went *craz-zy!* Fans would try like hell to grab her on stage, to try and sneak backstage, *anything* to see her. It was phenomenal! I remember one night, as we were taking our final curtain calls, this girl jumped on stage. The curtain came down and she was still there. Liza screamed, 'Run, Chita!' I didn't know what was going on, and before I knew it, Liza was out of the damn theater! Then, this girl grabs *me!* I figured she wanted Liza's autograph, but no, she was holding scrapbooks of *my* career! What a hoot! I later told Liza and we laughed for *days.* Who would think someone wanted *me?* In those days, honey, *everyone* wanted Liza."

One of the severest flaws in A Matter of Time *was in its editing. Upon completion of the film, the producers withdrew it from Vincente's supervision. Thus, he was not allowed final cutting of* A Matter of Time, *and everyone's performance, including co-star Ingrid Bergman's, suffered. Liza was under great pressure during the filming. "I was afraid of kidnap threats so I had more security than anyone else," she recalls. Vincente was also protected. "I arranged it with the studio, but Daddy never knew it," Liza adds.*

116

For the first time in cinema history, the Minnelli team worked together: Liza as star, Vincente as director. "I always wanted to work with Daddy," Liza says. "And why not? He's a genius at what he does. He's a perfectionist and it shows in his work. From watching Daddy on the set, I learned not only about film, but about life."

(On the following page) Liza, looking amazingly like Judy, belts out the "Theme from New York, New York" in New York, New York. The number—one of the film's highlights—is a perfect example of Liza's style: a growl, a purr, a flick of the hand, a toss of the head and a thrust of the pelvis.

Rivera also remembers getting an acting lesson from Liza "I've been in musical theater a long time," she says, "and I figured I knew how to bow. Wrong! When Liza came in *Chicago*, she showed me how to *really* bow. You see, there are bows; then there are Liza bows."

At the end of her run, Liza threw a "closing night" party for the *Chicago* company at New York's St. Regis Hotel. Entertainment writer Earl Wilson estimated that the bash cost Liza anywhere from $10,000 to $15,000. Hundreds of people showed up and the party lasted until the wee hours of the morning. Liza says, "I had expected just a little intimate party, but we ended up in Versailles!" To show their appreciation for her help, the cast and crew gave Liza a silver onyx triangular pendant. The inscription read: "With love from *Chicago*." But it was Fred Ebb's that meant more to Liza: a solid gold charm in the shape of a Lifesaver.

A Matter of Time

Vincente Minnelli wanted to make a film with his daughter. He read Nancy Milford's best-selling book *Zelda*, and envisioned Liza as the tragic literary heroine. "The film had to be something right," says Vincente, "and *Zelda* was right; it was important." But it seemed that Vincente and Liza were not important enough—*Zelda* was unavailable for their use.

A little while later, father and daughter chanced upon *The Last Flapper*, a somewhat thinly disguised tale about (again) Zelda Fitzgerald, written by her husband, F. Scott Fitzgerald. Liza would star; Robert Redford would co-star. This too fell through. "The project was weighed down by unsolvable problems," recalls Vincente, "and it just couldn't get off the ground."

Some time later, along came *Film of Memory*. "When I first read the English translation of the Maurice Duron book, I felt it would make a marvelous picture," recalls Vincente. "The book had been optioned by several film producers over the past years, and whenever I got my offer in, it was either too little or too late. I had given up hope that I'd ever be involved with that lovely story. Then, in early 1973, it became available again. And though I hadn't seen Liza in the role at first," he adds, "she had grown to the point where the part would show still another facet of her extraordinary range. Liza, too, was crazy about the idea."

Interjects Liza: "I had been waiting to do a film with Daddy ever since I was five years old. It was a matter of finding the right subject. When I heard about *Film of Memory*, it was like a dream come true." Unfortunately, the dream would later turn into a nightmare.

Pre-production on *A Matter of Time*—the film's working titles had been *Carmella* and *Nina*—began in the fall and winter of 1973. Actual filming, however, did not take place until early winter, 1975. In the film, Liza plays doe-eyed Carmella (Nina), a nineteen-year-old hotel chambermaid who befriends an aging Contessa, who once was the toast of Europe. The Contessa spends her last days in the decaying squalor of a seedy Rome hotel, living on the memories of yesteryear, and living vicariously through Carmella, who eventually becomes a big film star. Ingrid Bergman played the Contessa, though it was reported both Katherine Hepburn and Pola Negri wanted the role.

Vincente Minnelli was sure *A Matter of Time* would be a huge success. Why not? Geoffrey Unsworth, the genius cameraman from *Cabaret*, was on the film's crew; Charles Boyer would have a cameo (it would be his last film) and John Kander and Fred Ebb were writing two new songs for Liza (she also would sing the Gershwin classic, "Do It Again"). John Gay was writing the screenplay; he had to, Terrence Rattigan's original manuscript was unsuitable. Perhaps that's when Vincente should have smelled trouble.

A Matter of Time ran into more problems in Italy where strikes and delays added months of extra work to the production schedule. "The film labs decided not to work before the holidays," Liza remembers, "and they ruined six days' worth of film. For the first time in my life, I saw Daddy blow his top." In addition to the Italian problems, Liza would be away from the set for days at a stretch. She was in America trying to salvage *Lucky Lady*.

When she was on the set, Liza handled her free time well. She rushed all over Rome, sending her three burly bodyguards into quick pursuit. One day she popped into Perugina for some chocolate; the next day she would be at Wendy's munching a fast-order burger. Still on other days, she feasted on champagne and crêpes suzette at the elite Excelsior Hotel. She even found time for social obligations. One night she partied till dawn at Donald Sutherland's villa, where she also sang for three hours, much to the shocked delight of the other invited guests. Husband Jack Haley, Junior, felt he had nothing to worry about: Sutherland, like Roger Moore—who spent several Roman evenings with Liza—was no threat.

Liza enjoyed filming New York, New York. *Not only did she have a chance to play a character she liked—big-band singer Francine Evans—but she also had the opportunity to star opposite Robert DeNiro (above). Though he had a reputation for being a recluse, DeNiro became close friends with Liza. Her relationship with him remained platonic. DeNiro and Liza again teamed up for the 1982 film,* The King of Comedy. *In* Comedy, *DeNiro starred as aspiring comic Rupert Pupkin, who just happened to keep a cardboard cutout of Liza in his basement. In the film, Liza received credit for playing herself. In* New York, New York, *DeNiro learned to "finger" play the saxophone from music master George Auld (left). DeNiro grew so obsessed with the sax that his wife Diahnne Abbott, who also appeared in NY, NY, remarked: "I thought Bobby was going to climb into bed with that horn!"*

Liza would call Jack on Sundays. "It was cheaper that way," she explains. Yet Liza never really felt away from home: her dressing room walls were covered with family photographs and, at night, Liza slept on luxurious, expensive Porthault sheets.

The biggest problem with *A Matter of Time* came at post-production—the editing. The producers withdrew the film from Vincente's supervision after the first assemblage (it was running nearly three hours long) and the director was not allowed the final edit. Subsequently, he disowned the film.

It is no wonder the critics disowned it too. David Sterritt in *The Christian Science Monitor*: "Liza sings her three songs strongly, does a lot of wide-eyed mugging and wears plenty of fancy outfits. But she never becomes more than Miss Bergman's second banana. *A Matter of Time* falls flat and it looks choppy. Even Rome looks stale. The Minnelli team is a losing one."

The film opened at Manhattan's Radio City Music Hall on October 7, 1976. Vincent Canby, in *The New York Times*, was a bit kinder: "The film is full of glittery costumes and spectacular props. Its principal star is Liza Minnelli, whose appearance recalls her father and whose voice and mannerisms recall her mother. She has talent of her own, but it comes through to us through the presence of others. Liza's eyes seem to have been widened surgically to play this part. *A Matter of Time* has moments of real visual beauty, but because what the characters say to each other is mostly dumb, it may be a film to attend while wearing your earplugs."

Upon completing the film, the late Ingrid Bergman said, "I can take my name off it, but I can't take my face off it." The film was never shown in France, Charles Boyer's native land. With the release of *A Matter of Time*, Liza had two film flops behind her. One more, she thought, and I'm out.

However, Liza did have some consolation. That year she had made a cameo appearance in Mel Brooks' film *Silent Movie*, a June–July, 1976, release. In the slapstick farce—which was much better received than *A Matter of Time*—Liza played a parody of herself, one of the five stars Mel Funn (Brooks) tries to sign for his upcoming silent epic. Paul Newman, Anne Bancroft, James Caan and Burt Reynolds were the other four *Silent Movie* cameos.

As she is trying to eat her lunch, Liza is pounced upon by Funn, Marty Eggs (the late Marty Feldman) and Dom Bell (Dom DeLuise)—the trio is dressed in armor. Penelope Gilliatt, in *The New Yorker*, called this scene "a joy to the kids in the audience." Liza's appearance in *Silent Movie* is so short (she receives no screen credit) that many of her fans do not even know she is in it.

※　※　※

On the surface, Liza and Jack seemed happy. They house-hunted together. Jack's California bachelor pad was too small for both of them, and their Central Park South penthouse apartment wasn't sufficient enough. Liza eventually bought jewelry designer Kenneth J. Lane's Murray Hill townhouse on East Thirty-eighth Street for $390,000—but Liza sold it before she ever moved in! Jack did everything for his wife and met all her whims. When Liza missed her cocker spaniel puppy, Hedy (after Miss Lamarr), Jack flew the dog to her. Jack and Liza even shared billing on Liza's red Rolls-Royce: the license plate read LIJACK.

Both Liza and Jack were well aware of the gossip that was being spread behind their backs. And both were ready to fight it.

Liza and Jack began by announcing their desire for children. "Any woman who's in love with a man wants to have his children," Liza said. "Jack gave me the greatest gift a man can give a woman—his name. I want to carry it on. And though this may sound old-fashioned, I'm happy being married to the most wonderful man in the world." Yet sometimes Liza's domestic avowals seemed rather forced: "Jack and I sit home a lot and watch TV. I also like to cook for him. I enjoy cooking because that's part of being a woman and wife."

Still, the Haleys were separated for long periods of time. Jack's new position as president of Twentieth Century-Fox Television kept him away from Liza quite frequently. "When we were first married," Jack recalls, "we had to be apart while Liza made *Lucky Lady*. Then she went to Rome for *A Matter of Time*. I had to stay in Los Angeles and only saw her occasionally. It was a strain—a physical hurt—but we knew it had to be this way. We knew [the separations would] never be pleasant," he adds, "but we never thought they'd be intolerable."

"Start Spreading the News..."

New York, New York. It is one of Liza's favorite cities. "I love it so much," she says. "It's the only place where I can be totally anonymous. It's full of new people, new ideas, new brainwaves. There's that onslaught of glamor, all the great parties and, of course, that New York sense of humor. Then, when I found out that Elizabeth [Taylor] was moving back to New York, I knew that was it. After all, I *knew* Elizabeth wouldn't stick around a dull place."

New York, New York is also one of Liza's favorite films. "Martin Scorsese [the film's director] mentioned *New York, New York* to me more than two years before we made it," Liza recalls. "At that time, it was a man's story, telling how he went from bandleader to record producer in the early years of rock 'n' roll. I told Marty I'd be interested in the film if the girl's role was beefed up. I wanted to see what went on *behind* the bandstand."

Scorsese agreed, and *New York, New York*, an $8.5 million tale of a post-World War II romance between a big-band singer (Liza) and a jazz saxophonist (Robert DeNiro) was born.

Liza began researching her role as Francine Evans in 1975. During breaks from filming *Lucky Lady*, Liza would breeze through the stacks of 1940s movie magazines that were piled in the living room of her oceanside cottage, studying the looks and fashions of the time. Scorsese also offered guidance; he occasionally flew to Guaymas to discuss the script. Some say this is when their romance began; the romance that climaxed with *The Act*.

Liza remembers the rest of her *New York, New York* research. "I borrowed Sammy Davis, Junior's collection of albums from that era," she says, "and listened to them for hours. I also studied film clips of big bands and talked to lots of knowledgeable people so I could get my brain completely immersed in the forties."

Liza also watched dozens of old movie musicals, including her mother's and father's collaboration, *The Clock*. "I saw all of Daddy's films," Liza proudly says, "and many of Mama's." Godmother Kay Thompson also helped by offering Liza long-distance singing lessons. Liza supplemented those "by borrowing a lot from singers like Lena Horne, Doris Day and Helen O'Connell. But I never tried to imitate any of them. They just, well, gave me a sound."

Liza also found inspiration in British jazz singer Cleo Laine. Laine—whose long marriage to saxophonist John Dankworth is, some say, the basis for *New York, New York*—remembers the day Liza called her. "Lisa," Laine says in her heavy guttural accent (she's the only one who can get away with calling Liza "Lisa"), "told me she was studying our records as she made the picture."

Robert DeNiro also researched his role. The actor was taught by music master George Auld how to hold and properly finger a saxophone. In March, 1976, DeNiro and Scorsese (along with the film's other musicians) went to study Liza in concert during her Lake Tahoe gig. Later, DeNiro and Scorsese escaped to her dressing room, where they spoke notes into a tape recorder.

Liza liked her role of Francine. "For the first time in my life," she says, "I didn't play a kook. Francine was just a nice, intelligent girl-woman, who also happened to be tough and ruthless. I understood her because I knew women like her in Hollywood. Yet Francine was never crazy. Bobby [DeNiro] was the wacky one for a change!"

Filming began in early 1976 and *New York, New York* took nearly twenty-two weeks to complete. "The script wasn't right at first," Liza recalls, "so Marty asked us to improvise. We had to think the story out as we went along, and for weeks, all we did was rehearse while Marty videotaped us. He then took the best moments from those tapes and gave us that dialogue. We were all under great duress, three people going bananas every day. It was exciting," but Liza adds, "it was also exhilarating. I can't even remember sitting down for the whole time. I always said, 'If I drop dead making this movie, it'll be a great way to go.'"

Liza lost twenty-two pounds while filming and sometimes had to film her close-ups at 4 A.M. During one scene in which Scorsese showed DeNiro how to slug a "pregnant" Minnelli, the action was so intense that all three ended up in a hospital's emergency room with accidental injuries. No one was seriously injured, and filming continued the next day.

Despite its rigorous schedule, *New York, New York* was a pleasant experience for Liza. Some of the film was shot on Stage 29, the same stage set where Judy Garland filmed *The Pirate*. Liza also had her mother's old M-G-M dressing room. One spacious room was totally furnished in green—from the sofa to the rug to the wallpaper. Sally Bowles would have been proud.

Her hair was being styled by Sidney Gulleroff, who first did Liza's hair when she was six. "I could not believe how closely Liza resembled Marilyn Monroe," Gulleroff recalls. "They had the same nose, same smile, same expression in the eyes. It was eerie."

Theodora Van Runkle was designing Liza's costumes.

"Thea's clothes—with the pagoda shoulders—were so feminine," Liza says, "and so flattering."

Liza also became close to DeNiro, who has a reputation for being a recluse, during the making of *New York, New York*. "Everyone thought Bobby was so introverted," Liza explains, "but it was just that he saw things a little bit differently than we did." There were rumors that Liza was having an affair with DeNiro. Not true. DeNiro was happily married to Diahnne Abbott, a black singer who had a cameo in *New York, New York*. Abbott was also pregnant at the time.

New York, New York promised to be a grandiose picture, a movie's movie, an icon of Hollywood and a lavish throwback to the forties. Liza would sing lots of songs—from "The Man I Love" to "You Are My Lucky Star" to "Just You, Just Me." Kander and Ebb also wrote several new songs for Liza, including "But the World Goes 'Round" and the tune that would become her trademark—her "Over the Rainbow"—"New York, New York." Ironically, Liza's single of "New York, New York" never made the charts. Frank Sinatra later recorded the song on his *Trilogy* album, and many people considered it "his" song. When Liza found out that "New York, New York" was not nominated for an Academy Award for Best Song, she was deeply hurt.

New York, New York did not open quietly in New York City; rather it premiered lavishly, just like a real 1940s musical. On June 22, 1977, the eighth anniversary of Judy's death, *New York, New York* was shown at a fund-raising gala for the Film Society of Lincoln Center. After the screening, the star-studded audience dined and danced at the Rainbow Grill, before winding up the event, the next morning, at a breakfast party Halston threw at Studio 54. That night, Liza, dressed in a transparent red dress and locked on the arm of Jack Haley, Junior, was awarded a Steuben Glass Apple Award for her contributions to the entertainment industry. Nevertheless, all the glitter could not blind the critics to the film's flaws. *New York, New York* was greeted by mixed reviews; most of them tipped to the negative. The *Saturday Review*: "At two hours, thirty-five minutes—an hour too much—*New York, New York* doesn't come off. But it does offer Liza Minnelli at her most charismatic (with moments as a reincarnation of her mother, Judy Garland) and enough niceness to provide passable entertainment."

New York, New York was indeed long, but now when one considers that the rough cut was originally almost twice as long. When Scorsese trimmed the film, he edited out some of Liza's dance sequences, including the $350,000, twelve-minute production number, "Happy Endings." (The mini-epic co-starred Larry Kent and boasted a cameo by Liza's father-in-law, Jack Haley, Senior.) For awhile, the film's co-producer, Irwin Winkler, toyed with the idea of releasing "Happy Endings" as a short.

On Friday, June 19, 1981, United Artists rereleased *New York, New York* with the "Happy Endings" number intact. For a second time, the reviews were tepid, and United Artists promptly pulled it from distribution. (To this day, Liza maintains *New York, New York* is "my best work.")

Other *New York, New York* reviews: Penelope Gilliatt in *The New Yorker*: "Martin Scorsese has made some very fine pictures, but this is not one of them. There is the initial plagiarism of a title and an era, the facetiousness of the dialogue and the ersatz nourishment that the story offers filmgoers homesick for the movies of thirty years ago. Liza Minnelli [does] a shameless copy of her mother. *New York, New York* is *Ho Hum, Ho Hum*."

Stanley Kauffmann in *The New Republic*: "*New York, New York* is one more of the current avalanche of disappointing U.S. films. They tried to make a tough sentimental show biz story with lots of period songs and some new songs… but the sentiment doesn't take, and what's left isn't tough, it's occasionally repellent, but mostly tedious and trite. The picture, faults and all, might have been pleasant if it had some charm. Liza Minnelli has none, ever."

Liza feverishly insisted that she would never exploit her mother, yet in *New York, New York* she does. In the final number, "New York, New York," Liza looks shockingly like Judy, and in other sequences, she is a near-perfect facsimile of Judy from *The Clock* and *Meet Me in St. Louis*. Critics picked up on this repeatedly, including Kauffmann in *The New Republic*.

"Martin Scorsese," he wrote, "says that some people complain that Minnelli reminds them of her mother, Judy Garland, but there's nothing he can do about that. Two things he could have done in her last song are: not give her, or permit, hyperdramatic Garland gestures; not give her a costume that strongly suggests Garland's costume from the 'Get Happy' number of *Summer Stock*."

When confronted with this excessive amount of Garland necrophilia, Scorsese becomes abrupt. "You put a wig on Liza," he shouts, "and she looks like her mother! What can I tell you!" Some people insist that Scorsese was so obsessed with Judy Garland that he purposely directed Liza, both in *New York, New York* and *The Act*, as if Liza were Judy.

Still, there were some critics who loved *New York, New York*. "Minnelli is overpowering in a scene in which she's recording 'But the World Goes 'Round,'" wrote *Newsweek* magazine's Jack Kroll. "Here the double focus is perfect: the dynamic singer is both Liza Minnelli and Judy Garland, it's not pastiche, but a moving synthesis of old and new. Liza is a human Art Deco doll, and *New York, New York* is a flawed gem." The film has now reached a cult status among select film fans, who see the work as a prime example of musical *film noir*.

Liza reflects on *New York, New York*: "In 1975, I figured I could afford to do the movie. Then, suddenly, I started it and realized that if *New York, New York* was a turkey, I would be in a lot of trouble because, oh Mama! in Hollywood, you're not allowed to have three bad pictures in a row."

Liza carefully decided to get her act together. That's why, during the shooting of *New York, New York*, she decided to do a Broadway musical called *The Act*. She felt it would pacify her if and when *New York, New York* fell flat on its face.

Getting Her Act Together

The Act had its early beginnings in 1975. George Furth, the man responsible for writing the Broadway hits *Twigs* and *Company*, had written a backstage drama about a once-famous singer named Michelle Craig. During her Las Vegas nightclub act debut, Craig flashes back to her personal and professional triumphs and failures; the book was an ambiguous *roman à clef* about any number of stars, including Judy Garland. It boasted sex, abortions, extramarital affairs, homosexuality and death; all the proper ingredients to assure a success. Furth showed the book to Marvin Hamlisch, who agreed to write the score. Stars like Doris Day, Mary Tyler Moore, Debbie Reynolds, Shirley MacLaine and Cloris Leachman were mentioned for the lead.

While filming *New York, New York*, Liza heard about Furth's work. Now, however, there were some changes: Hamlisch was out, Kander and Ebb were in and Ron Lewis was signed to make his theatrical choreography debut. Liza wanted in. "It was the best Broadway part for a woman in years," she says.

Furth rewrote the script, tailoring the role of Michelle to fit Liza. (Michelle Craig was now a 31-year-old singer.) Liza had one additional demand: she wanted Martin Scorsese to direct.

While he began work on *The Act*, Scorsese was also putting final touches on *New York, New York* as well as editing his rock documentary, *The Last Waltz*. Scorsese also wanted to make *The Act* a sequel to *New York, New York*, but quickly regained his senses.

By the time *The Act* rehearsals were underway in Los Angeles (the show was then called *In Person*), Liza was deeply involved with Scorsese—he was married at the time to *New York, New York* writer, Julia Cameron.

Jack Haley, Junior insisted there was no romance (he believed Liza when she called him "my only man"), and was said to have bought his wife a bauble every time a columnist linked Liza and Martin. The affair was confirmed in August of 1977—the morning after *The Act* opened in Los Angeles—when Julia Cameron sued her husband for divorce. Liza was cited in her court petition. No one was surprised, though they suspected Liza and Martin would now marry. It was Cameron, then pregnant with Scorsese's child, who had taught Liza her "pregnancy lessons" for *New York, New York*.

Troubles began with *In Person* in Chicago, where the show, now called *Shine It On*, opened on July 4, 1977. Critics hated the show. "They were the worst goddamn notices," recalls Cy Feuer, one of the show's producers. *Shine It On* was produced through the facilities of the Los Angeles and San Francisco Civic Light Opera Companies.

Theodora Van Runkle, who had so successfully designed the costumes for *New York, New York*, again clothed Liza, but this time her creations were deemed "sadistic." When this criticism broke, Liza quickly summoned Halston to the rescue, at a tune of nearly $100,00. While her new costumes were being made, Liza performed in other Halston creations—straight from her personal wardrobe.

Stanley Lebowsky, the musical conductor for the show, recalls Van Runkle's original costumes. "Thea was not a stage designer, but a film designer," he says. "When she was told to design costumes for the show's gypsies [slang for the dancers in a Broadway show], Thea actually designed costumes for *real* Spanish gypsies! She had no idea what she was doing, so you can imagine how hideous Liza's clothes were."

After the onslaught of devastating reviews, more work was called for. Song and dance numbers were shifted; new dialogue was added. Furth wrote at least one dozen revisions of his original script. A new set—adding approximately $80,000 to the show's costs—was built.

Recalls Wayne Cilento, one of the show's dancers and the

Liza and New York, New York *director Martin Scorsese may have begun their affair while the film was in production. Liza was still married to Jack Haley, Junior and denied a romance, although Julia Cameron, Scorsese's wife at the time, later named Liza in her divorce court petition. Scorsese and Robert DeNiro flanked Liza at the lavish world-premiere of* NY, NY *at Manhattan's Lincoln Center in June, 1977 (right). Scorsese later directed Liza in the musical* The Act *(following page). When the lackluster show limped onto Broadway, their romance was just about over, and Liza was basking in the adulation of other celebrities, including backstage visitors Jacqueline Onassis, Irving "Swifty" Lazar and Bianca Jagger (below).*

man who later co-choreographed Liza's Carnegie Hall triumph, "So much went on that we were always forgetting whether we were going forward or backward!" Even with the biting notices, the Chicago run was a complete sell-out—for only one reason: Liza.

The show then moved to San Francisco; the flaring tempers, reworked material, sold-out performances and bad reviews followed. Stanley Eichelbaum of the *San Francisco Examiner* declared *Shine It On* in need of "major overhauling."

It received some from Michael Bennett and Ron Field. The two prominent Broadway directors were called in to take a look at *Shine It On* while it was still playing in San Francisco. They attended opening night and sat in side aisle seats in the twenty-third row. They did not like what they saw.

A few nights later, Field and Bennett met with Liza, Scorsese, Kander and Ebb and others involved with *Shine It On*. They stayed up well past dawn, devising methods to salvage the show. Director Scorsese took notes but, several days later, incorporated his own ideas into the show. They did not work. "Marty is a terrific little guy," says Cy Feuer, "but he's a *film* genius. *The Act* was theater." The show marked Scorsese's theatrical directorial debut.

One of the major stumbling blocks with the show was that Liza refused to let Scorsese be replaced. "If he goes," Liza supposedly said, "I go too." Rumors of their romance grew stronger; there were reports of hand-holding in local San Francisco restaurants, and investors began to worry. Would the show make it to New York?

"Liza's contract gave her the final say on *everything*," recalls one production head who requires anonymity, "including whether Scorsese was canned. At first, people wanted him off the show; later those same people thought it might be a good idea if he stayed around because of their relationship. It was like Liza was out there working for Marty. The only problem was that she was excessively loyal, and loved, perhaps, too blindly."

After its San Francisco run, *Shine It On*—now called *The Act*—moved into Los Angeles's Dorothy Chandler Pavilion. Disaster—in the form of criticism—struck again. KNBC-TV: "George Furth tries to give us some insight on how Michelle got unemployed, but there was more insight on *Ozzie and Harriet*. After three hours, not only does the show need a new book, but you need a new backside."

One of the more stinging barbs came from *Los Angeles*

Times writer Dan Sullivan: "*The Act* is the dumbest backstage musical ever, even to the point where you figure they've got to be kidding."

Three weeks into the sold-out Los Angeles engagement, Scorsese was out of *The Act*. He had suffered a severe asthmatic attack—some say the timing was perfect although the attack was merely mild—and the late Gower Champion was called in to doctor the ailing show. "Marty's illness was handy," admits producer Feuer, "so we decided to use it."

"I had nothing to do with Marty going," Liza insists. "He came in and told me, 'I know you're going to trust me. I will not let you open in New York as anything less than super. You've never worked with Gower, but we need help. Gower can add something terrific and I want only the best for you.' It's not," Liza adds, "like Marty stormed off somewhere to Italy [where the director had gone on a film deal]. The show was always on his mind."

Gower Champion received no credit for his contribution to *The Act*, although he was responsible for its new look. After watching the September 24 matinee and evening performances, he rehearsed the cast the following day, and on Monday night, September 26, inserted several changes. A new opening and the show-stopping finale of "City Lights" were in. Out were Michelle Craig's abortion scene, the scenes in which she loses two Oscars, and eleven minutes of the overture. The Los Angeles run completed, Champion felt ready for New York. Liza was still unsure.

The Act in New York: Liza's Illnesses

New York was waiting for Liza. Advance ticket sales were estimated at $2 million; a staggering amount even though *The Act* was charging $25—a first in theater history—for its top-priced ticket. It seems everyone wanted to catch Liza in the act; after all, they had been reading about the show's out-of-town tribulations for months.

At the time, not everyone was happy with the expensive ducats. "As much as I like Liza," said theater *wunderkind* Joseph Papp, "I think you have to draw a distinction between Liza's show and serious theater." At the time *The Act* opened, other Broadway shows were charging about $8 less per ticket. A British playwright remarked: "That's what happens when movie stars bring their greedy ways to the theater."

The Act opened at the Majestic Theater on Saturday, October 29, 1977. It was a night to remember; a night right out of

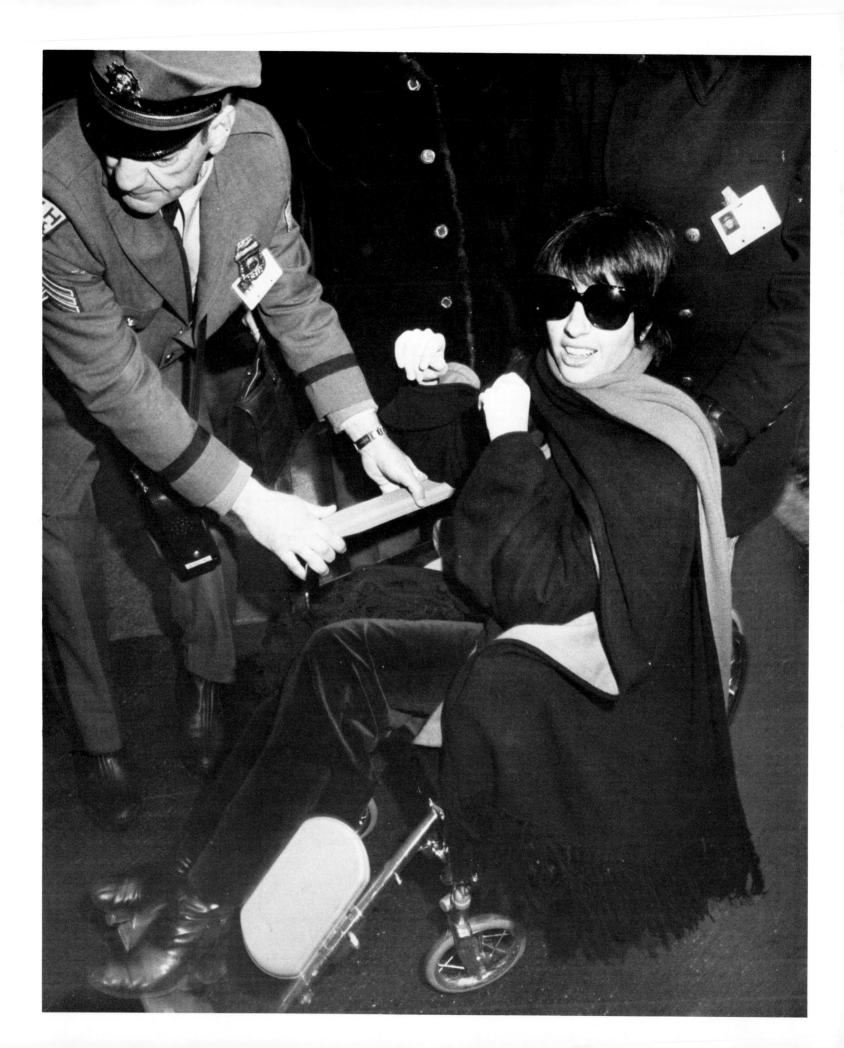

It took a long time for Liza to get her act together. Late night partying, combined with The Act's exhausting numbers, led to a breakdown in Liza's health. On January 18, 1978, Liza—still looking every inch the star—was wheeled into New York Hospital (left). It was only one of Liza's many sicknesses during the run of the show. "Was Liza burning out like Judy?" the public asked; the producers said "no." They "proved" it by showing a recovered Liza reading her fan mail in the Majestic's dressing room (above). What many fans didn't know was that by 1978, Liza rarely saw—let alone answered—fan mail.

Day of the Locust. Mounted police struggled with the shrieking hoards of fans and autograph hounds seeking glimpses of the luminous first-nighters: Elizabeth Taylor, Bob Fosse, Ethel Merman, Sammy Davis, Junior, Martha Graham, Dick Cavett, Phyllis George, Andy Warhol, Desi Arnaz, Junior, Jule Styne, Jack Haley, Senior (and Junior), Pete Hamill and Halston.

After the standing ovations that greeted Liza's final curtain, these select guests, along with nearly 600 others, attended the $40,000 black-tie opening-night party at Central Park's Tavern on the Green. The bash was paid for by *The Act*'s presenters, the Shubert Organization. Tickets for the fete went for $35 each; Halston bought twenty-seven for his pals.

Liza, wearing a black diaphanous gown and accompanied by three bodyguards, arrived at exactly 1 A.M. and was immediately greeted by a standing ovation. She looked stunning and, later, admitted she was relieved that *The Act* finally made it to Broadway—even if it limped there.

At 3:30 A.M., when she noticed that the band was preparing to leave, Liza convinced them to stay until 5:30 A.M. As a thank-you, Liza sang "More Than You Know" and foxtrotted with a guest.

"Have you ever seen me better?" she asked the crowd. "I was absolutely at my best tonight!" No one disagreed. Elizabeth Taylor: "She was beautiful!" Halston: "She revived theater that night!" Jack gave his wife a 14-karat gold Valium. Only Bob Fosse reserves comments about Liza's *The Act* opening. "I'm such a pushover for her that I can't be objective," he explains. "There were things I didn't like, but they weren't her fault."

Martin Scorsese kept his promise and also caught the show. "The evening was quite beautiful," he recalls, "really quite beautiful." Liza's romance with the director was ebbing at this point; in fact, towards the end of the opening-night party, she and Jack joined Scorsese and his guests—his parents and daughter Catherine—at his table.

Liza insists she was not nervous on opening night, despite all the pressures around her. "I just put my mind in the right place," she remembers. "But seeing the funny side was important too. The week I opened, Donny and Marie Osmond were on the cover of *People*. Everywhere I went, I passed newsstands and smiling up at me were the Osmonds. So, on opening night, I got the usual crate of good luck telegrams, but my favorite one read, 'Do it for Donny and Marie!'"

Liza worked hard in *The Act*. She sang eleven of the score's twelve songs, and was on stage for all but four minutes of the show. Shortly after *The Act* opened, one song, "Hollywood, California," was cut. As she did with her one-woman show *Liza* at the Winter Garden three years earlier, Liza also used "lip-sync" in *The Act*.

Critics greeted Liza's performance with enthusiasm, but few found *The Act* worthy of praise. Richard Eder in *The New York Times*: "*The Act* is precisely what its name implies," he wrote, "and it displays the breathtaking presence of Liza Minnelli. But George Furth's book is not just thin, it pretends to be there. It has little development or characterization of its own; and except for a stray line or two, [it has] only the most trite and synthetic dialogue. Still, Minnelli's voice comes tearing out exuberantly in the opening 'Shine It On,' it comes out in the tearing, bitter 'The Money Tree' and in the quiet 'There Where I Need Him.'"

Rex Reed called the show "an exhausting triumph"; John Simon, in his scathing *New York* review, dubbed it "Liza with a Zzzz." Douglas Watts, in the New York *Daily News*, found great fault with Liza's talents. "She is only a fair singer," he wrote. "She began as a flagrant imitator of Barbra Streisand, and gradually leaned more and more to her mother's style so that she's now an amalgam of the two. She's only a fair dancer and, let's face it, not exactly a knockout."

Nevertheless, Liza's fans loved the show, even if they saw it as nothing more than Liza in concert (no one ever really followed the "plot"). At just about all performances, people would scream "We love you, Liza!" and "Sing 'Cabaret!'." More than once, Liza would step to the apron of the stage and announce, "My name is Michelle Craig." John Kander observed, "It was very difficult for the audience to separate Michelle from Liza." There were even reports that while she sang the Garlandesque "City Lights," some people screamed "We love you, Judy!"

The problems began on Thursday, December 8, just after *The Act* opened. Liza was sleeping (in the nude) at her penthouse apartment at Forty Central Park South when a fire broke out in the draperies at 12:42 P.M. Firefighters quickly had the fire—which did little damage—under control. When they arrived—Liza had picked up the phone and told the operator what was happening—Liza exclaimed "Wait! I have no clothes on!" She then rushed into the bathroom while they extinguished the flames.

Liza's publicist at the time insisted the fire was caused by faulty wiring; others insisted (just as loudly) that Liza had fallen asleep with a cigarette. Liza suffered smoke inhalation and, upon her doctor's request, could not sing for twenty-four hours. Liza was thus forced to cancel that night's performance of *The Act*.

It was the first of many missed shows. On Wednesday afternoon, December 21, Liza showed up for the matinee performance of *The Act*. She had a temperature of 104°. When the backstage crew saw how ill she was, a doctor was summoned, and he immediately sent Liza home. Liza—in bed with a virus and a bronchial infection—missed one week of performances.

The management began to sweat. *The Act* was a star vehicle; Liza could not be replaced. So they announced that they would either refund tickets, switch them for another Broadway show or exchange them for a future *The Act* performance. One ticket holder was Jacqueline Onassis, who was supposed to see the show on Wednesday night, December 21. When she heard Liza was ill, she chose to see the comedy *Sly Fox* instead. A few weeks later, she made it back and caught Liza's act.

Liza's one-week illness cost *The Act*'s producers nearly $193,000. At this time, Liza also requested Monday nights off—she claimed the demands of eight performances a week were too stressful for her. But tickets had been sold so far in advance that Liza's request had to wait.

On January 14, 1978, the "flu bug" bit Liza again—she missed two performances that day; her no-show total was now twelve—and producers, losing nearly $30,000 a show, decided to close *The Act* for two weeks. The shut-down brought the losses to over $750,000, and ads were placed in newspapers guaranteeing Liza's January 30 return.

Liza moved out of her Central Park South penthouse apartment and into a hotel suite. "My doctors advised me to keep away from anybody I didn't want to give the flu to," she told reporters. Gossip columnists suggested that Liza was indeed sick—of Jack, and thus the move.

On the morning of January 18, Liza was whisked off to New York Hospital to determine the underlying cause of her lingering illness. Liza thought she had pneumonia because of the excessive amounts of mucus in her chest. Fans would call the hospital every hour of the day; the more devoted sent letters and flowers.

Only Jack Haley, Junior, and Lois Smith (Liza's press agent at the time) were allowed to visit. Haley would pop into Liza's tower room (it had a magnificent view of the East River) almost every day, bringing his wife lollipops in the shape of hearts and other tokens of his affection. After Jack left, Liza would watch television or read.

While at New York Hospital, Liza did not want to wear the obligatory hospital gown, so she changed into lace-trimmed cream-colored pajamas. She knew she was going to be brought in for a battery of tests—from an EKG to blood tests to X-rays—and Liza wanted to look every inch the Star.

When the tests were read, it was discovered that Liza was suffering from a severe viral infection. "Liza was so sick," Jack Haley, Junior, recalls, "that she didn't even know the days of the week."

On January 23, less than one week after her New York Hospital stay, Liza flew to the Greenhouse, an exclusive $1,500-a-week spa near Dallas, Texas. She returned to New York—and to *The Act*—one week later, looking radiant from her twelve-pound weight loss.

"The people at the Greenhouse didn't bother me," Liza remembers. "I slept, ate [she was on a 500-calorie-a-day diet] and relaxed." Liza immediately went into rehearsals and Halston refitted Liza's gowns.

The Act's producers milked Liza's return for all its worth. Liza was photographed in her Majestic dressing room, reading fan mail; local news stations covered the major event. The hype worked—ticket sales remained on a standing-room-only basis.

Even when Liza returned to *The Act*, there were still problems. At times she would forget her lyrics and start the songs over. Then, on several occasions, Liza arrived so late at the theater that the 8 P.M. curtain was held for thirty minutes. Immediately the press picked up on her actions and, less than kindly, suggested that she was "burning out" just like Judy. On Thursday, March 2, Liza suffered from a gastric infection so severe, she says, "that it left me too weak to stand." Ann-Margret and Walter Cronkite had tickets that night. Again, *The Act* was cancelled. Miraculously, Liza returned the next night. Ann-Margret did not.

There are those who suggest Liza's bouts with sickness during the run of *The Act* were not always true; some swear they saw her dancing at Studio 54 the same night she had called in sick. Liza defends herself by insisting she never went to

Studio 54 as often as people reported. "I'm a party person," she says.

Barry Nelson, Liza's co-star in *The Act*, maintains that all of Liza's illnesses were real. "There were times when she was so sick that we had to restrain her from going on. She always felt guilty if she missed a show. Liza's job was a lot harder than mine—she carried double the volume of work. Somebody once said that a performer leaves bits of flesh on the stage after a show, I say Liza left some bones too."

Liza's involvement with *The Act* was worth the trouble she went through. On May 15, 1978, she was nominated for her third Tony Award as Best Actress in a Musical. On the night she heard the news, Liza popped into Charlie's, a theatrical restaurant across the street from the Majestic Theater's stage door, and dined on Bullshots (next to Grand Marnier, a Bullshot—beef broth and vodka—is Liza's favorite drink). Just before showtime, she crossed West Forty-fifth Street and walked the short distance to the theater. She entered through the stage door, signed in and nodded to the stage manager. His name was Mark Gero.

Leaving Jack

After months of speculation, Liza Minnelli and Jack Haley Junior, officially separated on February 24, 1978. They had been married for nearly four years and lawyer Mickey Rudin proclaimed the separation "amicable." Liza's friends insisted her workout in *The Act* caused the split. Others blamed Liza's love affair with ballet superstar Mikhail Baryshnikov. Liza met Misha during the run of *The Act*. Not only did she find him breathtakingly beautiful, but Liza was enraptured by his agile dancer's body. Soon after they met, the couple began a whirlwind, secretive romance. While Misha was performing in Washington, D.C., Liza would complete her show, fly to D.C., arrive back in New York the following day, catch some sleep, repeat *The Act* and, again, fly to Washington.

The reckless ritual continued for some time until Misha realized he just could not sacrifice his career for Liza's more undisciplined life style. Misha would later have a widely-publicized romance with actress Jessica (Tootsie) Lange, who gave birth to Baryshnikov's illegitimate daughter, Alexandra, in March, 1981.

Jack Haley, Junior, moved out of the Central Park South penthouse and sublet another apartment—in the same building! Liza did not want to stay in the same building,

however, so she slept at her old East Fifty-seventh Street apartment. Although Jack and Liza called their breakup "temporary," Jack filed a court petition for dissolution of their marriage on April 20.

He had had—and had seen—enough. Much of Liza's behavior throughout her four-year marriage to Haley had been thoughtless. Jack, however, had been tolerant. He supported Liza through four of her biggest career moves—*Lucky Lady*, *A Matter of Time*, *The Act* and *New York, New York*—but there came a time when his patience dissolved into intolerance. That year, 1978, was the time.

Liza Meets Mark Gero

People began linking Liza with Mark Gero from the first time they were photographed together, shortly after *The Act* opened. But Liza was still married to Jack Haley, Junior, at the time, and as she has always done in the past, the actress vehemently denied a romance.

Liza recalls that, at first, their whole relationship was based on Gero's stage call: "Hello. Good evening. Five minutes." Mark's father, Frank Gero, had been one of the stage managers on Liza's first Broadway show, *Flora, the Red Menace*. Then, in 1978, Mark and Liza shared a limousine on the way to Studio 54, where they were going to celebrate Liza's final performance as the Narrator in Martha Graham's production of *The Owl and the Pussycat*. "That's when we talked to each other for the first time," Liza says. When *The Act* closed, "We kept finding excuses to have lunch together," she adds. Then Fred Ebb innocently (so he claims) hired Mark as stage manager for Liza's 1978–79 concert tour. "From then on," Liza says, "we lived and worked together."

In mid-1979, Mark followed Liza to England, where she taped *The Muppet Show*. "I was a musical star who hired Kermit to solve a murder mystery," Liza recalls. "It was great fun." While in London, Liza, on Monday, July 23, opened in *The Owl and the Pussycat* at Covent Garden. Liza was repeating her role as the Narrator as a favor to the *grande dame* of dance, Martha Graham. In 1976, Halston had introduced her to Liza.

"One day Martha came to see *The Act*—I think it was her third time—and recited 'The Owl and the Pussycat' to me," Liza remembers. "I knew right there it was essentially a love story, and when she asked me if I wanted to dance and speak to it, I nearly fell on the floor! My eyeballs literally twirled

around in my head! I've always considered myself a dancer first, and this role was a perfect way to show off." Liza also claims she lives by Graham's adage: "Act your age."

In January, 1979, Liza publicly strengthened the romance rumors by appearing in Eric Bentley's off-Broadway drama, *Are You Now or Have You Ever Been?* Mark's father, Frank, was appearing in the show as Abe Burrows; and Mark, while his lover was working onstage, was officially working backstage. *Are You Now . . .* is a riveting dramatization of the

On December 4, 1979, Liza May Minnelli Allen Haley became Liza May Minnelli Allen Haley Gero. The winter wedding, held in Manhattan, was small, intimate and emotional. When Liza and Mark (here with Mark's dad, Frank Gero) left the church, they were greeted by rice-throwing Minnelli fans. One week after the wedding, Liza miscarried.

House Un-American Activities Committee's 1947–1956 investigation of Communist activity in the entertainment industry, and Liza cameoed as Lillian Hellman. Dressed in simple street clothes, Liza appeared toward the end of the play reading Lillian's letter to the committee. The task took less than five minutes, and critics did not officially review Liza's performance.

Mark Gero remembers his first meeting with Liza. "She told me I looked just like Robert DeNiro," he says, "and she asked me if I wanted to be his stand-in. I said, 'No, that's not my kind of job.'"

It took time for Liza to warm up to Gero. He recalls: "Several times I invited her to dinner, but she was always too tired. I never got the time of day from her until much later. We had our first date after *The Act* closed, and Liza was the first girl I ever waited that long to go out with. I loved her from the very beginning." It also did not bother Mark that he was five years Liza's junior.

Liza and Mark officially announced their engagement at the New Orleans Thanksgiving party she hosted for the cast and crew of her road show. Less than one month later—and less than eight months after her divorce from Jack Haley, Junior—Liza married Mark.

The Wedding at St. Bartholomew's

The wedding was, like Liza's previous ones, a small, private

affair. It took place at Manhattan's St. Bartholomew's Episcopal Church on December 4, 1979. Thirty of Liza and Mark's closest friends attended. The church's altar was decorated with pink and white lilies, roses, lilacs and narcissus. Fifty candles cast their soft glow on the gold mosaic dome. Mark Gero, chainsmoking, paced nervously in a small anteroom. It was his first marriage. It was Liza's third. She was also two months pregnant.

Wearing a full-length fur coat, Liza arrived for the 8 P.M. ceremony forty-five minutes early. She slipped in a side door to avoid the many fans and reporters, who had gathered outside. Though the police tried their best to keep the uninvited outside, some fans managed to watch as they hid behind pillars.

Liza wore a *bois de rose* chiffon dress with a capelet top and an asymmetric hemline, designed by, of course, Halston. The Reverend Peter Delaney, the man who had married Judy Garland and Mickey Deans, officiated. Two other clergymen were also present.

As the clock approached 8 P.M., organ music began bellowing throughout the church. Delaney read a passage from I Corinthians . . . "faith, hope and love, but the greatest of these is love."

Liza looked at Mark; Mark smiled broadly. They exchanged rings. Matron of honor Lorna Luft dabbed at her eyes; Vincente Minnelli, who gave the bride away, was "full of wonder." Best men Jason and Jonathan Gero were speechless. They were still delighted by the fact that Liza Minnelli was becoming their sister-in-law.

A half-hour later, the ceremony was over. As the newlyweds left the church, a legion of Liza's fans threw rice at their idol. "We love you, Liza!" they shrieked.

Later that evening, Halston threw a black-tie reception for Liza and Mark at his cavernous East Sixty-third Street house for about fifty guests. Andy Warhol was there, as was

Some of Liza's more memorable work in recent years has been done on television. In 1980, she starred with Goldie Hawn in the CBS special, Goldie and Liza Together *(left). The two actresses still like to clown around. No one had to pull Liza's strings to get her to guest star on* The Muppet Show. *"It was great fun," Liza recalls. Liza's favorite Muppet? Miss Piggy. "I cried like her all through my wedding [to Mark Gero]," she admits.*

Steve "Studio 54" Rubell, Faye Dunaway, Fred Ebb, Lois Smith and Elizabeth Taylor, who said she had stood in for Judy Garland at the wedding. When Liza arrived at the party, she climbed the staircase to the third floor of Halston's house, turned her back and flung her wedding bouquet to the group of cheering women gathered below. It was caught by Lee Anderson, Vincente Minnelli's long-time lover.

꙰ ꙰ ꙰

Liza still gets teary when she talks about the wedding. "Everyone else was supposed to cry," she says, "but *I* cried throughout my whole wedding! It was so embarrassing. I went to say

my vows, and I sounded like Miss Piggy! I've been married before," Liza adds, "but I've never been *married* before. Mark comes the closest to all the stuff I read about romance. Before Mark came along, I don't think I ever loved before."

On their second month anniversary, Mark surprised his wife with a small dinner party. He cooked the pasta himself —he even served the same wine he and Liza discovered in the Greek Isles—and invited a handful of guests, including his parents and Lorna Luft and her husband, rock musician Jake Hooker. For dessert, Mark played a cassette of their wedding vows. Everyone dissolved—once again—into tears.

Liza also gave Mark little things. For his thirtieth birthday party, Liza threw a star-studded bash at their East Sixty-ninth

Street apartment, inviting everyone from Robert DeNiro to Bianca Jagger to Ryan O'Neal and Farrah Fawcett. Gregory Peck showed up, as did Vincente Minnelli and Al Pacino. Everyone had a grand time—even if Liza did not cook the pasta herself.

Liza and Mark now live in a fourteen-room apartment on East Sixty-ninth Street. The apartment is a stupendous journey into a world of glamor. The floors are white marble, contrasting with black, white, silver and crimson accents. Upon entering, visitors are met by a display of Mark's marble sculptures and Andy Warhol's silk-screen portraits of Martha Graham, Judy Garland and Liza herself. Posters from Vincente's films dominate the walls of a small sitting room; the room also boasts a breathtaking view of New York City. Next to the sitting room is what Liza calls "Mark's poker room"—a big bar and card room painted a brilliant red. Then there is the music room (complete with a grand piano, zebra-striped chairs and white rugs), the master bedroom (copied after the bedroom in *Gigi*, done in red), and another sitting room, filled with white leather furniture. Vases filled with red carnations are placed artfully throughout the rooms; the lingering floral scent greets visitors. Liza—assisted by Halston and interior designer Tim MacDonald—decorated the apartment. Mark was pleased when he saw his wife's undertaking.

Liza at Carnegie Hall

The black-and-white ad first appeared in the Sunday *New York Times*. The announcement was concise: "Liza/In Concert/At Carnegie Hall." Tickets, starting at $7.50 and escalating to $25.00, would go on sale the next day at 10 A.M.

What was most striking about the ad was the length of Liza's engagement: eleven days. No one in the history of Carnegie Hall ever played the hall for so many nights. On September 4, 1979, Liza became the first performer to ever sell out such an extended engagement. Even Judy Garland, when she played the prestigious hall in 1961, didn't top Liza.

Liza did not want to come back to New York with the same nightclub act she had been doing for years. She wanted something more. With the help of her dedicated staff—including Fred Ebb (who would write, produce and direct the show), Wayne Cilento and Ron Lewis (who would choreograph), and Lawrence Miller (who would design the multi-tiered set)— Liza set about to knock New York on its backside. She also hired Mark Gero as her production manager.

"I wanted to make my Carnegie Hall shows a piece of presentational theater," Liza recalls. "I wanted each song to be an acting piece; a complete character. I wanted Carnegie Hall to be my baby."

Liza gave birth on September 4, 1979. She had succeeded in her plan; the critics loved her. "The show has three or four high points in which the power and excitement pouring out of Minnelli is almost frightening," wrote *Newsday*'s Jerry Parker. "She is terrific, maybe the greatest musical-hall artist going today. Are there any other performers these days who knock themselves out for an audience the way Liza does?"

Patricia O'Haire in the New York *Daily News*: "As Liza begins to sing 'How Long Has This Been Goin' On?,' the musicians file in one by one and take their places on the various platforms. From then on, energy, pure and simple, takes over. It's a dazzling display."

Jacques LeSourd, writing for the Gannett Newspapers: "The show is dynamite from start to finish. Liza galvanized the venerable hall in a way that I have never seen. She dispenses enough controlled energy in two hours to power the entire metropolitan area for a decade. She glitters and dazzles in Halston sequins. It's a job splendidly well done and a truly memorable night."

Halston hosted Liza's opening-night party at Studio 54, which happened to coincide with Mark's birthday. Guests included Joel Grey, fashion doyen Diana Vreeland, Michael Bennett and the late author Anita Loos. At one time, Jack Haley, Junior, was interested in Loos' memoirs, *Kiss Hollywood Goodbye*. He wanted Liza to play Loos. When she was asked what she thought about the casting, Loos cried: "Perfect! Liza has my bangs. That's all she really needs."

Liza eventually toured with her Carnegie Hall show. When she was in New Orleans she had her performance videotaped for cable-television airplay. She also recorded the two-disc *Liza at Carnegie Hall* for Altel Records. Liza owns the copyright on the disc package; she recorded for an unknown label so her sales profits would be larger than if she went with a more commercial company. Altel is also the company which does the sound for Liza's concerts.

Shortly after Liza's final Carnegie Hall performance, on September 14, the superstar flew to Los Angeles to tape a CBS special with another superstar. Her name was Goldie Hawn.

At the time they filmed *Goldie and Liza Together*, Goldie Hawn and Liza Minnelli were both superstars in their own rights. Both performers boasted kooky onscreen images, yet both had also proven themselves capable of dramatic appeal: Goldie after she crossed over from television laugh-ins; Liza when she stepped further away from Judy's shadow.

Liza could have based her friendship with Goldie on their common professional backgrounds, but it was her co-star's maternal instincts that solidified their relationship. And Liza is very generous when she praises Goldie: "Goldie and I are two cartoon characters. She's the blond airhead. But Goldie's as much an airhead as Einstein. I've worked with other women and it was tough, but it was different with Goldie. If there was something wrong with my dress, she would fix it. I know people who would have let me go on covered in lint. The basis of the show we did was to prove you don't have to be better than anyone else, you just have to be as good as you are."

Liza knew she was pregnant when she was taping the special, and she confided in Goldie. The blonde actress already had two children of her own and Liza found inspiration in this.

"I hadn't had a girlfriend in so long," Liza recalls, "that Goldie was the first one I told I was pregnant. She cried silly! She told me to have lots of children and how much fun it was to be pregnant. I guess that before I met her, everyone else thought it was hip to complain about kids."

"I'm so glad I did that special with her," Goldie says. "Liza and my kids became buddies. I told her having children would be the most important, beautiful thing that would ever happen to her. Liza is so sweet."

Liza has always wanted to have a baby, and when she found out she was pregnant from Mark, she was overjoyed. She even had the names picked out: Savannah Kay ("Savannah just because I like it; Kay for Kay Thompson") or John Joseph ("Joseph for my brother; I'd call the baby Joey").

However, on Monday, December 10, 1979—barely one week after her marriage—Liza was rushed to New York Hospital–Cornell Medical Center with intolerable stomach pains. She registered under the name of her manager, Deanna Wenble. Later that day, Liza, two months pregnant, suffered a miscarriage.

"Mark and I were heartbroken," says Liza. "It was a big setback for us. But I remember refusing to be depressed; I knew it wasn't a disaster because I was otherwise fine." Liza and Mark were forced to cancel their Jamaican honeymoon because of Liza's hospitalization.

Liza In Concert: *this program sheet says it all. Joe Eula, the artist responsible for creating Liza's Winter Garden advertising logo, also designed Liza's Carnegie Hall program. Liza loved the Eula work so much that in 1983, she was still using it to promote her concert tour* By Myself.

Liza was true to her word: she refused to let the miscarriage keep her down. Nearly one week later, she went on a Christmas shopping spree at Hammacher-Schlemmer, where she spent several hundred dollars on two New Zealand sheepskins for her bathroom, a Lucite bath tray, a tissue box, a Swedish massager and a white wastebasket.

Again, less than a year later, on October 4, 1980—a few hours after she had finished a nightclub appearance with Joel Grey in Framingham, Massachusetts—Liza was rushed to Massachusetts General Hospital with severe stomach cramps. A day later, it was announced that Liza's cramps were caused by a second pregnancy. This time, doctors, knowing Liza was a high-risk patient, ordered her off her feet. Liza cancelled concert appearances in Boston and Philadelphia and secluded herself in her beachfront glass house in Lake Tahoe, Nevada. She had purchased the house because of the state's low taxes.

Liza spent weeks resting, confident she would carry the baby to full term. But on New Year's Day, 1981, Mark rushed Liza to a Reno hospital where she underwent minor surgery for a pregnancy complication. That day, Liza lost the baby. For Liza and Mark, it was not the happiest New Year.

Goldie and Liza Together aired on February 19, 1980, competing with ABC's Winter Olympics coverage. Most critics found the show to be sixty minutes of amusing diversion. Goldie, backed by an all-male chorus, performed the gay theme song "YMCA," while Liza, backed by a female chorus, danced and sang her way through Donna Summer's hit "Bad Girls." The couple also dueted together on "One Step," "The Other Woman," "All That Jazz" and "Together, Wherever We Go," the song Liza and Judy performed on several occasions.

The New York Times critic John J. O'Connor summed up the special best: "Two attractive, talented women have put together a nice show. Not spectacular, but nice."

Nearly two months after Liza and Goldie's special aired, Liza and Mikhail Baryshnikov, on April 24, were back together—but only for an hour, and only for his IBM/ABC special *Baryshnikov on Broadway.*

The sixty-minute special was a salute to the American musical theater. Liza—officially billed as the Special Guest Star—assisted her former love on several numbers. They dueted together on "Sunrise, Sunset" and "Shall We Dance" and later they brought down the house with the specially-written

Ironically, Liza never saw the initial showing of *Baryshnikov on Broadway*; the night it was aired, she was performing at the Metropolitan Opera House in *The Owl and the Pussycat*. And five months after the special aired, Liza found herself back on a film set. The movie was called *Arthur*.

Arthur

Liza liked the script of *Arthur*. It made her laugh. It would be her first film since the disappointing *New York, New York*, and her first *real* comedy role since the fetid *Lucky Lady*. The film would star Dudley Moore — "I knew we'd make each other laugh," Liza now says — and she was sure she could make her role work, even if she didn't have a song to sing.

Arthur is a love story. It is, actually, a love story between Arthur Bach, a rich, immature drunkard, and his crusty, Jeevesian valet, Hobson. But the commercial love story was between Arthur and Susan Johnson, a dreary upper-class debutante who wants to marry Arthur and his $750 million inheritance, and Linda Marolla, a lovely, lower-class waitress who shoplifts on the side.

Filming began in late summer, 1980. Except for a few bedroom interiors shot at Astoria Studios in Queens, and some footage shot in Old Westbury, Long Island, all of *Arthur* was filmed in Manhattan. "Filming could have been hell," says Steve Gordon, *Arthur*'s writer and director. "After all, we were shooting in New York at the height of the mid-summer heatwave. But Dudley, Liza and John made it a joy. From the first day, they treated me like I knew what I was doing." It was Gordon's first directorial job and Liza referred to him as "Boss."

One of the first scenes shot was a crucial one that took place on Fifth Avenue. It involved a shoplifting attempt by Linda (Liza), who (after stealing a necktie from Bergdorf Goodman's and being questioned by the store detective) is "rescued" by Arthur. He then persuades her to hop into his waiting Rolls-Royce in lieu of a Queens-bound bus. It is an important scene —and one of the film's best—because it sets the mood of their relationship. It also took nine takes to complete.

Steve Gordon remembers the scene. "By mid-morning," he says, "we were surrounded by thousands of people. Then, someone in the crowd decided to break into the movies without being asked, right during a tight two-shot between Liza and Dudley. Someone else tried to hold him back...you know how it is on a hot day in Manhattan, tempers blow. My

Kander and Ebb tune, "Show Stoppers." The song was a lead-in to a Broadway show-tune medley.

Liza recalls the special. "Misha and I had talked about working together for years," she says, "but that TV special was our first real chance. When I think about it now, I realize what an unlikely combination we must have been. I bet lots of people tuned the show in just to see what the hell we were going to do! But Misha? A warm, gentle man. A genius. A hell of a dancer and a great human being."

Baryshnikov on Broadway was better received than Liza's previous special. This time John J. O'Connor said: "The show is a smash hit, a marvelously imaginative format. Miss Minnelli proves invaluable as guide, narrator and supporter. In fact, her name deserves to be in the title. Her singing is stirring—especially on 'Music That Makes Me Dance'—and her dancing is splendid. She performs with rare and admirable generosity. All concerned deserve a standing ovation."

Liza loved filming *Arthur*. "The movie had some of the funniest dialogue that I have ever read," she explains. "It was kind of like a Frank Capra comedy." Liza also loved *Arthur* because it offered her the opportunity to work with two of her favorite stars: Dudley Moore and New York City. Liza on Dudley: "A genius! Sexy! *Arthur* was so easy to make because Dudley is so *naturally* funny." Liza on New York: "Manhattan is like a diamond, clear and full of glass and things that go Rrrrr as they come up from the ground. I love New York because of its energy."

main concern was protecting Dudley. After all, he's not the easiest guy to find. The next thing I knew, police were swarming all over the place."

Not a day went by that the set of *Arthur* wasn't besieged by the curious. "We became a tourist attraction," laughs Gordon. "People would say, 'Let's visit the Plaza Hotel and the Statue of Liberty, and on the way back, let's stop at *Arthur.*'"

Fans of Liza would wait in the 90-degree weather in hope of catching a glimpse of their idol. They rarely did. When she was not needed on the set, Liza was safely tucked away in her air-conditioned trailer—oblivious to the groupies outside.

Those who *did* visit the set—relatives of the film's crew and officials from Orion Pictures—found themselves attracted to Liza. Recalls Gordon: "These people would fall down laughing at Dudley, but they wanted to reach out and touch Liza. It's as if some bit of her magic would rub off on them."

Even Dudley Moore found Liza enchanting. "It was easy to be in a good mood while making *Arthur*," he says, "because I was usually around Liza. Her confidence attracted people."

Steve Gordon on Liza: "I think she's wonderful, a great example of a giving actress. She gave Dudley the kind of comic relief he needed. Everything you think she is, she isn't. She knows nothing and then she knows everything."

In May, 1981, shortly after she finished her concert engagements in Nashville and Philadelphia, Liza was summoned back to New York for last-minute *Arthur* retakes. She worked at a feverish pace; the film was set to be released that July.

Most critics responded to *Arthur* with lukewarm reviews. Some liked Dudley Moore's performance; almost everyone hated Liza's.

David Ansen, *Newsweek* magazine: "*Arthur* is not the best comedy of the season, which is a pity because it has the best comic team—Dudley Moore and Liza Minnelli. Liza is not to be blamed for the film's derailment; she's never had a chance."

Stanley Kauffmann, *The New Republic*: "*Arthur* has spots of amusement, one of which is not Liza Minnelli's performance as a waitress. She manages to turn any moment, any place—a Queens kitchen, for instance—into Las Vegas show biz full of 'heart.'"

Pauline Kael, *The New Yorker*: "A larger idea that doesn't work is the casting of Liza Minnelli. Moore and Gielgud bounce off each other...they have common ground. But when Minnelli turns up, she doesn't bounce off anybody, and there's no common ground under the three of them. I haven't a clue what Linda is supposed to be and I doubt if Minnelli had much of a clue. When she needs to be appealing, she's electrifying: her gamine eyes pop open as if she'd just seen a ghost. Yet you feel Arthur would be better off marrying Hobson."

But it was John Simon, who so venomously described Liza's looks in *The Act*, who was the harshest. In the *National Review* he wrote: "[As Susan] Jill Eikenberry is an able, attractive actress, here deliberately made to look as dreary as possible, but even so...she is a thousand times more preferable than Liza Minnelli. Miss Minnelli, though relatively restrained, still exudes her special brand of physical and spirited repulsiveness."

Arthur was a disappointment for Liza, but disappointment has become an integral part of Liza's life today. She has never made a musical with her father; she has been waiting to film *Chicago* (presumably with Goldie Hawn) since 1975; Franco Zeffirelli has promised her the film musicalization of *Much Ado About Nothing*; Liza tested for—and lost—the coveted role of Eva Peron in the film version of *Evita*; she longs for the baby that may never come.

What did come—following *Arthur*'s release—was a concert tour of Australia, Japan and Manila. Liza and Mark concluded their globetrotting with a stopover in Hawaii, where Vincente Minnelli and his wife vacationed with the Geros. When Liza finally returned to New York, she reshuffled her professional operations and signed a contract with International Creative Management, the show biz agency that handled Liza when she was young. Super-agent Sam Cohn was assigned to negotiate Liza's affairs.

But Cohn had little to do with a venture that Liza took part in on April 25, 1982. That was the month Liza repaid a professional debt. Liza knew a lot about debts: it is a lesson she learned in 1973, after she spent the year working in London nightclubs to pay off her mother's debts. When Judy died, she was virtually penniless and Liza took responsibility for her mother's estate.

Save It With Music was a two-and-a-half-hour benefit for the Nyack, New York, Tappan Zee Playhouse, the summer-stock theater where Liza and Elliott Gould had appeared in *The Fantasticks* nearly twenty years earlier.

At first, Liza did not want to do the show, but she was finally persuaded by Terry O'Neill, Faye Dunaway's husband

(one of the benefit's producers), to consider the performance a professional payback. Melba Moore, Helen Hayes and Dick Cavett also agreed to appear.

The day before the show, Liza rehearsed at the Carol Music Studio on Manhattan's West Forty-first Street. Twenty-four hours later, she was on the stage of Carnegie Hall, giving the audience what they paid up to $150 to see.

Liza was scheduled to be the last performer, but she surprised the crowd when she walked onstage with one of the show's other guests, Dudley Moore. Wearing a simple black and white outfit, Liza sang "Best That You Can Do"—the theme from *Arthur*—while Moore played the piano. It was the first time Liza publicly sang the song, some of which had been written by her ex-husband, Peter Allen. She didn't know the lyrics and read them from the sheet music she was carrying.

After the number, the set was changed and Liza—the Liza most concertgoers know—reappeared to wow the crowd with nearly an hour of razzle-dazzle. Unfortunately, the benefit was not as successful as the producers had hoped. In late 1983, it looked as if the Tappan Zee Playhouse would be closed for good.

Six months after *Save It With Music*, Liza arrived with her entourage of twenty-five (including twelve musicians and two male dancers) in apartheid Bophuthatswana, South Africa, where she opened a ten-day, eleven-performance engagement at the plush $85 million gambling resort, Sun City. Liza reportedly received $1 million for her work.

One clause of Liza's contract stipulated that blacks be al-

lowed admittance to her shows. Only a handful came, however—few could afford the $45 and $36 tickets, a price equal to the monthly wage of many Bophuthatswanans.

After her South African gig, Liza toured Europe, playing in Paris, Milan and Rome. The climax came on New Year's Eve in Vienna, Austria—for one night's work, Liza earned a whopping $300,000!

What Makes Liza Run?

Of all the events in Liza's life, perhaps the most enlightening one occurred when she was still a very small tot. The incident took place quickly. But Liza's reponse to it was prophetic of her determination, vulnerability and tenacity. It was an event Liza will never forget.

One day, while at a birthday party at Ira Gershwin's house, a woman pointed to Liza—who, at age two, was still crawling—and cooed, "Aren't you ashamed you haven't started to walk? My Johnny is only eight months and *he* walks!" The next day, Liza began walking.

When Liza relates the tale, she does so with a laugh. "Daddy told me it took that woman to get me angry enough to get up and walk," she remembers.

Today, when Liza gets upset, she doesn't walk away. She runs away. She runs away from probing reporters who get too close; she runs away from anger and pain; she runs away from change and the uncertainty it usually brings.

Magazines and newspapers often contradict themselves by describing Liza as either a power-hungry, hard-driving, pro-

Liza goes to bat. At the taping of The Night of 100 Stars *at Manhattan's Radio City Music Hall, Liza performed the "Theme from New York, New York" surrounded by who else but the New York Yankees (left, center, right). That night, the whole team scored! After the show, Liza and ex-husband Peter Allen, who also participated in the gala, danced for the cameras. Neither looks happy.*

miscuous woman bent on perfection or a vulnerable street-urchin, barely able to fend off predators.

Few people see Liza's emotional outbursts; she keeps a tight rein on them. Liza doesn't like to deal with pain, change, hurt and anger; so those around her often carry the burden for her. She latches onto friends, draining them of energy. It is a taxing chore and one that does not sit easily with some of Liza's friends. Liza also calls pals when she's alone and no one is nearby: Liza doesn't reach out and touch someone; she reaches out and grabs. Like a drowning woman at sea, Liza clings.

But it's all done very quietly and in private. Judy may have exposed her soul on stage—lacerated scars and all—but Liza is more discreet.

"Mama and I went after different things," Liza explains. "On stage, Mama always said, 'Love me, want me, need me,' But with me, it's more 'Love me, want me, need me...but only if you want.' I can't show pain on stage like Mama did. That's like masturbating in public."

"They All Want Dirt"

Who is Liza May Minnelli Allen Haley Gero? Liza comes to the buying public as a guaranteed package of gamine charm and boundless talent, usually wrapped by Fred Ebb, polished by Bob Fosse and sold by press agents everywhere. She always sells out: The public sees to that.

Say the name Liza—practically anywhere in the world—and people will know who you are speaking about. She needs no surname; like Marilyn or Judy, Liza is a product of familiarity. Liza is a four-letter superstar.

Not surprisingly, many of Liza's best friends are also superstars. Perhaps one of her closest is Elizabeth Taylor, who has a need to protect Liza. When Elizabeth speaks about Liza, she inevitably mentions Judy—who also was her close friend—and more often than not, Elizabeth ends her conversation the same way: "I'll never end up like Judy."

You'll never read that Elizabeth Taylor has died of a drug

overdose. She has found her niche in life. Her weight may fluctuate, her marriages may crumble, but Elizabeth's sense of stability has long been grounded.

But what about Liza? Is she really happy? Has she finally freed herself of Judy's tarnished reputation, or does that image persist—like a refrain from one of Judy's songs? Liza inherited Judy's sense of humor and determination...has she also inherited the art of self-destruction?

Liza claims she no longer takes drugs. "One day," she recalls, "I smoked this funny stuff and everybody and every-thing I didn't want to see, I saw." Liza insists that her only addictions today are occasional Valiums and her endless chain of Marlboros.

Yet Liza will drink Bullshots, or Grand Marnier mixed with Coke. And the "in crowd" at Studio 54 constantly whispers... *Did you hear about Liza's sexual acrobatics in the bathroom? Have you heard her new nickname, The Snow Queen? Is it true she and Mark have split?*

Liza listens to it all. "Dirt," she says with disgust. "They all want dirt."

Liza and two of her avant-garde show biz pals, artist Andy Warhol and Bianca Jagger. When Warhol painted a pair of pop-art Minnelli portraits, Liza was so impressed that she bought them—for $25,000.

Two more Minnelli chums. Michael Jackson (left) had his name added to Liza's list of all-time best friends only recently. Like all Liza fans, Jackson found Liza huggable when he congratulated her after her 1983 Los Angeles concert engagement. An older pal of Liza's is Baby, better known as Halston (right). "Liza is everybody's pal," he says. "She's great fun, a great talent and a great lady to dress."

"Liza embodies all of the talents of her gifted parents and adds her own measure of pizzazz," says Elizabeth Taylor, one of Liza's closest Hollywood friends (left). Elizabeth stood in for Judy at Liza's wedding to Mark Gero. "Liza," Elizabeth adds, "is like my daughter." Liza reciprocates: "I love Elizabeth! She's great fun and such a beauty!" Liza and halfsister Lorna Luft (right) did not get along very well as children. Today, however, the two women are close. Liza even supports Lorna's show biz yearnings. "Poor Lorna has to deal with Mama and me," Liza says. Lorna, who failed to slide into stardom in Grease II, *may costar with Liza in the new film* Pipeline.

Vincente Minnelli always threw lavish birthday parties for his little Liza, so Liza—along with Vincente's third wife, Lee Anderson—did the same. In February, 1983, Liza and Lee helped Vincente celebrate his eightieth birthday. His birthday coincided with the film tribute Liza hosted at the Palm Springs Desert Museum. Vincente has been ill these past few years, and Liza will do anything to see him happy. "Daddy is my best friend," she says. "He gave me my dreams. I'll always be Daddy's little girl."

Epilogue

There is no ending to *Liza! Liza!* There can't be. Liza has to write one herself. In the meantime, she is keeping busy.

In early 1983, Liza began a nation-wide concert tour, unofficially titled *By Myself*. The highlight of the two-hour show was supposed to be a twenty-five-minute tribute to her father's films, which Liza sang before an illuminated caricature of Vincente. When *By Myself* opened at Los Angeles's Universal Amphitheater in April, the critics ripped the show apart. It was easy to see why.

Liza's overwhelming energy and awesome zest controlled every number—even the quiet love songs—and she bombarded the listener with a cuteness that, after a while, made her performance somewhat annoying.

The tribute to Vincente was inappropriate. Liza narrated the homage to music that sounded suspiciously like "Roxie" from *Chicago* (music which had no bearing on Vincente's career) and most of the tunes were performed with a rock 'n' roll beat. And when Liza sang "The Boy Next Door" and "The Trolley Song," two of Judy's greatest numbers from *Meet Me in St. Louis*, she pushed her hair away from her face in such a finely orchestrated movement that some audience members swore Judy had come back to life. The gesture may have been forgiven had Liza chosen not to sing "The Trolley Song" as if it were written for a punk-rock opera. All of Judy's melodic charm had been replaced by Liza's unmodulated energy.

Yet the critical outlash did not matter: the shows were immediate sell-outs. Some writers even dared to disagree with reviewers. Gossip columnist Liz Smith, a long-time friend of Liza's, called *By Myself* "the best personal appearance of her career."

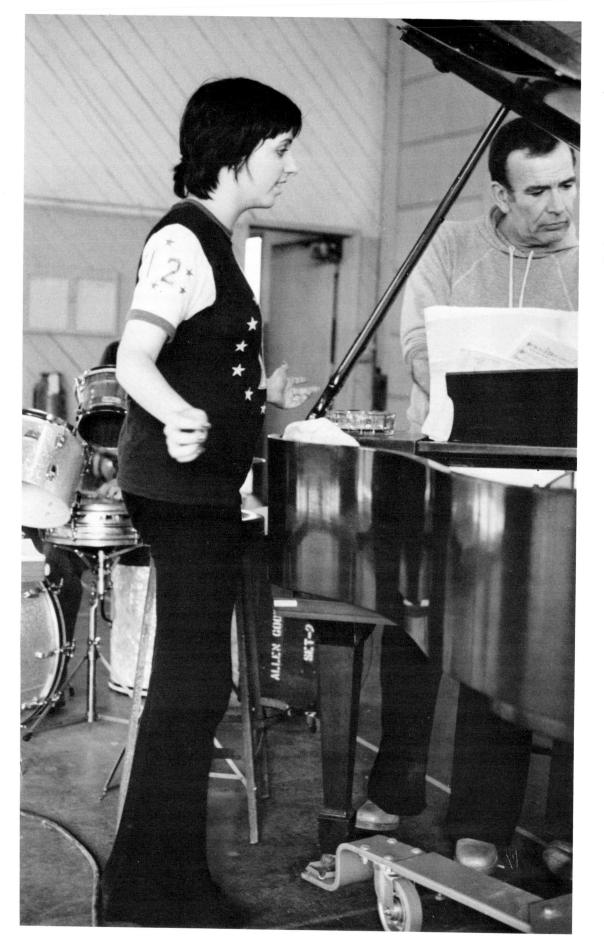

Photographer Nancy Barr, a long-time friend of Liza's, insists Liza is just fat in this rehearsal shot with Fred Ebb (left). Others, however, insist—just as loudly—that Liza was pregnant. The time was May, 1976, just about the time Liza was beginning to film New York, New York. The Minnelli family en masse (right). Mark and Liza Gero joined Vincente and Lee Minnelli for a quiet dinner at the Beverly Hills' restaurant, La Scala, in April, 1983.

As a thank-you for the Smith praise, Liza appeared at the June 13 "Broadway Salute to Liz Smith" at Manhattan's Shubert Theater. The show, which benefited the Literary Volunteers of New York City, Inc., was directed by Michael Bennett. Carol Channing opened the show; Liza closed it. In between were Lena Horne, Treat Williams, Susan Sarandon, Tommy Tune and Bernadette Peters.

In May, Liza interrupted her concert tour and took *By Myself* to London's Apollo Victoria Theatre. The British reviews were the total antithesis of the California ones: Liza was brilliantly received and all nineteen performances were sold out. Audience response to *By Myself* was so great that Liza has said she would eventually like to bring an extended version of the show to Broadway.

After her London engagement, Liza and Mark flew to France where Liza was awarded the Distinguished Achievement Award in the Art of Cinema at the Cannes Film Festival. Despite the fact that her last four films have been busts in the United States, Liza is a box-office smash in Europe.

Between concert engagements, Liza took time to again pay homage to her father. On March 8, 1983, Liza honored Vincente at a film tribute at Manhattan's Museum of Modern Art. Earlier, on February 19, Liza hosted a similar tribute at the Palm Springs Desert Museum in California.

Although Vincente could not make the trek to New York — he was confined to a Los Angeles hospital with his wife by his side — the evening was a huge success. Vincente sent a telegram, which Liza read out loud. "My darling Liza," it began, "first of all, as your father, let me remind you to stand up straight and speak slowly." The audience applauded wildly.

Almost 250 guests attended the tribute which raised more than $100,000 for the museum's film preservation project. After sipping cocktails and watching clips from some of Vincente's greatest films, the crowd gathered at a supper dance held at the Hotel Pierre. Liza was a radiant hostess and greeted each guest cordially. Some of the invited included actresses Joan Bennett, Cheryl Tiegs, Hermione Gingold, Kitty Carlisle Hart, Polly Bergen, Farrah Fawcett and Lorna Luft. Lucie

Arnaz and her husband Larry Luckenbill, Andy Warhol, Bianca Jagger and Halston were also there. Screen legend Lillian Gish stole the evening when she turned to Liza and said, "You're Vincente's greatest production!" At the end of the celebration, a huge birthday cake was wheeled out and pianist Peter Duchin played "Happy Birthday."

It is not surprising that Liza is still close to Vincente in his old age. "I've always been Daddy's little girl," Liza says. The thought that her father will soon die is painful to Liza. "Daddy's health is more important to me than anything else." He has been a strong but quiet force in her life, and she is devoted to him. She also owns all her own prints of his films, as well as those of her mother. "My parents drove me crazy," Liza said, "because they never collected anything. But I do. I love memories." When the Academy of Motion Picture Arts and Sciences presented the gala New York premiere of *A Star*

is Born at Radio City Music Hall on July 7, 1983—22 minutes of the film's original footage were restored—Liza and Lorna Luft lent their names to the festive proceedings.

As of mid-1983, Liza was planning to make two films: *Hang-ups* with rock star Elton John and *Pipeline*, a film which was written by one of Liza's brothers-in-law, Christopher Gero. *Pipeline*, which will be filmed in Alaska, will also star soft-porn star Koo Stark and, perhaps, Lorna Luft. There are also rumors that she will team with singer Linda Hopkins and pianist Dorothy Donegan to do a Broadway musical about great female singers from the 1920s to the 1950s. In June of 1983, theater producer Joseph Papp wanted Liza to star in *Non Pasquale*, a pop version of the Donizetti opera *Don Pasquale*, at Central Park's outdoor Delacorte Theater. Liza refused the role.

Still, Liza was hungry for more, and in September, 1983,

Liza shocked show biz insiders when she posed with her step-father Sid Luft (left, with his daughter Lorna) at the world-premiere of the restored film, A Star is Born, *in July, 1983. Sid and Liza are not friendly; their relationship came to a screeching halt in November, 1978, when Sid auctioned off close to 500 of Judy's personal belongings. Liza filed a court injunction to stop the sale, but her request was denied. Liza, as one of the three co-administrators of Judy's estate, claimed that the items—which included Judy's golf clubs, false eyelashes and 1953 Mercedes-Benz—were owned by the estate. Ironically, Lorna and Joey Luft were the other two co-administrators, and both refused to support Liza's injunction. Though the sale went on ($250,000 was raised), Liza's actions against Sid proved she's no boob. But what about singer Elton John? Elton and Liza will team for the film* Hang-ups, *something Elton obviously doesn't have. He and Rod Stewart's wife, Alana, seem to be bosom buddies (below), even if Stewart doesn't think so.*

Mark Gero is not only a successful theatrical producer—some of his better-known works include Extremities, Some Men Need Help and On Golden Pond—but he is a talented sculptor as well. Most of his abstract work is done in marble. At the June, 1980 opening of Mark's work at Manhattan's Point Rouge Gallery, Liza and Halston stop to discuss with Mark one of his works.

(On the following page) Love, Gero style. A bearded Mark Gero caught in a romantic moment with his wife. When Liza first met Mark, she told him he looked like Robert DeNiro. He told her she looked beautiful. Soon afterward, they became inseparable. The Gero-Minnelli marriage appears secure—even if stories abound to the contrary. Liza and Mark have fame, success and wealth; all they want now is a child. "I want a baby of my own before we adopt," says Liza. After all, the legend has to continue.

72 Market Street, a restaurant in Venice Beach, California, was scheduled to open. Liza has a part of the culinary venture, along with Dudley Moore, restaurateur Julie Stone and actor Tony Bill—the man with whom Liza was involved in her 1970 motorcycle accident.

Liza and Mark, 1983

Liza's desire to be a mother has not changed. As recently as 1983, Liza was informing the press that she would like to have a baby. But as she nears forty, the chances seem slim. Liza has already thought about alternatives: if she cannot have a baby, she will adopt.

One of the major reasons Liza has been able to accept her miscarriages has been her husband's strength. Unlike Liza's previous husbands, Peter Allen and Jack Haley, Junior, Mark Gero is a strong—almost bossy—individual who rarely lets Liza wander off-course. Even more rarely does he allow her to feel sorry for herself. Mark is a quiet man, but a man of strong convictions.

Mark never has to worry about being called "Mr. Liza Minnelli." He has his own commanding personality and much of his autonomy is linked to his strong family ties. He is not afraid of Liza's success—rather he welcomes it, calling it "a three-ring circus"—because of his own profitable careers. Not only is Mark a sculptor (he prefers working in marble and creates abstract designs), but he is also one of today's best young theatrical producers. Along with his father, Frank, Mark and his three brothers run Gero Communications, the company responsible for producing such successful off-Broadway shows as *Key Exchange*, *Extremities*, *On Golden Pond* and *Some Men Need Help*. And when Mark needs help, he has Liza, who shows up on opening night, smiling for the photographers and greeting the theater patrons. Liza is the show, Mark is the business—it is a marriage that seems to be thriving.

"Take Care of Liza"

Singer-actress Lainie Kazan won a Golden Globe nomination as Best Supporting Actress for her role in the 1982 film *My Favorite Year*, but actually Lainie's favorite year still is 1967. That was when she first met Judy Garland.

"Judy loved me," Lainie recalls, "and I was often invited to her house to sing. Liza was always there...sweet, quiet and looking very much like a young Judy. One night, Judy pulled me aside and whispered, 'Lainie, take care of Liza for me.' I can still see the tears in Judy's eyes," Lainie adds. Less than one year later, Judy Garland was dead.

It may come as a surprise to Lainie Kazan, but no one has to take care of Liza Minnelli. She takes care of herself. She may cling to the men in her life—Fred Ebb, Bob Fosse, Mark Gero—but Liza is also fiercely independent. It is an autonomy that borders on defiance, and one that she developed through all the tribulations of living with her mother. Give Liza one person, herself.

"I have the only friend I'll ever need, *me*," she explains. "People want to put me into their grinder; they want to shred me so they can get to my bones. They bone-picked Mama, but they're not going to bone-pick me. Everyone thinks I'm as frantic as a ping-pong ball. Well, I'm *not* crazy, and as long as I'm around, I can be my own protector."

Liza takes a deep breath. "I fight to be Liza Minnelli on stage, and I fight to be Liza Minnelli off stage. God gave me a talent, and I'm not going to spit in His eye. People are trying to prove that history repeats itself. But Mama always told me history doesn't have to repeat itself. Mama always complained and fell apart on the job. Well, I'm not like that. I have different goals than Mama did. For me, living is having peace of mind. I don't think Mama ever had that."

Filmography

In the Good Old Summertime (1949). Directed by Robert Z. Leonard; screenplay by Albert Hackett, Francis Goodrich and Ivan Tors, based on Miklos Laszlo's play *The Shop Around the Corner* (original screenplay by Samuel Raphaelson); produced by Joseph Pasternack; camera, Harry Stradling; editor, Adrienne Fazan; music director, George Stoll. Cast includes: Judy Garland (Veronica Fisher); Van Johnson (Andrew Delby Larkin); S. Z. "Cuddles" Sakall (Otto Oberkugen); Spring Byington (Nellie Burke); Clinton Sundberg (Rudy Hansen); Buster Keaton (Hickey); Lillian Bronson (Aunt Addie); Marica Van Dyke (Louise Parkson) and Liza Minnelli (Veronica and Andrew's little girl). Color, 102 minutes. Released through Metro-Goldwyn-Mayer.

Journey Back to Oz (1962). Directed by Hal Sutherland; screenplay by Fred Ladd and Norman Prescott, based on characters by L. Frank Baum; additional dialogue, Bernard Evslin; produced by Norman Prescott and Lou Scheimer; animation, Andy Paliwoda; special effects, Horta-Mahana Corporation; editor, Joseph Simon; songs by Sammy Cahn and Jimmy Van Heusen; music director, Walter Scharf. Cast includes: Voices of Milton Berle (Cowardly Lion); Herschel Bernardi (Woodenhead Stallion III); Mel Blanc (the Crow); Paul Ford (Uncle Henry); Margaret Hamilton (Aunt Em); Jack E. Leonard (the Signpost); Paul Lynde (Pumpkinhead); Ethel Merman (Mombi, the Bad Witch); Liza Minnelli (Dorothy); Mickey Rooney (the Scarecrow); Rise Stevens (Glinda, the Good Fairy) and Danny Thomas (the Tinman). Color, 88 minutes. Released through Filmation. *Note: Journey Back to Oz*, also titled *Return to Oz*, was not distributed until 1974, when it was shown as a television special.

Charlie Bubbles (1968). Directed by Albert Finney; screenplay by Shelagh Delaney, from an original story by Miss Delaney; produced by Michael Medwin; camera, Peter Suschitsky; editor, Fergus McDonnell; music, Misha Donat. Cast includes: Albert Finney (Charlie Bubbles); Colin Blakely (Smokey Pickles); Billie Whitelaw (Lottie); Liza Minnelli (Eliza); Timothy Garland (Jack) and John Ronane (Gerry). Color, 91 minutes. Released through Regional Films.

The Sterile Cuckoo (1969). Directed and produced by Alan J. Pakula; screenplay by Alvin Sargent, based on the novel by John Nichols; camera, Milton R. Krasner; editors, Sam O'Steen and John W. Wheeler; music, Fred Karlin. Cast includes: Liza Minnelli (Pookie Adams); Wendell Burton (Jerry Payne); Tim McIntire (Charlie

Schumacher); Austin Green (Pookie's father); Sandra Faison (Nancy Putnam); Jawn McKinley (Helen Upshaw) and Elizabeth Harrower (the Landlady). Color, 107 minutes. Released through Paramount.

Tell Me That You Love Me, Junie Moon (1970). Directed and produced by Otto Preminger; screenplay by Marjorie Kellogg, based on her novel; camera, Boris Kaufman; editors, Henry Berman and Dean O. Ball; music, Philip Springer with original songs by Pete Seeger and Pacific Gas and Electric. Cast includes: Liza Minnelli (Junie Moon); Ken Howard (Arthur); Robert Moore (Warren); James Coco (Mario); Kay Thompson (Gregory); Fred Williamson (Beach Boy); Emily Yancy (Solana); Ben Piazza (Jesse); Leonard Frye (Guiles); Anne Revere (Miss Farber); Clarice Taylor (Minnie); Barbara Logan (Junie Moon's mother); Nancy Marchand (Nurse Oxford) and Lynn Milgrim (Nurse Holt). Color, 113 minutes. Released through Paramount.

Cabaret (1972). Directed by Bob Fosse; screenplay by Jay Presson Allen, based on the musical play *Cabaret* by Joe Masteroff, John Van Druten's play *I Am a Camera* and *The Berlin Stories* by Christopher Isherwood; produced by Cy Feuer; camera, Geoffrey Unsworth; editor, David Bretherton; music direction and orchestrations, Ralph Burns; songs by John Kander and Fred Ebb. Cast includes: Liza Minnelli (Sally Bowles); Michael York (Brian Roberts); Joel Grey (Master of Ceremonies); Helmut Griem (Maximilian von Heune); Marisa Berenson (Natalia Landauer); Fritz Wepper (Fritz Wendel) and Elisabeth Neumann-Viertel (Fräulein Schneider). Color, 123 minutes. Released through Allied Artists.

That's Entertainment (1974). Directed, written and produced by Jack Haley, Junior; executive producer, Daniel Melnick; cameras, Gene Polito, Ernest Laszlo, Russell Metty, Ennio Guarnieri and Allan Green; editors, Bud Friedgen and David E. Blewitt; additional music adapted by Henry Mancini. Guest Narrators: Fred Astaire, Bing Crosby, Gene Kelly, Peter Lawford, Liza Minnelli, Donald O'Connor, Debbie Reynolds, Mickey Rooney, Frank Sinatra, James Stewart and Elizabeth Taylor. Color and black-and-white, 137 minutes. Released through United Artists. *Note: That's Entertainment* is a compilation of scenes from M-G-M movie musicals from 1929–1958. Liza narrated the Judy Garland sequence.

Lucky Lady (1975). Directed by Stanley Donen; screenplay by Willard Huyck and Gloria Katz; produced by Michael Grushkoff; camera, Geoffrey Unsworth; editors, Peter Bolta and George Hively; music, Ralph Burns with songs by John Kander and Fred Ebb. Cast includes: Liza Minnelli (Claire Dobie); Burt Reynolds (Walker); Gene Hackman (Kibby); Robby Benson (Billy Webber); Geoffrey Lewis (Captain Aaron Mosley) and John Hillerman (Christy McTeague). Color, 118 minutes.

Silent Movie (1976). Directed by Mel Brooks; screenplay by Mel Brooks, Ron Clark, Rudy DeLuca and Barry Levinson, based on a story by Mr. Clark; produced by Michael Hertzberg; camera, Paul Lohmann; music, John Morris; editors, John C. Howard and Stanford C. Allen. Cast includes: Mel Brooks (Mel Funn); Marty Feldman (Marty Eggs); Dom DeLuise (Dom Bell); Bernadette Peters (Vilma Kaplan); Sid Caesar (Studio Chief); Harold Gould (Engulf); Ron Carey (Devour); Henny Youngman (Fly-in-the-soup Man) and Charlie Callas (Blind Man). Color, 87 minutes. Released through Twentieth Century-Fox. *Note:* Liza Minnelli, Paul Newman, James Caan, Burt Reynolds and Anne Bancroft appeared in cameo parodies of themselves.

A Matter of Time (1976). Directed by Vincente Minnelli; screenplay by John Gay, based on Maurice Droun's novel *Film of Memory*; produced by Jack H. Skirball and J. Edmund Grainger; camera, Geoffrey Unsworth; editor, Peter Taylor; music, Nino Oliviero with original songs by John Kander and Fred Ebb. Cast includes: Liza Minnelli (Nina); Ingrid Bergman (The Contessa); Charles Boyer (Count Sanziani); Spiros Andros (Mario Morello); Tina Aumont (Valentina); Fernando Rey (Charles Van Maar) and Isabella Rossellini (Sister Pia). Color, 97 minutes. Released through American International. *Note:* The producers withdrew *A Matter of Time* from Vincente Minnelli's supervision after the final assemblage. He was not allowed the "final cut" of the film and subsequently disowned it.

New York, New York (1977). Directed by Martin Scorsese; screenplay by Earl Mac Rauch and Mardik Martin, based on a story by Mr. Mac Rauch; produced by Irwin Winkler and Robert Chartoff; camera, Laszlo Kovacs; supervising film editors, Irving Lerner and Marcia Lucas; editors, Tom Rolf and B. Lovitt; original songs by John Kander and Fred Ebb. Cast includes: Liza Minnelli (Francine Evans); Robert DeNiro (Jimmy Doyle); Lionel Stander (Tony Harwell); Barry Primus (Paul Wilson); Mary Kay Place (Bernice); George Auld (Frankie Harte) and Diahnne Abbott (Harlem Nightclub Singer). Color, 153 minutes. Released through United Artists. *Note:* In 1981, *New York, New York* was rereleased with the 12-minute "Happy Endings" number added.

Arthur (1981). Directed and written by Steve Gordon, produced by Robert Greenhut; camera, Fred Schuler; editor, Susan Morse; music, Burt Bacharach; title song written by Burt Bacharach, Christopher Cross, Carol Bayer Sager and Peter Allen. Cast includes: Liza Minnelli (Linda Marolla); Dudley Moore (Arthur Bach); John Gielgud (Hobson); Jill Eikenberry (Susan Johnson); Stephen Elliott (Burt Johnson); Ted Ross (Bitterman); Barney Martin (Ralph Marolla) and Anne DeSalvo (Gloria). Color, 96 minutes.

New York Stage Appearances

Best Foot Forward. Opening night Tuesday, April 2, 1963 at Stage 73 Theater. Directed and choreographed by Danny Daniels; produced by Arthur Whitelaw, Buster Davis, Joan D'Incecco and Lawrence Baker, Junior; book by John Cecil Holm; music and lyrics by Hugh Martin and Ralph Blane; musical director, Buster Davis; sets and costumes, Robert Fletcher; lighting, Jules Fisher; stage manager, Tony Manzi. Ran for 224 performances; original cast album released on Cadence. Cast included: Ronald Walken (Clayton "Dutch" Miller); Paul Charles (Fred Jones); Edmund Gaynes (Monroe "Hunk" Hoyt); Gene Castle (LeRoy "Goofy" Clarke); Don Slaton (Harrison "Satchel" Moyer); Edwin Cooper (Doctor Reeber); Kay Cole (Minerva Brooks); Susie Martin (Lois Street); Karen Smith (Debbie Baxter); Renee Winters (Linda Ferguson); Liza Minnelli (Ethel Hofflinger); Jill Choder (Winnie McKaye); Jack Irwin (Old Grad); Glenn Walken (Bud Hooper); Grant Walden (Jack Haggerty); Paula Wayne (Gale Joy); Truman Smith (Chester Billings); Tony Manzi (Professor Lloyd); Karin Wolfe (Helen Schlessinger) and Paul Kastl (Chet Evans).

Flora, the Red Menace. Opening night Tuesday, May 11, 1965 at the Alvin Theater. Directed by George Abbott; produced by Harold Prince; book by George Abbott and Robert Russell, based on Lester Atwell's novel *Love is Just Around the Corner*; music and lyrics by John Kander and Fred Ebb; dance and musical numbers staged by Lee Theodore; musical director, Harold Hastings; sets, William and Jean Eckart; costumes, Donald Brooks; lighting, Tharon Musser; stage managers, John Allen, Frank Gero and Bob Bernard. Ran for 87 performances; original cast album released on RCA-Victor. Cast included: Art Carney (Voice of FDR); Liza Minnelli (Flora Meszaros); Bob Dishy (Harry Toukarian); Louis Guss (Comrade Galka); Mary Louise Wilson (Comrade Ada); Clark Morgan (Comrade Jackson); Cathryn Damon (Comrade Charlotte); Stephanie Hill (Elsa); Joe E. Marks (Mr. Weiss); Marie Santell (Katie); and Jamie Donnelly (Lulu).

Liza. Opening night Sunday, January 6, 1974 at the Winter Garden Theater. Directed by Bob Fosse; produced by The Shubert Organization in association with Ron Delsener; written by Fred Ebb; original music material, John Kander and Fred Ebb; musical director, Marvin Hamlisch; music conductor, Jack French; choreography, Bob Fosse and Ron Lewis; lighting, Jules Fisher. Ran for a limited engagement of 24 performances; original cast album recorded on Columbia. Cast: Liza Minnelli in a one-woman show, assisted by Pam Barlow, Spencer Henderson, Jimmy Roddy and Sharon Wylie.

Chicago. Opening night Tuesday, July 1, 1975 at the Forty-Sixth Street Theater. Directed and choreographed by Bob Fosse; produced by Robert Fryer and James Cresson; book by Fred Ebb and Bob Fosse, based on Maurine Dallas Watkins's play, *Chicago*; music and lyrics by John Kander and Fred Ebb; settings, Tony Walton; costumes, Patricia Zipprodt; musical director, Stanley Lebowsky. Cast included: Chita Rivera (Velma Kelly); Gwen Verdon (Roxie Hart); Christopher Chadman (Fred Casely); Barney Martin (Amos Hart); Mary McCarthy (Matron); Jerry Orbach (Billy Flynn) and M. O'Haughey (Mary Sunshine). Ran for 923 performances; original cast album recorded on Arista. Liza Minnelli replaced Gwen Verdon for five weeks starting August 5, 1975.

The Act. Opening night Saturday, October 29, 1977 at the Majestic Theater. Directed by Martin Scorsese; produced by The Shubert Organization in association with Cy Feuer and

Ernest H. Martin; book by George Furth; music and lyrics by John Kander and Fred Ebb; choreography, Ron Lewis; settings, Tony Walton; costumes, Halston; lighting, Tharon Musser; musical director, Stanley Lebowsky; stage managers, Robert Corpora, Mark Gero and Richard Lombard. Ran for 239 performances; original cast album on DRG. Cast included: Christopher Barrett (Lenny Kanter); Liza Minnelli (Michelle Craig); Barry Nelson (Dan Connors); Roger Minami (Arthur); Mark Goddard (Charley Price); Gayle Crofoot (Molly Connors); Carol Estey and Laurie Dawn Skinner (The Girls) and Wayne Cilento, Michael Leeds, Roger Minami and Albert Stephenson (The Boys).

Are You Now Or Have You Ever Been. Opening night Sunday, October 15, 1978 at the Promenade Theater. Directed by John Bettenbender; produced by Frank Gero and Budd Block; book by Eric Bentley; sets, Joseph E. Miklojcik, Jr.; costumes, Vicky Rita McLaughlin; lighting, Kathryn M. Pinner; stage managers Donald E. Peterson and Kevin Motley. Ran for 149 performances. Cast included: Tom Brennan, Robert Nichols and Jim Haley (Committee Members); Jerry ver Dorn (The Investigator); Gene Terruso and Mary Beth Fisher (The Narrators); Jim Haley (Sam G. Wood); Joseph Rose (Edward Dymtryk/Martin Berkeley); Benjamin Bettenbender (Ring Lardner Junior/Tony Kraber); W. T. Martin (Larry Parks); Frank Gero (Abe Burrows); Raymond Baker (Sterling Hayden/Elliot Sullivan); David Francis Barker (Elia Kazan/Marc Lawrence); Kevin Motley (Jerome Robbins); Colleen Dewhurst (Lillian Hellman); Tom Brennan (Lionel Stander) and Avery Brooks (Paul Robeson). Liza Minnelli appeared as Lillian Hellman for three weeks starting January 9, 1979.

Major Television Appearances

Pontiac Star Parade Presents The Gene Kelly Show, April 24, 1959, CBS

The Hedda Hopper Showcase, January 10, 1960, NBC

The Jack Paar Show, March 15, 1963, NBC

The Ed Sullivan Show, April 21, 1963, CBS

The Tonight Show, June 3, 1963, NBC

Talent Scouts with Merv Griffin, July 2, 1963, CBS

The Keefe Brasselle Show, July 23, 1963, CBS

April in Paris Ball, October 27, 1963, NBC

The Judy Garland Show, November 17, 1963, CBS

The Arthur Godfrey Thanksgiving Day Special, November 28, 1963, NBC

The Judy Garland Show, December 22, 1963, CBS

The Ed Sullivan Show, May 24, 1964, CBS

Mr. Broadway (Nightingale for Sale episode), October 24, 1964, CBS

The Ed Sullivan Show, January 3, 1965, CBS

Hullabaloo, January 19, 1965, NBC

What's My Line?, May 16, 1965, CBS

The Today Show, May 18, 1965, NBC

The Ed Sullivan Show, May 23, 1965, CBS

Fanfare (The Al Hirt Show), August 14, 1965, CBS

The Dangerous Christmas of Red Riding Hood, November 28, 1965, ABC

Ice Capades of 1966, December 1, 1965, CBS

The Danny Kaye Show, January 5, 1966, CBS

Perry Como's Kraft Music Hall, March 28, 1966, NBC

The Match Game, April 3–7, 1967, NBC

The Carol Burnett Show, September 18, 1967, CBS

Kraft Music Hall: Give My Regards to Broadway, October 4, 1967, NBC

Kraft Music Hall: Woody Allen Looks at 1967, December 27, 1967, NBC

The Today Show, January 2, 1968, NBC

The Tonight Show, January 9, 1968, NBC

The Carol Burnett Show, February 5, 1968, CBS

The Best on Record, May 8, 1968, NBC

The Ed Sullivan Show, December 8, 1968, CBS

That's Life, December 17, 1968, ABC

The Ed Sullivan Show, January 19, 1969, CBS

The Ed Sullivan Show, October 26, 1969, CBS

Movin', February 24, 1970, CBS

The Ed Sullivan Show, March 22, 1970, CBS

The Forty-second Annual Academy Awards, April 7, 1970, NBC

Liza Minnelli, June 29, 1970, NBC

Rowan and Martin's Laugh-In, November 8, 1971, NBC

The Forty-fourth Annual Academy Awards, April 10, 1972, NBC

Liza with a Z, September 10, 1972, NBC

Royal Variety Performance, January 3, 1973, ABC

The Forty-fifth Annual Academy Awards, March 27, 1973, NBC

The Forty-sixth Annual Academy Awards, April 2, 1974, NBC

The 1974 Tony Awards, April 21, 1974, ABC

Love From A to Z, April 30, 1974, NBC

That's Entertainment: Fifty Years of M-G-M, May 29, 1974, ABC

Rona Looks at Raquel, Liza, Cher and Ann-Margret, May 28, 1975, CBS

60 Minutes, August 3, 1975, CBS

The Dick Cavett Special, August 16, 1975, CBS

The Mac Davis Special, November 13, 1975, NBC

Bell Telephone 100th Anniversary Jubilee, March 26, 1976, NBC

Life Goes to the Movies, October 31, 1976, NBC

The American Film Institute Tribute to Bette Davis, March 21, 1977, CBS

The Today Show, February 15, 1978, NBC

Gene Kelly...An American in Pasadena, March 13, 1978, CBS

Goldie and Liza Together, February 19, 1980, CBS

Baryshnikov on Broadway, April 24, 1980, ABC

The Today Show, December 25, 1980, NBC

Gala of Stars, March 22, 1981, PBS

The Tonight Show, May 26, 1981, NBC

The Tomorrow Show, June 2, 1981, NBC

The Today Show, December 25, 1981, NBC

The Night of 100 Stars, March 8, 1982, ABC

The Today Show, December 24, 1982, NBC

The Fifty-fifth Annual Academy Awards, April 11, 1983, ABC

The President's Command Performance, May 29, 1983, SYNDICATED

Hour Magazine, May 30, 1983, SYNDICATED

Discography

Best Foot Forward (Original Cast Recording). Cadence CLP-24012, released in 1963. Rereleased by DRG, DS-15003, in 1977 and Pic-A-Dilly in 1980. Contents: "Wish I May," "Three Men on a Date," "Hollywood Story," "The Three B's,"(Liza, Kay Cole and Renee Winters), "Ev'ry Time," "Alive and Kicking/The Guy Who Brought Me," "Shady Lady Bird," "Buckle Down Winsocki," "You're Lucky," "What Do You Think I Am?" (Liza, Edmund Gaynes, Kay Cole and Ronald Walken), "Raving Beauty," "Just a Little Joint With a Juke Box" (Liza, Gene Castle, Don Slaton and Paul Charles), "You Are For Loving" (Liza), Finale.

Liza! Liza! Capitol ST-2174, released in 1963. Rereleased by Capitol in an abridged version as *Maybe This Time*, ST-11080, in 1972. Contents: "It's Just a Matter of Time," "If I Were in Your Shoes," "Meantime," "Try to Remember," "I'm All I've Got," "Maybe Soon," "Maybe This Time," "Don't Ever Leave Me," "The Travelin' Life," "Together, Wherever We Go," "Blue Moon," "I Knew Him When."

It Amazes Me. Capitol T-2271, released in 1965. Contents: "Wait Till You See Him," "My Shining Hour," "I Like the Likes of You," "It Amazes Me," "Looking at You," "I Never

Have Seen Snow," "Plenty of Time," "For Every Man There's a Woman," "Lorelei," "Shouldn't There Be Light'-ning," "Nobody Knows You When You're Down and Out."

Flora, the Red Menace (Original Cast Recording). RCA-Victor LOC-1111, released in 1965. Rereleased by RCA, ABL-12760 in 1978. Contents: Overture, "Prologue/Unafraid"(Liza, Students and Ensemble), "All I Need (is One Good Break)" (Liza and Artists), "Not Every Day of the Week"(Liza and Bob Dishy), "Sign Here"(Liza and Bob Dishy), "The Flame," "Palomino Pal," "A Quiet Thing"(Liza), "Hello Waves" (Liza and Bob Dishy), "Dear Love" (Liza), "Express Yourself," "Knock Knock," "Sing Happy" (Liza), "You Are You" (Liza, Joe E. Marks and Company).

Judy Garland and Liza Minnelli Live at the London Palladium. Capitol SWBO-2295, released in 1965. Rereleased as a single disc by Capitol, ST-11191 in 1973. Contents: Overture, "The Man That Got Away" (Judy), "The Travelin' Life" (Liza), "Gypsy in My Soul" (Liza), "Hello, Dolly!" (Duet), "Together, Wherever We Go" (Duet), "We Could Make Such Beautiful Music Together" (Duet), "Bob White" (Duet), "Hooray for Love" (Duet), "After You've Gone" (Judy),

"By Myself" (Liza), "'S Wonderful" (Judy), "How About You?" (Duet), "Lover, Come Back to Me" (Liza), "You and the Night and the Music" (Judy), "It All Depends on You" (Duet), "Who's Sorry Now?" (Liza), "Smile" (Judy), "How Could You Believe Me When I Said I Love You When You Know I've Been a Liar All My Life?" (Liza), "What Now My Love" (Judy), Liza's medley: "Take Me Along," "If I Could Be With You," "Tea for Two," "Who," "They Can't Take That Away From Me," "By Myself," "Take Me Along," "Mammy"; "Make Someone Happy" (Judy), "Pass That Peace Pipe" (Liza), "The Music That Makes Me Dance" (Judy), "When the Saints Go Marching In" (Duet), "He's Got the Whole World in His Hands" (Duet), "Never Will I Marry" (Judy), "Swanee" (Duet), "Chicago" (Duet), "Over the Rainbow" (Judy), "San Francisco" (Duet).

There is a Time. Capitol T-2448, released in 1966. Rereleased by Capitol in an abridged version, SM-11803, in 1978. Contents: "There is a Time (Le Temps)," "I (Who Have Nothing)," "M'Lord," "Watch What Happens," "One of Those Songs," "The Days of the Waltz," "Ay Marieke," "Love at Last You Have Found Me," "Stairway to Paradise," "See the Old Man,"

"The Parisians."

The Dangerous Christmas of Little Red Riding Hood (Original Television Soundtrack). ABC 536, released in 1966. Contents: Overture, "We Wish You a Happy Yule," "My Red Riding Hood" (Liza), "Snubbed," "Woodsman's Serenade," "Granny's Gulch," "Along the Way," "I'm Naïve" (Liza and Cyril Ritchard), "Red Riding Hood Improvisation," "We're Gonna Learn How," "Ding-a-Ling" (Liza and Cyril Ritchard), "Poor House," "Granny" (Liza and Cyril Ritchard), Finale.

Liza Minnelli. A&M SP-4141, released in 1968. Contents: "The Debutante's Ball," "Happyland," "The Look of Love," "(The Tragedy of) Butterfly McHeart," "Waiting for My Friend," "Married," "You'd Better Sit Down, Kids," "So Long Dad," "For No One," "My Mammy," "The Happy Time."

Come Saturday Morning. A&M SP-4164, released in 1970. Contents: "Come Saturday Morning," "Raggedy Ann and Raggedy Andy," "Leavin' on a Jet Plane," "Wailing of the Willow," "Nevertheless (I'm in Love With You)," "Wherefore and Why," "Love Story," "On a Slow Boat to China," "Don't Let Me Lose This Dream," "Simon," "MacArthur Park/Didn't We."

New Feelin'. A&M SP-4272, released in 1970. Contents: "Love for Sale," "Stormy Weather," "Come Rain or Come Shine," "Lazy Bones," "Can't Help Lovin' That Man of Mine," "(I Wonder Where My) Easy Rider's Gone," "The Man I Love," "How Long Has This Been Goin' On?,"

"God Bless the Child," "Maybe This Time."

Cabaret (Original Motion Picture Soundtrack). ABC, ABCD-752, released in 1972. Contents: "Willkommen," "Mein Herr" (Liza), "Two Ladies," "Maybe This Time" (Liza), "Sitting Pretty," "Tiller Girls," "Money, Money" (Liza and Joel Grey), "Heiraten (Married)," "If You Could See Her," "Tomorrow Belongs to Me," "Cabaret" (Liza), Finale.

Liza Minnelli Live at the Olympia in Paris. A&M SP-4345, released in 1972. Contents: Introduction, "Everybody's Talkin'," "Good Morning Sunshine," "God Bless the Child," "Liza With a Z," "Married/You'd Better Sit Down, Kids," "Nous On S'Aimera," "I Will Wait For You," "There is a Time (Le Temps)," "My Mammy," "Everybody Loves My Baby," "Cabaret."

Liza With a Z (Original Television Soundtrack). Columbia KC-31762, released in 1972. Contents: "Yes," "God Bless the Child," "Liza With a Z," "It Was a Good Time," "I Gotcha," "Ring Them Bells," "Son of a Preacher Man," "Bye Bye Blackbird," "You've Let Yourself Go," "My Mammy," Medley from *Cabaret*: "Willkommen," "Married," "Money, Money," "Maybe This Time," "Cabaret."

The Liza Minnelli Foursider. A&M, SP-3524, released in 1973. Contents: "Everybody's Talkin'," "Good Morning Starshine," "Liza With a Z," "I Will Wait For You," "Cabaret," "The Man I Love," "Love Story," "Married," "You'd Better Sit Down, Kids," "Leavin' on a Jet Plane," "Come Saturday Morning," "Nevertheless (I'm

in Love With You)," "Lazy Bones," "Come Rain or Come Shine," "My Mammy," "Waiting For My Friend," "MacArthur Park/Didn't We," "Maybe This Time," "God Bless the Child."

Note: The Liza Minnelli Foursider is a compilation of *Liza Minelli, Come Saturday Morning, Newfeelin'* and *Liza Minnelli Live at the Olympia in Paris.*

The Singer. Columbia KC-32149, released in 1973. Contents: "I Believe in Music," "Use Me," "I'd Love You to Want Me," "Oh, Babe, What Would You Say?," "You're So Vain," "Where is the Love," "The Singer," "Don't Let Me Be Lonely Tonight," "Dancing in the Moonlight," "You Are the Sunshine of My Life," "Baby Don't Get Hooked on Me."

Muscle of Love. Warner Brothers BS-2748, released in 1974. Contents: "Big Apple (Hippo)," "Never Been Sold Before," "Hard Hearted Alice," "Crazy Little Child," "Working Up a Sweat," "Muscle of Love," "Man With the Golden Gun," "Teenage Lament '74," "Woman Machine." Liza sings background vocals on "Man With the Golden Gun" and "Teenage Lament '74" on this Alice Cooper album.

Liza Minnelli Live at the Winter Garden (Original Cast Recording). Columbia PC-32854, released in 1974. Contents: Overture, "If You Could Read My Mind/Come Back to Me," "Shine on Harvest Moon," "Exactly Like Me," "The Circle," "More Than You Know," "I'm One of the Smart Ones," "Natural Man," "I Can See Clearly Now," "And I in My Chair (Et Moi Dans Mon Coin)," "There is a Time (Le Temps)," "A Quiet Thing,"

"Anywhere You Are/I Believe You," "Cabaret."

Lucky Lady (Original Motion Picture Soundtrack). Arista AL-4069, released in 1976. Contents: "Too Much Mustard," "While the Getting is Good" (Liza), "Christy McTeague," "Young Woman Blues," "The Guaymas Connection/Dizzy Fingers," "Lucky Lady Montage" (Liza), "If I Had a Talking Picture of You/All I Do Is Dream of You," "Ain't Misbehavin'," "Hot Time in the Ole Town Tonight," "Portabello Waltzes," "When the Saints Go Marching In," "Lucky Lady" (Liza).

New York, New York (Original Motion Picture Soundtrack). United Artists LA-750-L2, released in 1977. Contents: Main Title, "You Brought a New Kind of Love to Me" (Liza), "Flip the Dip," "V.J. Stomp," "Opus Number One," "Once in a While" (Liza), "You are My Lucky Star" (Liza), "Game Over," "It's a Wonderful World," "The Man I Love" (Liza), "Hazoy," "Just You, Just Me" (Liza), "There Goes the Ball Game" (Liza), "Blue Moon," "Don't Be That Way," "Happy Endings" (Liza and Larry Kert), "But the World Goes 'Round" (Liza), "Theme from New York, New York," "Honeysuckle Rose," "Once Again Right Away," "Bobby's Dream," "Theme from New York, New York" (Liza), Orchestral Reprise of New York, New York.

Tropical Nights. Columbia PC-34887, released in 1977. Contents: "Jimi Jimi," "When It Comes Down to It," "I Love Every Little Thing about You," "Easy," "I'm Your New Best Friend," "Tropical Nights/Bali Ha'i," "Take Me Through/I Could Come to Love You," "Come Home Babe," "A Beautiful Thing."

The Act (Original Cast Recording). DRG 6101, released in 1978. Contents: "Shine It On" (Liza, Boys and Girls), "It's the Strangest Thing" (Liza), "Bobo's" (Liza), "Turning (Shaker Hymn)" (Liza, Boys and Girls), "Little Do They Know," "Arthur in the Afternoon" (Liza), "The Money Tree" (Liza), "City Lights" (Liza, Boys and Girls), "There Where I Need Him" (Liza), "Hot Enough for You?" (Liza, Boys and Girls), "Little Do They Know" (Reprise), "My Own Space" (Liza), "Walking Papers" (Liza, Boys and Girls).

Journey Back to Oz. Morton Norwich, released in 1980. Contents: Overture, "A Faraway Land" (Liza), "Signpost Song," "Keep a Happy Thought" (Liza), "The Horse on the Carousel," "B-R-A-N-E," "An Elephant Never Forgets," "H-E-A-R-T," "N-E-R-V-E," "You Have Only You," "If You're Gonna Be a Witch," "Return to Oz March," "That Feeling For Home" (Liza), Entre Act Overture.

Liza Minelli Live at Carnegie Hall. Altel, released in 1981. Contents: "How Long Has This Been Goin' On?/It's a Miracle," "My Ship/The Man I Love," "Some People," "Come in From the Rain," "London Town," New York City Medley: "I Guess the Lord Must Be in New York City," "Take Me Back to Manhattan," "Manhattan," "New York City Rhythm," "42*nd* Street/Lullaby of Broadway," "On Broadway," "New York, New York," "Every Street's a Boulevard," "Theme from New York, New York"; "Someone to Watch Over Me," "Twelve Fellas," "You and I/The Honeymoon's Over/Happy Anniversary," "City Lights," "Cabaret," "Shine on Harvest Moon," "But the World Goes 'Round."

Selected Bibliography

Most of the research for this book came from interviews with people who have worked with or known Liza Minnelli throughout the years. I also relied on several books for vital background information. Gerold Frank's *Judy* is, by far, the definitive Garland biography to date. Vincente Minnelli's *I Remember It Well* was extremely useful in helping recreate Liza's childhood.

Various film and theater reviews have been cited, and some material comes from the sixty-five pounds of research material I have amassed over the last fourteen years. The following articles and books were also helpful:

Davis, Junior, Sammy. *Hollywood in a Suitcase*. New York: William Morrow, 1980.

Deans, Mickey. *Weep No More, My Lady*. New York: Hawthorn, 1972.

DiOrio Junior, Al. *Little Girl Lost*. New York: Arlington House, 1973.

Finch, Christopher. *Rainbow: The Stormy Life of Judy Garland*. New York: Grosset & Dunlap, 1975.

Frank, Gerold. *Judy*. New York: Harper and Row, 1975.

Garland, Judy. "The Real Me." *McCall's* magazine, April 1957, p. 78.

——. "There'll Always Be Another Rainbow." *McCall's* magazine, January—February, 1964, p. 54.

Halliwell, Leslie. *The Filmgoer's Companion*. New York: Hill and Wang, 1977.

Harmetz, Aljean. *The Making of The Wizard of Oz*. New York: Knopf, 1977.

Laufe, Abe. *Broadway's Greatest Musicals*. New York: Funk and Wagnalls, 1977.

Minnelli, Vincente. *I Remember It Well*. New York: Doubleday, 1974.

Morella, Joe and Epstein, Edward. *Judy: The Films and Career of Judy Garland*. New York: Citadel Press, 1969.

Parish, James Robert. *Liza!* New York: Pocket Books, 1975.

Prince, Hal. *Contradictions*. New York: Dodd, Mead, 1974.

Streebeck, Nancy. *The Films of Burt Reynolds*. Secaucus, New Jersey: Citadel Press, 1982.

Willis, John. *Screen World*. New York: Crown, volumes 20, 22, 24, 27, 29.

——. *Theater World*. New York: Crown, volumes 19, 21, 30, 32, 33.

Yates, Penny, ed. *The Films of Vincente Minnelli*. New York: The Thousand Eyes, Ltd., 1978.

Index

I say *Live*, *Live* because of the sun,
the dream, the excitable gift.
                              Anne Sexton

About the Author

ALAN W. PETRUCELLI has been a celebrity journalist since 1976. His work has appeared in such publications as *After Dark*, *Flair*, *In Cinema*, *Photoplay* and *Showbill*. During his three-year tenure as Associate Editor of *Us* magazine, he garnered several exclusive stories. Some of these include profiles on Connie Francis, Lainie Kazan, Dr. Elisabeth Kübler-Ross, Amanda Plummer, Helen Reddy and Grace Slick. His 1982 interview with singer Johnny Mathis brought Alan worldwide attention; for the first time ever, Mathis discussed his homosexuality with great candor.

Educated at Iona College, Alan lives in Bronxville, New York, with his two cats, Bonnie (after Miss Raitt) and Lainie (after Miss Kazan). He is at work on his second book.